THIS BOOK BELONGS TO:

Sew Cloth Grocery Bags

Make Your Own in Quantity
For Yourself, For Gifts, and For Sale

Sew Cloth Grocery Bags

Make Your Own in Quantity
For Yourself, For Gifts, and For Sale

Teresa Peschel

PESCHEL PRESS ~ HERSHEY, PA.

SEW CLOTH GROCERY BAGS: MAKE YOUR OWN IN QUANTITY FOR YOURSELF, FOR GIFTS, AND FOR SALE. Copyright 2019 Teresa Peschel. All rights reserved. Printed in the United States of America. No part of the notes or essays may be used or reproduced in any manner without written permission except in cases of brief quotations in an article or review. For information, email peschel@peschelpress.com or write to Peschel Press, P.O. Box 132, Hershey, PA 17033.

Cover and book design by Bill Peschel.

Sign up for our newsletter at www.peschelpress.com

ISBN-13: 978-1-950347-08-7
ISBN-10: 1-950347-08-7

Library of Congress Control Number: 2019914891

First printing: September 2019

Table of Contents

What Can Readers Do With This Book?...............7

PART I: PRELIMINARY NOTES

1. Why Cloth Grocery Bags?........................ 9
2. A Tale of Two Bags............................... 11
3. Choosing the Right Fabric 13
4. Preparing and Washing Fabric............. 16
5. Useful Tools... 18
6. The Bag-Making Process 22
7. About the Trim-Line 25
8. Making the Straps 27
9. Outsourcing Tasks 31
10. Cutting Layouts and Measurement Charts.. 32

PART II: BOXED BAGS

11. Making Boxed Bags 36
12. Boxed Bags With the Flange On the Inside . 48
13. Boxed Frankenstein Bags.................... 51
14. Making Boxed Bags With One-Way Cloth 54

PART III: TAILORED BAGS

15. The First Pass 57
16. The Second Pass 62
17. The Third Pass 64
18. The Fourth Pass 67
19. The Fifth Pass 70
20. The Sixth Pass 72
21. Tailored Frankenstein Bags................ 74
22. Layout Example #1: Brown Floral and Paisley Bags 76
23. Layout Example #2: Blue and Gray Building Bags 80

PART IV: PRODUCTION SEWING AND SELLING

24. Production Sewing 87
25. Selling at Craft Shows........................ 91
26. Know Your Competition.................... 98
27. Afterword..101

APPENDIX

Stitching Diagrams 102
How to Use the Pattern Layouts 108
Boxed Bag Layouts 111
Tailored Bag Layouts 116
    With 13" x 15" Panels........................... 116
    With 14" x 16" Panels...........................136
About the Author 145
Peschel Press Catalog..............................146

WHAT CAN READERS DO WITH THIS BOOK?

All of the material in this book is copyrighted by Teresa Peschel.

The publisher, Peschel Press, grants the book's purchasers a royalty-free license to use the patterns, instructions, and layouts contained within to sew bags for commercial or non-commercial purposes.

Purchasers can redesign the bags to suit their needs and tastes. Go wild.

However, purchasers can NOT resell the patterns, layouts, and instructions in their own publications. Go write your own book.

Nor should purchasers repost the information on their websites except for brief quotations in an article or review. Short excerpts for review purposes are fine.

Are we clear? If not, please email Teresa at Peschel Press (peschel@peschelpress.com) and ask.

And if anyone asks where you learned to make your fabulous bags, please tell them about this book. We appreciate reviews. Good reviews, even simple one-sentence reviews ("I love this book!") sell books and selling books keeps our household afloat.

Part I: Preliminary Notes

1. Why Cloth Grocery Bags?

We all use grocery bags, but we never think about the price we pay for using them. We buy our groceries, get them bagged, take them home and go on with our lives.

But what do we do with the bags? Most of us throw them away. Some of us recycle them, reuse them at the store until they tear, or find other uses for them.

If the bags are made from paper, they're reused as gift-wrap, book covers, underlayment under patio pavers, trashcans liners, or composted.

Plastic bags, however, don't have as many reuses. They can't be composted or used in the garden. They can be reused as trashcan liners or for collecting poo during dog walks. Some people crochet things with them. Thrift stores will take your bags if they are clean, dry, and empty.

But no matter what you do with the bags, you're still paying a price for the convenience. Grocery stores have to pay for these one-use wonders, and they pass the cost to us.

Then there's the hidden cost to our environment. Brown paper bags are manufactured from wood pulp, a renewable resource that uses vast quantities of energy and fresh water to turn trees into paper bags. Plastic bags are made of petroleum by-products. You cannot grow oil like you can trees. They can be recycled, but not nearly as easily as the industry would like you to think. They do not rot on their own, ever. They are easy to spot in the winter, caught in shrubbery like airborne jellyfish. Animals like sea turtles eat them and starve; their stomachs full of indigestible plastic.

There are many reasons to avoid one-use bags.

Alternatives

So, what should you use? Many stores sell reusable shopping bags for 99¢. They'll sometimes give them away as advertising. These are better than paper or plastic, but still not good. They are very cheaply made of petrochemicals so they can't be recycled easily. They don't rot. They cannot be washed or repaired. They tear almost as easily as flimsy plastic bags. Some even use lead-impregnated petrochemicals via the stenciled design advertising the store. Mmm, I love lead in my food, don't you?

The solution is to make your own grocery bags from cloth. Cloth bags can be washed. They can be repaired. They will last for years. They are not hard to make, if you have a sewing machine and some basic skills. You don't even need a pattern, just a yardstick and chalk.

Designed For Groceries

This book will show you how to make grocery bags, not tote bags. Tote bags are very different from grocery bags. They come in a variety of sizes. They are often lined. They have pockets and compartments. They may have zippers, toggles, buttons, snaps or other closures. Tote bag instructions assume you are only making one at a time; in the layout, the cutting, and in the sewing.

My grocery bag design doesn't have pockets, closures or linings. It is designed to be sturdy, with long straps and sized to hold two gallons of milk. A bag that is larger will be overfilled by an enthusiastic bagger, making it impossible for my 78-year-old mother to carry it. A bag that is smaller won't hold enough groceries, which also irritates me and my mother.

Production Sewing Methods

I emphasize production sewing because you will need a lot of bags. Depending on the size of your household, you may need a dozen or more. How many plastic bags come home with you from the grocery store? That's how many bags you need, plus a few extra if you buy more than usual.

Production sewing is nothing like sewing one-offs. You lay out the patterns, whether for cloth grocery bags, stuffed toys, or pajamas, very differently than you do for a single item. A single item means waste fabric. The goal of production sewing is to use the fabric as efficiently as possible, leaving zero scrap fabric, while sewing as fast as possible. Too much time spent sewing is also counted as waste.

Another factor to consider is cost, especially if you plan on selling your bags. Fabric isn't often free, so you'll learn how to lay out your fabric for maximum economy, while using the cheapest fabric that is heavy enough to do the job.

This means that you don't want to spend more than a few dollars per yard. Less is better. Free is best of all. A typical customer, looking over your beautifully sewn cloth bags, does not understand the time and skill that went into a bag that will last a lifetime. They see that you want $10 for a bag that is superficially similar to the 99¢ supermarket brand. If a person needs a dozen bags, $12 is a small up-front cost for supermarket bags, but $120 for a dozen lifetime bags made of cloth is not. To compete, you'll have to source your fabric wisely.

Even if you don't intend to sell them, you may want to make bags for your family, your relatives (Christmas is coming), teacher gifts and other such occasions. Your cost still counts and so you still want to spend as little as possible on the cloth.

In this book, I talk about what fabrics to use and what to look for when shopping. I discuss how to make in quantity the two styles of bags – the efficient boxed bag and the more intuitive tailored bag. I show how to get the best use of an 8-yard piece of fabric. I also show how to take scrap home-decor fabric and repurpose it into bags that will last a lifetime, despite looking like Dr. Frankenstein sewed them together.

I have sewn hundreds of cloth grocery bags. My kids gave them to teachers as gifts. I give them to friends and relatives. I sell them at craft shows, and give them away with our books. I learned from my customers and friends what works and what doesn't. I made so many bags that I learned how to streamline the production process so that I can make many of them at one time

"Sew Cloth Grocery Bags" will show you how to do what I do, but easier and faster than how I learned it. After you've made a dozen for yourself, the only problem you'll have will be remembering to take them with you to the store.

2. A Tale of Two Bags

My book will teach you how to make two kinds of bags: an intuitive design I call tailored, and a more efficient version I call boxed. We'll be using those terms throughout the book — tailored and boxed — so keep them in mind.

When I started making cloth bags, I couldn't find a pattern that satisfied me, so I made my own. I worked out my design based on a picture I saw and my understanding of a cube. I sized it to hold two gallons of milk. It was the perfect size: not too big and not too small.

These tailored bags consist of three pieces — front panel, back panel, and gusset — plus a trim-line and two straps.

I made hundreds of bags with this pattern. I gave them away as gifts, gave them away with the purchase of a book at our Peschel Press booth at craft shows, and even sold some. These tailored bags worked so well that I decided to write this book to teach other people how to make them.

Then my dear husband asked if there were other, less complex ways to sew the bag. I wasn't sure. After all, I didn't make these grocery bags any other way. Why would I change? He persisted and pointed out that showing other methods of sewing cloth grocery bags could make a better, more complete book.

A Friend's Suggestion

Then fate intervened. My neighbor and friend, Lisa, also sews cloth grocery bags, so I asked her how she made hers.

That is how I learned about boxed bags. She uses one piece of cloth, instead of my three, to make the body of the bag. You take a long rectangle of fabric, fold it in half and sew up both sides.

At that point, you have a sack. Then you work a bit of magic by folding the bag like a

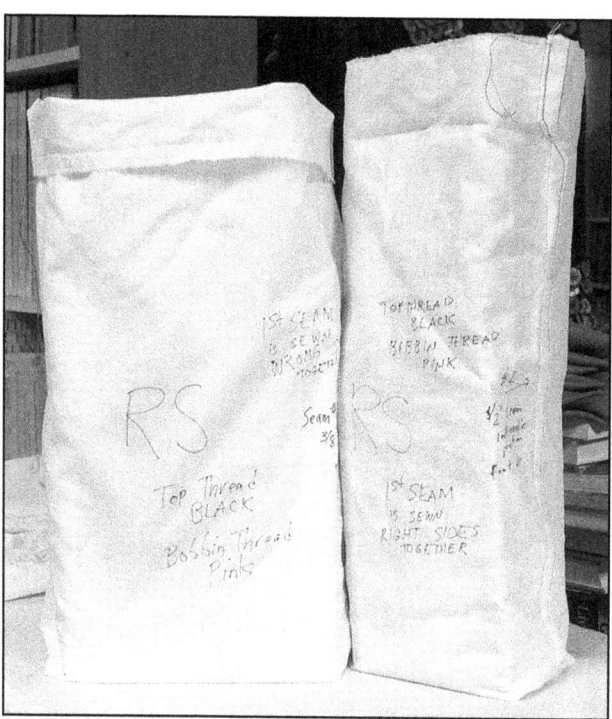

Two of the four muslin prototypes I made. I wrote notes on the bag to keep track of my progress. I used odd-sized rectangles of muslin, hence the oddly shaped prototypes. This proved both the concept and showed that the starting panel's dimensions mattered a lot.

piece of origami and sewing across a triangle on each side.

Fold in the triangles, sew them down, and — voila! — a boxed bag with a bottom and four sides.

Finish the top, add straps, and you have a finished grocery bag.

To teach myself how Lisa made her bags, I made several muslin prototypes, refining the seam finishing and figuring out how to handle those triangles.

These prototypes let me figure out the order of operations to make the seam margins behave. I wanted these boxed bags to be as well-finished as my tailored bags, useable inside and out, with not a raw edge to be seen anywhere. I also didn't want to reinvent the wheel with the straps or how I finished the top.

There are similarities between the two bag styles:
- Both last for years.
- Both can be repaired and hand-washed.
- With a careful layout, both bags are essentially zero-waste although boxed bags are better in that respect. You won't have much fabric left over if you bought the right amount of yardage and any excess can be repurposed as straps, trim-lines, panels, and gussets.

DIFFERENCES BETWEEN THE BAGS

There are significant differences between the two styles:
- Once you learn their origami-like construction, boxed bags are much easier and faster to lay out, cut, and sew. This is an important consideration if you are selling them.
- The boxed-bag design has to be sewn in the right order to ensure the seam margins end up with no raw edges. They do not create their own structure, unlike the tailored bags.
- **Boxed bags** require a single, larger piece of fabric — 19 by 36 inches — than the tailored bags do. Since the tailored bags use smaller pieces of fabric, it is possible to make them from that heap of oddly sized upholstery remnants without piecing.
- The boxed bags work better with a stiffer fabric. The tailored bags can use a fabric with a softer hand — although still heavy enough to become draperies — since the seaming forces the bag to hold its shape.
- Fabric with a strong up-and-down motif is easier to manage with the tailored bags. You can use an up-and-down pattern with the boxed bags but that forces a choice. You can have the back side of the bag with the fabric motif upside-down or you can cut the fabric not quite at the halfway mark (so the seam is offset) and sew it back together with each side going in the right direction. This adds an extra step, uses more fabric, and adds extra bulk in seams where you don't want them.

HOW TO CHOOSE BETWEEN STYLES

Since both styles of bags function equally well, choosing between the two depends on the fabric.

If you have a lot of suitable material in your stash, figure out on paper first which style gives you the most bags from a given length of yardage.

Study the waste fabric carefully. Can it be used for tailored bag panels and gussets and give you another bag? Is that odd rectangle the right size for a boxed bag?

If you are using fabric that's been repurposed or from the stash, it is almost a guarantee that you will have leftover cloth. Knowing how to sew both kinds of bags will help you here. Tailored bags lend themselves to being cut from oddly shaped remnants better than a boxed bag, allowing you to squeeze out still another bag, without piecing.

If you are going to buy material, then the boxed bags are quicker to cut out sew. Stick with these for production sewing as time is money and your buying public may not be able to understand why you charge more for a tailored bag than a boxed bag. Both bag styles look almost identical to anyone who doesn't sew.

If you only sew tailored bags with odd remnants, you can keep the price the same since you are using up fabric that could have gone to waste.

3. Choosing the Right Fabric

What fabric is suitable for bags? The easy answer is the cheap kind, but this is not completely true. The weight and sewability of the fabric also matter.

Look for a woven fabric heavy enough for skirts, pants, draperies, or upholstery. Woven fabric can be found in the garment section of your fabric store. Denim, corduroy, and khaki work well, as do medium or heavier weights of twill and brocades.

Not all woven fabrics can be used for bags. A fabric for a gauzy summer blouse is too lightweight. If you can make a suit jacket with it, you're on the right track. If the fabric has an open weave, whether eyelets, lace, mesh, or openwork designs, it won't work for grocery bags. Every one of those little openings will catch on the corners of the boxes you put into the bags and tear into a bigger hole.

Don't use knits. Their stretchiness is useful for fitted garments but a big negative for a grocery bag. A heavy, stabilized knit, like polyester doubleknit gabardine, might work. If you have some already on hand in the stash, sew a test bag and see how it works hauling groceries. Then, if you are satisfied, make more.

Another useful fabric is the canvas type from the utility fabric section. Mattress ticking also works well. Fabric made for crewel embroidery can work, but not needlepoint canvas; those little holes work against you. You'd have to needlepoint your grocery bags to make it work.

Test the fabric to see if it's right by weighing it in your hand. Stiffness is an asset. Very soft, drapable cloth is a serious defect in a grocery bag. In a tailored bag, some softness is acceptable because the structural seams provide a supporting skeleton. A fabric that acts like it can stand on its own is best, as the seams will ensure it will hold itself up and open while in use. Slick, shiny fabric or fabric that snags just by looking at it are bad.

Another source of good material can be found in your fabric store's home-decor department. Drapery material has the right weight for bags. Upholstery, however, is more problematic. It works as a grocery bag. Its thickness holds the bag upright and open, making it easier to load at the grocery store. But a thick, heavy fabric is also hard to sew, leading to broken needles. If your sewing machine isn't sturdy enough for upholstery work, you may have to hand-sew the sections your sewing machine refuses to do; forcing the needle through eight layers of fabric. This is tedious work and hard on the hands. It's easier to choose a lighter weight of fabric.

SOLIDS VERSUS PRINTS

I have made grocery bags from solids and from printed material. I prefer printed fabric. The bags are more interesting and a dramatic, unusual print guarantees that my bags don't get confused with anybody else's.

When choosing a printed fabric, you'll have to make some design choices. Do you care which direction the print runs in the finished bag? Florals and geometrics don't generally have an up and a down. Designs that incorporate houses or people do have an up and a down and you may not like your bags having a motif that is obviously upside-down. Avoiding this issue requires a careful layout that will use up more expensive cloth, resulting in fewer bags and more waste fabric.

Stripes, plaids, and checks may look strange in a tailored bag if you don't go to the trouble to match them at the seams. On the other hand, you can always claim the design is avant-garde.

The size of the motif can matter as well. A

Choosing the Right Fabric

The bigger advantage of double-sided upholstery is that, since you can use either side out, it adds variety to your line of bags.

very large-scale motif may look strange when cut up. If someone notices, this is another opportunity to claim you're working at the bleeding edge of design. Try saying that you're emulating cubist and dada paintings.

How the print lays on the yardage matters because the most efficient layout may not be the one that shows the motif to its best advantage. That leads to wasting fabric that could be used to squeeze out another bag. This is a judgment call. Does the appearance of your grocery bag matter to you or do you want to get the most bags possible?

Another thing I look for in fabric is what the reverse looks like. Upholsteries are often woven using colored threads to form the design, as opposed to it being printed on one side. The wrong side of a piece of upholstery can be just as attractive and just as usable as the right side. This is important because my design requires folding over the top edge of the fabric by 2 inches. This stiffens and reinforces the bag's top so it stands up better and lasts longer. It also shows the reverse of the cloth as a contrasting border. The reverse side of upholstery adds another design element, more interesting than just the reverse side of regular printed material.

The bigger advantage of double-sided upholstery is that, since you can use either side out, it adds variety to your line of bags. For tailored bags, you can orient the side panels right-side-out and the gusset wrong-side-out. For both tailored and boxed styles, you can sew half the bags together one way and the other half in the reverse. The amount of cutting and sewing remains the same and the layout doesn't change. You get a wider range of bags for the same money and from the same piece of cloth.

How Much Should You Pay?

Making a dozen or more bags requires plenty of fabric. How much you need to buy depends on how many bags you want to make, and whether they're tailored or boxed.

For example, a 3¼-yard piece of fabric will make, depending on the width of the gusset strip, six to seven tailored bags. Boxed bags are more economical in their layout, often leaving zero waste fabric after cutting. Three yards of 45-inch-wide fabric will yield six boxed bags. Three yards of 60-inch-wide fabric will give you nine boxed bags.

How much should you pay? If you are making bags for resale, then you have to minimize the cost of fabric. You may have to sell your bags for $10 each to cover your fabric, webbing, trim, thread, sewing machine depreciation costs plus something for your time. With that in mind, I strongly recommend not paying more than $2 to $3 a yard. If you are sewing bags for yourself or as gifts, then spend what you like.

SHOPPING FOR FABRIC

Where do you get the fabric? Start at a fabric store. Check first for an independent store in your area. They can be very competitive on price, and they nearly always have a clearance table. There are a few national chains of fabric stores. As a group, they run good sales, they have a clearance rack, and they sometimes provide discount coupons. Sign up for the mailing list, look over their fliers, and you may get lucky.

Every Walmart used to have a fabric department. A lot of them don't, not anymore. But if your Walmart has a fabric department, then it probably also has a dollar bin. You never know what you will find, but the dollar bin at my local Walmart has been good to me and thus it is always worth checking out.

Depending on where you live, there may be local department stores that still carry fabric. Some craft stores do, as does every quilt shop. The trick is finding the heavy cloth you need at the price you are willing to pay. Every one of these places will have some kind of clearance rack, so search there first. The less fussy you are about the appearance of the fabric, the more likely you are to get lucky.

Next, there's the secondhand market. It's possible but unlikely to find raw yard goods at a thrift shop. The same is true of yard sales.

Here's a tip: Look for big pieces of the right weight of cloth that are disguised as something else. It can be tablecloths, draperies, bedspreads, or fabric shower curtains. In each case, look beyond what the fabric is currently being used as and envision it as something else.

Inspect carefully before you buy secondhand cloth. If the drapery panel or tablecloth is full of moth holes, shredded, or has obvious wear spots, then pass them by. If it has stains, then it depends on who's going to use it. You might overlook stains if they're your bags, but if you're selling them, you'll have to cut around the stains, wasting cloth. Even so, it might still be a good bargain.

Also check out Goodwill's Bargain Bins. These are super-cheap Goodwill stores. Everything there — clothing, coats, and household linens — is sold by the pound, and when you buy more than 20 pounds, the price drops to just over a dollar a pound.

A WORD ABOUT TASTE

When you are buying fabric for bags to sell, don't rely on your taste. You may hate that pattern of yellow pears on dark brown, but other people may like it very much. Concentrate on how much fabric is available for the price of that big piece. A wide variety of design motifs in your fabric selection means you have a better chance of appealing to a wider variety of shoppers.

THREAD CHOICES

I match my thread to the dominant color of the fabric for the bag body but I don't make myself crazy trying for an exact match. A few dozen bags uses a lot of thread and an exact match often means purchasing tiny, more expensive spools, raising my costs. Go for a less-perfect match so you can use larger spools that cost less per yard.

I match thread to the straps as well, which is another reason to stick to black webbing for straps.

Any good quality, general purpose thread, such as Coats and Clark or Gütermann, will work. If you're sewing hundreds of bags, cones of thread are far more economical and well-worth the purchase of a cone stand. Very cheap thread breaks, both in the sewing process and when the bags are being used, so avoid dollar spools at the discount store.

4. Preparing and Washing Fabric

Skip this section if you bought new fabric from the store.

The used fabric you are most likely to find for repurposing comes in two varieties: tablecloths and drapes. You'll need to restore them to raw cloth before cutting them up for bags.

TABLECLOTHS

Tablecloths come in all kinds of sizes, ranging from little side tables to banquet tables. Bigger is always better. Tablecloths usually don't have wide hems. Unpicking the hem will give you an inch or more of cloth on each side, but you won't get more than that. Measure carefully to see if you need that extra inch or so to lay out bags most economically. If you don't, don't bother unpicking the hems. Rectangular tablecloths give you the most usable cloth. Round tablecloths have a lot of waste. Oval tablecloths, depending on how big they are, vary widely in how much scrap you have left over. A small oval tablecloth isn't much better than a round one in terms of usable fabric. A long, wide oval can provide quite a lot of fabric.

DRAPES

Draperies come in sizes too. They are often quite long, seven feet or more. The width can vary wildly, from just the width of the original fabric to several widths seamed together. Unpick the deep hem, rod pocket or pinch pleats and you can get another foot of fabric.

Drapes are often lined, giving you a second piece of fabric (usually muslin but sometimes blackout lining) to use for something else. A muslin lining won't be heavy enough for bags although you can repurpose the muslin for straps. Blackout lining is thick, stiff, and heavy, but it doesn't like being punched full of holes by sewing machine needles. It doesn't like being washed either. Save it for lining drapes and window quilts.

What you don't want are drapes that have a flocked lining glued to the underside. That pseudo-lining makes them unusable for grocery bags. This plastic-y stuff is unpleasant to sew through, it gets sticky, and it will slowly degrade and rub off inside your grocery bags onto your food. Leave them for someone else. Drapes with this kind of lining may not even be made from cloth. I have seen some that were more like a plastic paper than any cloth I ever saw.

Drapery bottom hems and side hems are easy to unpick. They are often sewn with a lockstitch and if you snip the pulling end, the seam will unzip itself.

The top of the drapes can be more challenging. Rod pocket tops will have multiple stitch lines, separating the header ruffle from the rod pocket, giving you at least two rows of stitching to unpick. Tab tops need to be removed. They cannot be reused for grocery bags, even if you unpick every seam and iron the fabric sections. They are too small and full of needle-holes. Ring tops are the same. There may be a top hem to unpick, after you trim off the tabs or rings, giving you some extra cloth.

Pinch pleats give the full length of the pleats plus a fold under. The height of the pinch pleat determines the extra fabric you will be rewarded with: six-inch high pinch pleats will yield another six inches of cloth plus the fold unders. Eight-inch tall pleats give you another eight inches. Despite the pinholes in the cloth, it is well worth the tedious effort to undo the pleats, particularly if you are making bags for personal use.

To unpick pinch pleats, start by cutting the pleats apart. Examine the front and the back of the pleat. Look for the thread holding the pleats together. Snip this apart and remove every bit of thread. Do each pleat in turn, removing all the stitching. When the pleats are ripped, they should unfold, revealing a paper interior that should be discarded.

Once you have ripped all the seams, wash, iron and measure the resulting piece of cloth. You are ready to sew the secondhand cloth into bags, exactly as if you bought new fabric.

WASHING FABRIC

If you bought your fabric, should you wash it?

It depends.

If the fabric is new, unstained, odor-free, and clean, then no. Any sizing won't matter as it stiffens the finished bags. If you wash the finished bags, it should be by hand in the sink followed by line drying. This will not traumatize the bag.

If the fabric is dirty or smelly, then you should wash it. This is most likely with secondhand tablecloths and drapes, especially from the thrift shop. Don't dry-clean them. It's not necessary, and it's money spent on something that is supposed to be cheap. I prefer playing laundry roulette.

Tablecloths, heavy sheets, and rod-pocket curtains can be washed in cold water with a cold-water rinse and your usual detergent. Line-dry them, and the odors will be gone. If stains remain, then step up to warm water, but it can shrink curtain fabric. Don't worry about secondhand tablecloths. They have been washed before so somebody else shrank them.

Given the choice between the dryer and the clothesline, I prefer the latter. The dryer heat will shrink the fabric, so avoid it unless you want to ensure that your bags will never shrink again.

If the draperies have rings or other hardware, remove them before washing. Tab tops can go through the wash. Pinch-pleated drapes have to be unpleated and the papery stiffener inside them ripped out before washing. Otherwise, the stiffener will disintegrate and risk fouling up your plumbing.

Once you've washed the curtains or tablecloths, rip the seams if you have not already done so, iron them, and now you have clean, ready-to-use yardage to cut up and sew into bags.

Used tablecloths can provide plenty of material for bags. Opening the hem can give you an inch or more of cloth on each side.

5. Useful Tools

Here are some tools that will make the sewing process easier. You can find them at most fabric stores or online.

A SEWING MACHINE, NEEDLES, PINS, THREAD. You can sew a cloth grocery bag by hand, but a sewing machine makes the job light-years faster.

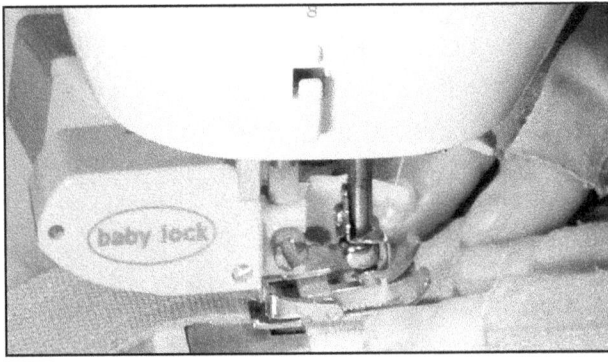

A WALKING FOOT. You don't <u>need</u> one, but it will make your life infinitely easier. I sewed hundreds of tailored bags before I bought one and afterwards, I wondered why I waited so long.

A walking foot controls the creep of fabric as it passes through the machine. Some fabrics stretch as they're sewed, leaving a trapezoid-shaped piece of gusset to trim off and a twisted tailored bag. Sewing very slowly controls this, but not as well as a walking foot does.

Warning: Even with the walking foot, you can get some fabric creep when making a tailored bag. Boxed bags don't seem to have the same issue.

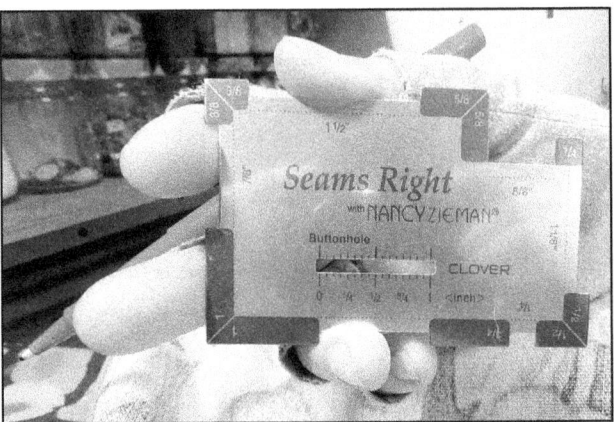

"SEAMS RIGHT WITH NANCY ZIEMAN" MEASURING GAUGE. Clover makes this wonderful little gadget that makes marking the pivot points on tailored bags easier than measuring by eye.

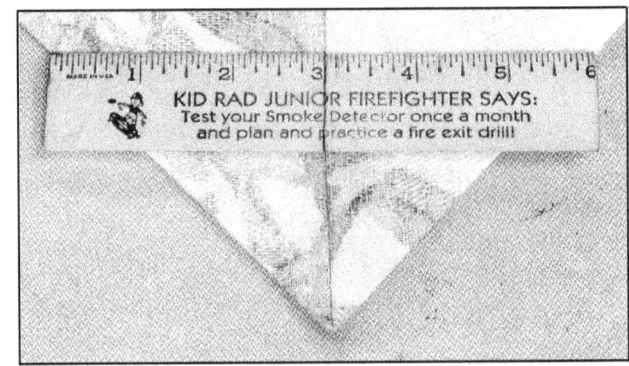

TRIANGULAR-WING SPACER FOR BOXED BAGS. Boxed bags require one additional spacer. Cut a rectangle from stiff cardboard or hardboard that is 6 inches long and 1 inch wide (or use a short child's ruler, like I did above). Draw a line down the center of the rectangle (short ways) at the 3-inch mark. The center line will be lined up with the crease in the bottom of a boxed bag when you mark the triangular wings.

Useful Tools

Spacers for tailored bags in place, with the handle pinned down.

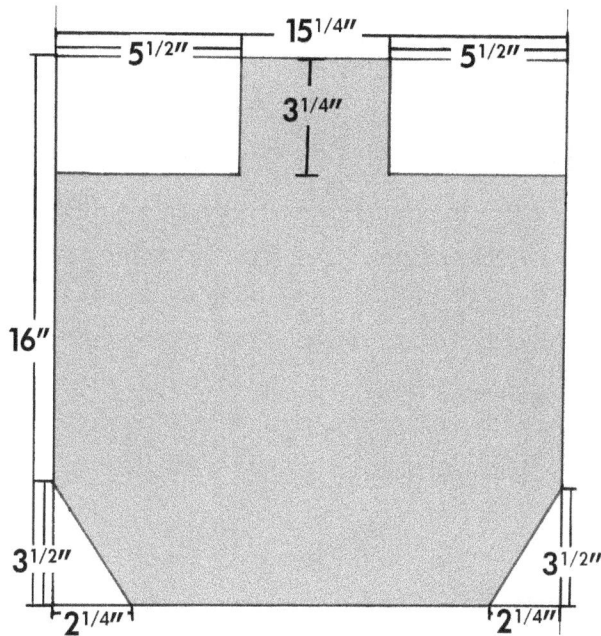

CARDBOARD SPACERS FOR STRAP PLACEMENT. Placing the straps is easier, faster, and more accurate with a cardboard spacer, especially if you are making dozens of bags. The two bag styles use different spacers: They are not interchangeable.

If you are making tailored bags, seen above, using 13-by-15-inch panels, cut two side spacers 1½ inches wide by 14 inches long. Cut the bottom spacer ½ inch wide by 14 inches long.

If you are making tailored bags using 14-by-16-inch panels, cut two side spacers 2 inches wide by 15 inches long. Cut the bottom spacer 1 inch wide by 15 inches long.

Boxed bags, as seen below, get a pair of rectangular spacers, each 4½ inches wide and 10 inches long. They do not need a bottom spacer.

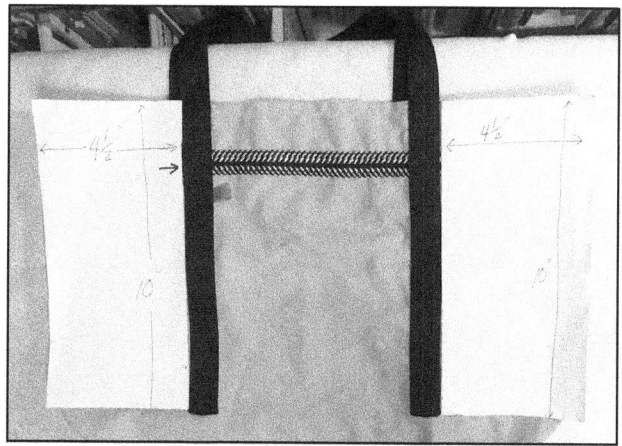

Spacers for boxed bags in place.

CARDBOARD INSERT FOR PINNING STRAPS. This keeps you from pinning the straps to the other side of the bag. After you pin your first bag without one, you'll understand why you need the insert. The boxed bag insert, shown above, is shaped to fit the inside corners.

Boxed bags need a shaped insert that fits neatly into the flat bag. The boxed-bag insert can also be used with 13-by-15-inch tailored bags so you may not want to make a separate insert. This insert has a lot of wiggle room if you use it for 14-by-16-inch tailored bags, but it will work.

Cut these inserts from heavy cardboard or, if you are going to make hundreds of bags, use ¼-inch-thick hardboard found at a building supply store. Use the kind with at least one smooth side.

If you are making only tailored bags using 13-by-15-inch panels, cut the insert into a simple rectangle 12 inches by 14 inches. The tailored bag insert does not require any other shaping.

If you are only making tailored bags using 14-by-16-inch panels, cut the insert into a simple rectangle 13 inches by 15 inches. No other shaping is required.

Useful Tools

60-INCH MEASURING TAPE. You'll use this a lot to mark boxed panels, tailored panels, gussets, and webbing. **120-INCH MEASURING TAPE.** When doubling up twill tape or ribbon to make straps, you have to measure an 84-inch-long section. A 60-inch measuring tape won't do the job.

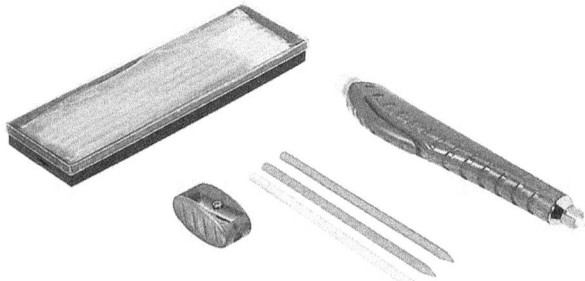

CHALK MARKER. I use the Bohin 91493 cartridge chalk marker. It gives a fine line and the wide variety of colors ensures finding a color that shows on the fabric. Pencil works, but chalk is easier to use when drawing long cutting lines on fabric. Your cutting lines will not show in the finished bag.

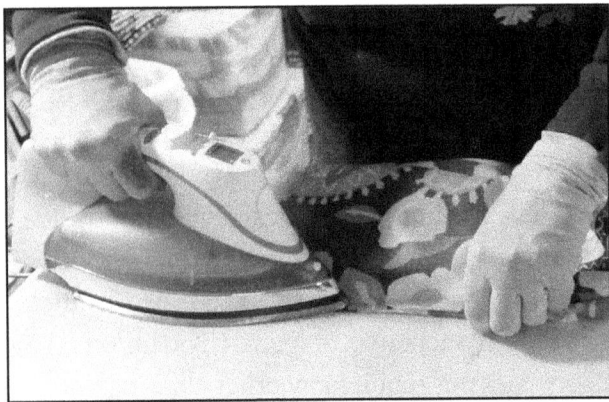

IRON AND IRONING BOARD. You'll use them a lot. The ironing board also makes a handy work surface.

YARDSTICK. For drawing straight lines across long lengths of fabric. Measuring tape will never give you a straight line. Three-foot-long yardsticks are common, but hardware stores often sell metal yard sticks that are 48 inches long (above). The extra foot is very useful.

ULTRA-FINE TIP FELT PEN. For marking the pivot point on tailored bags. Black is fine as the mark won't show in the finished bag. I also use this pen to mark the sewing line for the boxed bag's triangular wings. These marks won't show either.

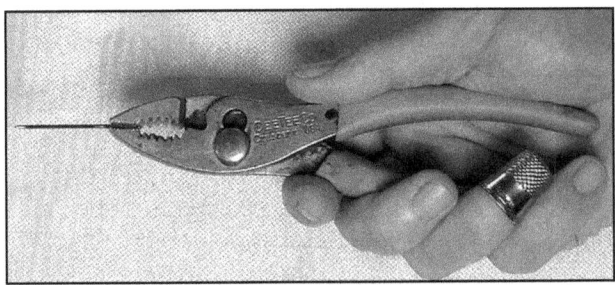

STURDY HAND NEEDLE, THIMBLE, AND PLIERS. You want these available in case the layered seam margins are too much for your sewing machine. If that happens, you have to sew the seam by hand and use the pliers to pull the needle through all the layers.

POINT TURNER. This wooden or plastic tool turns points such as the corners on boxed bags. It also lets you press in a temporary crease when you don't want to drag out the iron. A knitting needle works, too.

Useful Tools

JEAN-A-MA-JIG. Dritz makes this little gem. It lets your sewing machine handle the transition between two layers of cloth and thick built-up seam margins, the kind you get when sewing the foldover over top of the flanges. You're much less likely to get broken needles and skipped stitches. I don't usually need my jean-a-ma-jig unless I'm sewing a heavier fabric than usual.

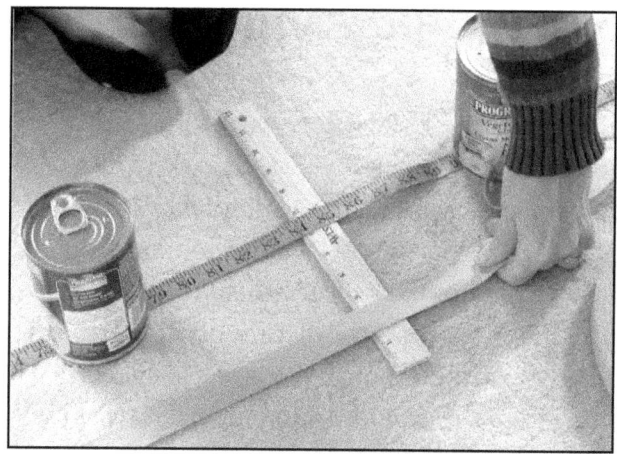

HEAVY SOUP CANS OR SIMILAR ITEMS. Used to weigh down the ends when cutting webbing and especially when cutting 84-inch lengths of twill tape or ribbon.

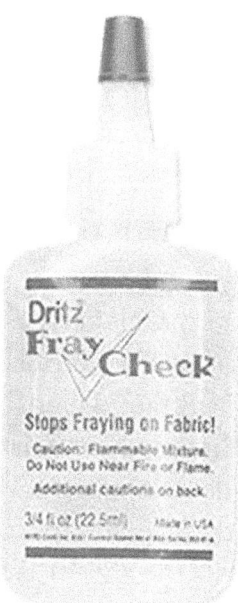

FRAY CHECK. This treats the raw edges of webbing so it doesn't unravel. I don't usually bother.

COMPRESSION GLOVES. I suffer from pain in my hands, so I wear these gloves for all my sewing and writing. They have saved my hands and made it possible for me to work. There are many brands of compression gloves available. Get them in any drugstore or in sewing and craft stores. If you can, try them on before you buy. You want a snug but not painful fit. Fingertip free gloves provide more support than fingerless and still let you sew. I can't recommend these enough.

6. The Bag-Making Process

I designed my cloth grocery bags with several goals in mind. I want my bags to look attractive and sturdy. I want them to last forever. I want them to support themselves and not flop around, so it's easier for the bagger to load them. I want the straps to last for the lifetime of the fabric. I want straps long enough to carry a loaded bag slung from the shoulder, but not so long that they get in the way. I don't want my bags to have raw edges, or spots that can snag and rip the fabric. I want the sewing to be efficient and straightforward.

Whether you make the boxed or tailored kind, these are the Cadillacs of grocery bags.

The list of steps is long, but they're quick to perform. When I sew several bags at a time — never less than three or four — I sew one complete step with all my bags before going to the next step. This finishes all of the bags at the same time.

MAKING BAGS: A SUMMARY

This is an overview of my bag-making process. It's designed to get you familiar with the basic procedure. Don't worry about trying to understand it all now. We'll go into more detail in subsequent chapters.

This is what I do:

1. Choose the fashion fabric. The bigger the piece, the more bags I can cut from it.

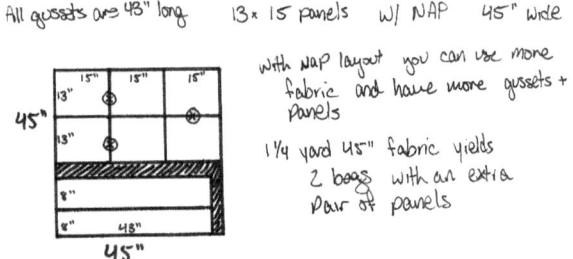

2. Design the layout on paper. This lets me figure out the most efficient use of the cloth before setting scissors to expensive fabric.

If I'm making tailored bags, I want to get pairs of side panels and gussets without waste and without ending up with too many side panels and not enough gussets or vice versa. If I'm sewing boxed bags, I want any fabric left over to be usable for panels, gussets, or trim-lines.

Note: I don't reserve fabric for straps. I use webbing. So my instructions and charts do not set aside fabric for making them. If you use fabric for straps, adjust your layout accordingly.

3. Cut out the side panels and gussets (tailored) or single panels (boxed). Keep the edges clean and true on grain. Straight-grain cuts ensure straight-sided bags, with no twisting or skewing in the fabric. It doesn't matter if you use the straight grain (the length of the yardage) or the cross grain (across the width) as long as you don't cut even the smallest bit on the bias. Clean cuts also mean fewer whiskers to trim later.

After this, the steps diverge depending on whether I am sewing boxed bags or tailored bags. They have commonalities: precision pressing, no raw edges, finishing one complete pass on all the bags before moving onto the next step, and the trim-line and strap sewing.

If You're Making Boxed Bags

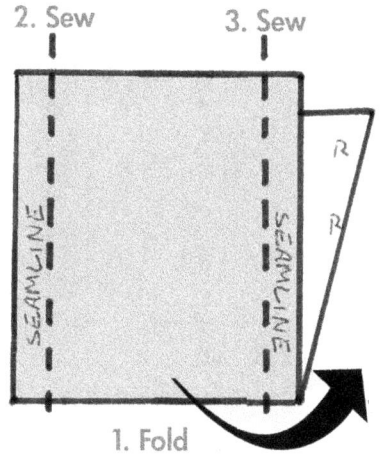

4. Fold the panel in half, right sides together, and sew up both sides with a 3/8-inch seam.

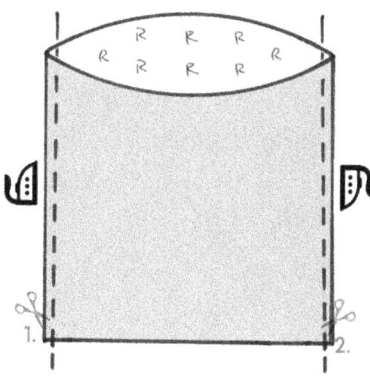

5. Iron the sack. Get a crisp edge with the seam line exactly at the fold on each side. Clip the corners and flip the bag right-side out.

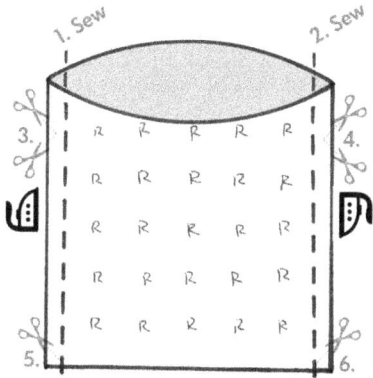

6. Sew a second 1/2-inch seam along both sides, creating the flanges. Cut notches in the flanges. Clip the corners. Iron down the flanges.

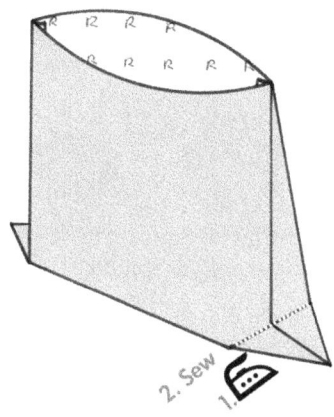

7. Flip the bags so the wrong side faces out. Press, mark, and pin the triangular wings, one pair for each bag. Sew the triangular wing seams.

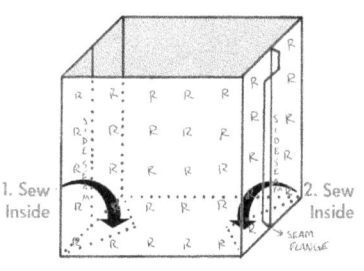

8. Flip the bag right-sides out. Working inside the bag, sew down the triangular wings onto the bottom of the bag.

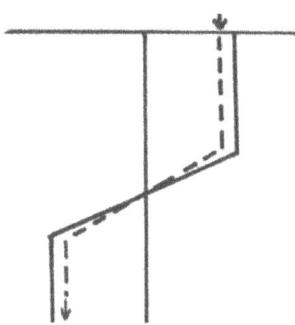

9. Working on the outside of the bag, sew the flanges in place on both sides to provide support for the bag.

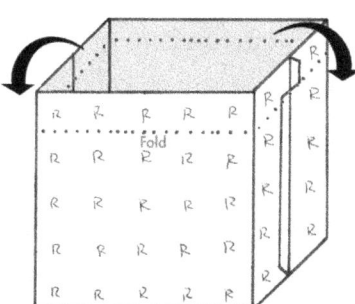

10. Fold and press the top foldover, sew it down, and trim loose threads.

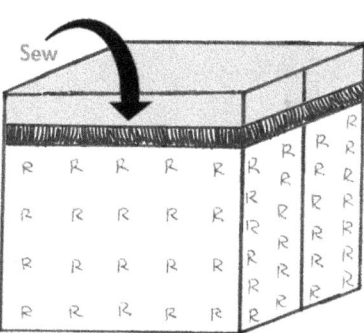

11. Sew trim-line to cover foldover edge.

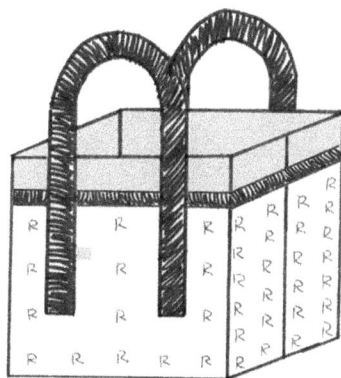

12. Pin and sew straps along with an optional label. Enjoy using the stylish, new bags.

The Bag-Making Process

IF YOU'RE MAKING TAILORED BAGS

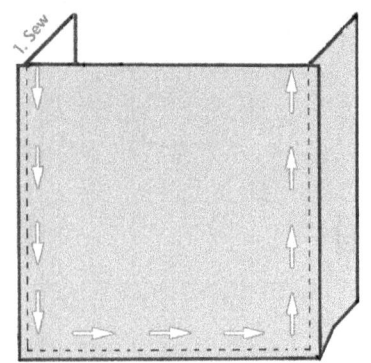

4. With the right panel sides together, sew a front panel to the gusset with a 3/8-inch seam.

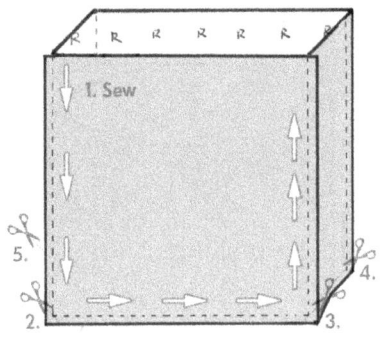

5. Sew the other side panel gusset with a 3/8-inch seam. Trim the gusset end and corners and turn the bag right side out.

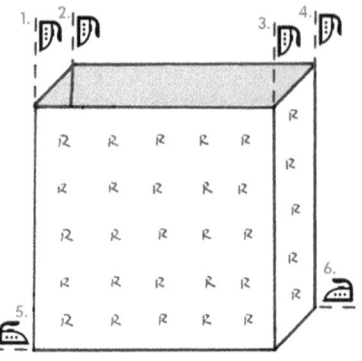

6. Iron the bags. The objective is a crisp knife edge with the seam line exactly at the fold.

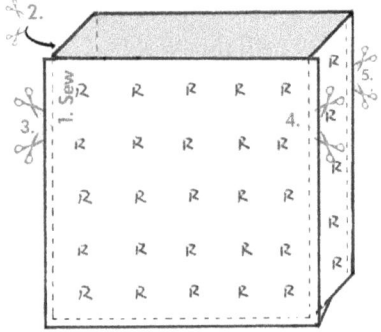

7. On the outside of the tailored bag, resew each seam, giving you a ½-inch flange around the sides of the bag. Measure 2 inches from the top of the bag and snip the flange to mark the foldover.

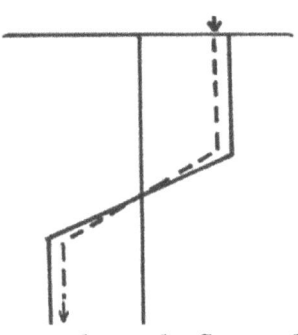

8. Sew down the flange all the way around, providing a supportive skeleton for the bag.

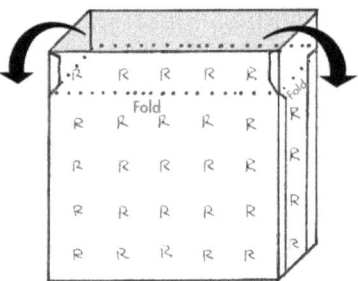

9. Fold and press the top foldover, sew it down, and trim loose threads.

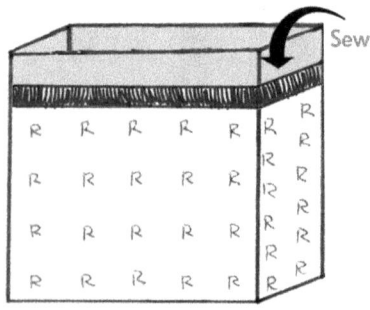

10. Sew trim-line to cover foldover edge.

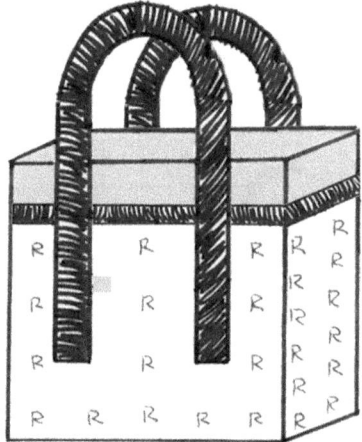

11. Pin and sew straps along with an optional label.

When you're finished, pour yourself a stiff drink or a restful cup of tea, depending on how aggravating you found the process. Then enjoy your stylish new grocery bags.

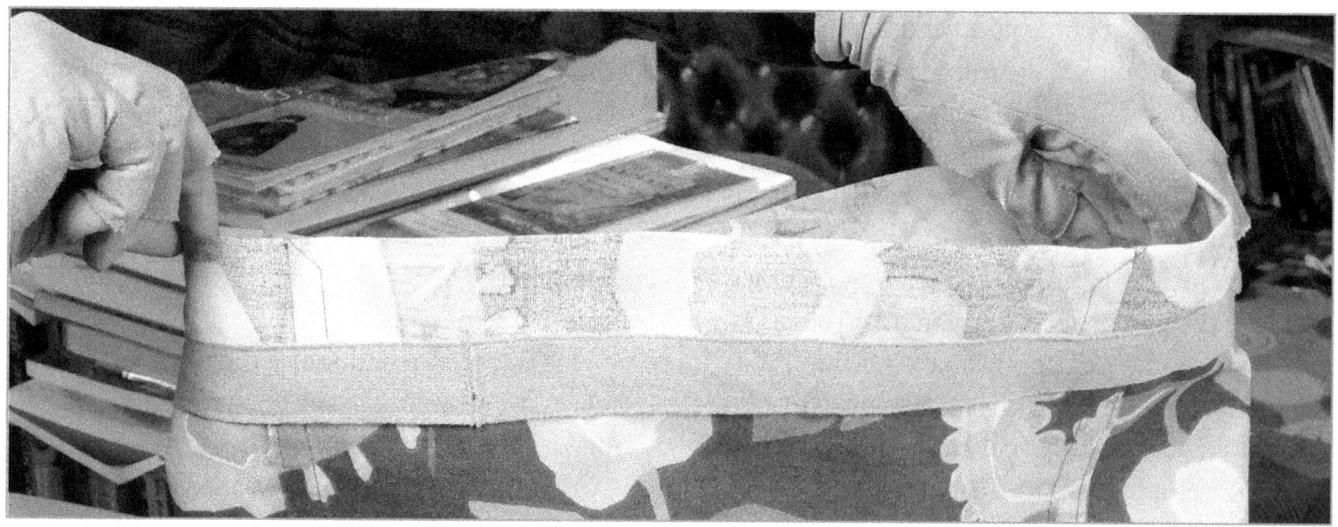

7. About the Trim-Line

My grocery bag design always includes adding a line of trim. This is not just because it looks nice. The trim-line fulfills several functions.

First, it covers up the raw edges of the folded-over top without adding bulk. The alternative is to fold under the raw edges by ½ inch, press them flat, and stitch the hem down. The difficulty lies with the thickness of the sewn-down flange. You are sewing through eight layers of thick cloth, plus another layer for the bag itself. Unless you have a heavy-duty sewing machine, you'll have to sew down this section by hand. A heavy needle, a thimble, and a pair of pliers to yank the needle through the layers will work, but it's time-consuming and hard on the hands.

Second, trim reinforces the bag's structure. This and the straps force the bag to stand upright and open when it is being filled.

Note that some trims work better than others in adding structural strength.

Third, trim is decorative. I like that band of color across the bag, whether it matches the straps or contrasts with them and the fashion fabric. Think of it as the squiggle of chocolate syrup that the restaurant puts on a slice of cake to justify charging $5. This extra bit of color helps sell $10 bags.

How much trim do you need? A tailored bag made of 13-by-15-inch panels will require 34 to 36 inches of trim per bag.

A tailored bag made of 14-by-16-inch panels will require 36 to 38 inches of trim. The exact length depends on the width of the gusset.

Boxed bags will use about 38 inches of trim.

WHAT KIND OF TRIM TO USE

For starters, don't use trim narrower than a half-inch. It won't be wide enough to cover and contain the raw edges, especially if they are uneven. Narrow trim also doesn't lay as well over the thick sewn-down flanges.

Your trim should be flat. Bumpy, irregular trim won't be easy to sew down. It is also harder to sew the straps over top of bumpy trim than smooth trim This rules out a lot of fancy braids and fringes. For example, ball trim may be wide enough, but you'd have to trim off the balls where the straps would go. The same is true of fringe.

That still leaves a lot of trims that are both wide enough and flat. I have used extra-wide single-fold bias tape, quilt binding, readymade bias hem facing, grosgrain and satin ribbon, twill tape,

About the Trim-Line

and lightweight webbing. It depends on what I have floating around. Sometimes, I will iron double-fold bias tape flat — transforming it into extra-wide single-fold bias tape — and use that.

For my Frankenstein bags — named because they're made from pieces of scrap fabric — I'll also use scraps of bias tape, butt the sections together, and hide the join under the straps. Tip: When piecing trim, choose trim that has the same weight and width. I'll piece bits of extra-wide single-fold bias tape, but not bias tape and twill tape on the same bag. I'll also try to color-match the pieces, but if I can't, I'll use what's available. The functionality is not affected.

Before making a set of bags, see if what you're using for straps will work. Grosgrain ribbon or twill tape, while it has to be doubled up for the straps, works as-is perfectly for trim. It will also match perfectly. Webbing is generally too heavy to use for trim, but when it is used, it alone will keep the bag open on the checkout counter.

If you make single-fold bias tape from fabric you already have on hand, the sky's the limit for your fabric choices as long as you can force the fabric through a bias tape maker. Make the finished bias tape an inch wide or so, after the raw edges have been turned under.

You can also make non-bias trim, but if you do this, cut the fabric perfectly on grain. You won't get any stretch and you need a deeper fold under to prevent any future unraveled edges. To do this, measure, mark and cut the woven fabric into 2-inch-wide strips. Press under ½ inch on each side, leaving a 1-inch-wide strip, with the fold-unders meeting in the middle but not overlapping. Obviously, a wider starting strip of fabric will leave you with a wider piece of trim. Don't make your fold-unders narrower than ½ inch.

It is easiest to cut fabric cross-grain, from selvage to selvage, so your finished lengths are long enough to be useful but not impossible to work with. They can be pieced so you don't end up with a lot of short lengths. Joins, if carefully sewn, aren't noticeable.

Don't use cloth that is sheer, open, lacy, gauzy or extra heavy when folded over. Otherwise, use whatever is hiding in the stash. If you are okay with the color match, then the cloth will work. If you're going to use a knit, test it on one bag before you cut and sew a whole pile of trim. Stretchiness is not an asset in a grocery bag.

If you make trim from your stash, rather than using readymade, make it <u>before</u> you sew the foldover so your trim is ready when you are. Having a stack of partially finished bags will also determine how much trim to make.

The trim-line finishes the grocery bag, making it more polished looking and more professional. It is another way to separate your bags from the run-of-the-mill grocery bags.

8. Making the Straps

In my continuing attempts to streamline my sewing procedures for grocery bags, I decided a long time ago to stop using fabric to make the straps.

There are a lot of reasons why. Fabric straps require careful cutting to keep them perfectly straight on grain. They require doubling the fabric to get the right weight and to enclose the raw edges. This consumes expensive fabric that could go into making panels and gussets. They are a lot of trouble to sew, ironing as you go, and the thickness ends up being uneven, with the turned-under hems on one side of the strap making four layers as opposed to the double layer at the fold. When you are using very heavy cloth, this extra thickness matters: in the sewing, in the orientation of the strap (which side do you place towards the outside?) and in how the strap feels in the hand.

I use far more fabric for a pair of straps than you would expect. I prefer long straps with plenty of play. Customers tell me they like carrying a bag over the shoulder and the longer straps let them do that.

I also use longer straps as stiffener for the bag's sides. I cut them 42 inches long, creating a handle that extends well above the top of the bag and extends almost to the bottom of the panel. This ensures that the strap can more easily support the weight of the groceries. Instead of a small, 1-inch square of support, I have 10-inch-long support mechanisms. More stitching equals more reinforcement and less chance of a bag tearing or failing and less chance of a strap ripping free.

Finally, it takes time to cut, press, and sew fabric straps.

One last tip: If you use fabric for your straps, pick something other than the heavyweight fashion fabric you are using for the grocery bags. You cannot substitute something else for the panels and gussets as you can with the straps. Reserve the home-decor weight cloth for the bags.

Using your stash to make fabric straps instead of webbing, twill tape, or grosgrain ribbon is a personal choice. It really depends on you: do you have the time to make them, do you have access to inexpensive 100-yard spools of webbing, or do you have plenty of short cuts of fabric laying around, looking to be used up for some project? If you don't want to spend the money on purchased webbing, then despite the additional sewing time, cloth straps work just fine.

ALTERNATIVES TO FABRIC

Straps can be made out of webbing, twill tape, or heavy grosgrain ribbon. These solutions save precious time because you just cut the straps and sew them down, rather than making the straps first. Cost does become a factor as you already have the fashion fabric on hand and webbing, twill tape or ribbon have to be purchased separately.

The easiest choice is to use 1- or 1½-inch-wide webbing that is used for belts and backpack straps. It is already the right width. It has clean edges and the same thickness throughout. The straps can be cut to any length. It also comes in a choice of colors, especially if you buy it online.

Webbing can be bought by the yard, but it's easier and often cheaper to buy the entire spool. Many fabric stores, for example, sell webbing in 15-yard spools. At 84 inches of webbing per bag — two 42"-long straps — that's enough for six bags with some left over. If the straps are cut 1 yard long per side, you'll get seven bags worth of

Making the Straps

One ideal source for straps is webbing used for belts and backpack straps. It's strong, comes in a choice of colors, and can be bought by the spool.

straps with a yard left over. I like longer straps — for security, functionality, and as part of the bag's appearance — but if money is an issue, shorter straps will work. Just don't make them too short.

Sometimes, you will find lightweight webbing or twill tape that is wider than the standard backpack width — 2 inches as opposed to 1 inch — or even wider. This webbing may be too lightweight to make a satisfactory strap. The solution is to fold it over and sew down the edges on one side and the fold line on the other. This strengthens the straps while keeping a uniform thickness.

I also use grosgrain ribbon, 7/8- to 1-inch wide. This ribbon has a nice feel and the ribbed texture makes it slip-proof. It is too lightweight as-is, so double it, press it, and sew down both edges. Like the folded-over webbing, it remains a consistent thickness throughout. Grosgrain ribbon comes in many colors and can be purchased in 100-yard spools. Since you have to double the ribbon, you don't get as many straps, but you still get plenty from a 100-yard spool. Make sure the grosgrain ribbon is made of washable cloth and made for sewing. Some craft ribbons are made of slick paper and will not work for straps.

Twill tape is like grosgrain ribbon. It is too lightweight for straps unless it is folded over and sewn down. Like grosgrain ribbon, it can be found in 100-yard spools and sometimes in a choice of colors and widths.

Webbing, twill tape, and ribbon can be found at fabric stores. They often sell the entire spool rather than by the yard. Use your discount coupons to reduce the cost. It is also worth looking for a discount fabric outlet. You don't know what you'll find, but the price will be right.

Ribbon spools, twill tape, and webbing can also be ordered online. Look for belting and backpack supplies. I purchased two 100-yard spools of black, 1-inch-wide webbing for $21 each. That's 20 cents a yard. Even better, the webbing is 600-pound test, so it doesn't have to be doubled over.

Sometimes, you get really lucky and instead of finding 100-yard spools, you get a 1,000-yard spool, the kind sold to the garment industry. If you plan on making thousands of bags, this is the way to go, since you'll pay the least amount per yard. For this kind of special deal, you will have to check regularly at fabric outlets and online.

One word of advice: When buying webbing or ribbon instead of fabric, consider the color carefully. One of my spools of 2-inch wide grosgrain ribbon is bright construction crew yellow.

The color is shockingly vivid, and for that reason, the store heavily discounted the 1,000-yard spool to get rid of it. I think it was $10, or a penny a yard. I use it whenever it looks acceptable with the fashion fabric, but it will take me a long, long time to use up all this ribbon. A 1,000-yard spool of dull forest green webbing was much easier to use up as it blended better with just about everything. Construction crew yellow does not blend with anything. It fills the foreground, demanding attention for a mile around.

To avoid this, stick to neutral tones like beige, tan, cream, brown or gray. White straps get dirty very fast so I don't recommend them. Black straps are striking and look good on most fabrics. In the end, the decision may be made for you based on what you can find and what you can afford.

MAKING STRAPS FROM CLOTH

If you are using cloth straps rather than purchased webbing, now is the time to make them. Dig through your stash and find those 45-inch-wide pieces of moderate-weight junk fabric in a reasonably coordinating color. Tear the fabric into 3-inch-wide strips from selvage to selvage. Fold each strip in half lengthwise, giving you a long, very skinny rectangle, press flat, and then fold in the raw edges ½ inch. Press again and then sew down <u>both</u> sides of the strap, tucking in the raw edges at the ends.

One yard of 45-inch-wide cloth will give you 12 straps, enough for six bags. Each of these strips will, because of the 45-inch-wide fabric, already be a good length for the bag, if a bit longer than my recommended 42 inches.

If you use wider cloth, then you will end up with strips that are too long. Cut the excess width down to 45 inches and proceed as above. Don't piece the fabric. That adds both bulk and a potential weak spot.

MAKING STRAPS FROM WEBBING

If you are using 1- to 1½-inch-wide webbing, measure and cut your strips.

Do this on a big table or on the floor. Place your measuring tape (the 60-inch one will work here) and pin both ends with a heavy soup can so it won't shift or move. Place the spool at one end, measure 42 inches and cut. Repeat until you have all your straps. This job is easier with a helper. If you don't have a helper, use another soup can to secure the loose edge.

If you like, treat the ends with fray check. I don't because I cover the raw edges with zigzag stitching.

MAKING STRAPS FROM WIDE GROSGRAIN RIBBON OR TWILL TAPE

If you are using 2-inch-wide ribbon or twill tape (or wider) and it is too lightweight, fold it in half, making it 1 inch wide. Do not cut the ribbon or twill tape in half down the middle. You will never be able to enclose and seal that raw edge and the ribbon is still too lightweight for straps.

As with 1-inch-wide webbing, measure 42-inch-long sections of your twill tape or ribbon.

Making the Straps

When you have cut all you need (one pair for each bag), move to the ironing board. Press each section flat, fold over the sides, and press the ribbon again, ironing towards the fold to push out the fullness. Press each section in turn. It does <u>not</u> work to fold over the entire length of ribbon, press it, and then cut off 42-inch long sections.

When all your sections are folded and pressed, go to the sewing machine.

REINFORCING STRAPS

Start at the narrow end of the ribbon, sewing close to the edge and working from the folded edge. Sew across the bottom edge, close to the raw edge. Pivot at the corner and sew the open sides together slowly, working down the length of ribbon or twill tape. Secure your stitching with a few .4mm stitches at the end if you are using a walking foot; otherwise backtrack.

Turn the ribbon or twill tape over and repeat with a line of stitching close to the raw, short end and then down the folded edge, taking care to sew close to the fold line. This forces the ribbon to lay flat. A line of stitching at both raw ends keeps the strap from fraying. Use a line of fray-check if you think it needs it. I don't bother as I enclose the raw edge with zigzag stitching.

When all of the ribbon or twill tape straps are sewn, press them again and set them aside.

MAKING AND REINFORCING NARROW TWILL TAPE OR GROSGAIN RIBBON

If you are using 7/8-inch or 1-inch-wide twill tape or ribbon, double the length so it can be folded over and sewn to the correct 42-inch length.

You will need your 120-inch measuring tape and a clean floor for this job. A helper will make this task <u>much</u> easier.

Stretch the 120-inch measuring tape on the floor, securing one end with a heavy soup can. Put another soup can at the midway point and a third near the end at the 90-inch mark, past where you will cut the ribbon.

Unspool your twill tape or ribbon and place it at the beginning of the tape measure. Secure the loose end with a soup can or have your assistant hold it. Pull the ribbon or twill tape to the 84-inch mark and cut. Repeat until you have a pair of straps for each bag.

When all these straps are cut, it's time to sew them to the correct length. They shouldn't need pressing.

Bring the two narrow edges together; make sure you don't introduce a twist in the ribbon. Sew across the bottom raw edge with a tight stitch. Pivot at the corner and sew up the long side, pushing the fullness towards the fold. Secure the stitch at the fold. Flip over the ribbon and repeat the process at the raw edge, sewing it again down the second side, pushing the fullness to the fold.

Repeat for all the straps. Sew very slowly if you don't use a walking foot, as you will get ripples. If extra fullness creeps in, gently push it under the presser foot. Tiny tucks work, too. A nail file works well for this.

Press the straps and set them aside.

If, despite your best efforts, you discover a twist in the ribbon at the end, don't despair. It can be fixed without ripping out the entire seam. Cut the ribbon apart at the fold and finish sewing to the end, just as if you had deliberately cut two separate pieces to start with.

When you set your straps aside, drape them over a chairback or table so they stay flat.

9. Outsourcing Tasks

You don't have to perform every task associated with sewing cloth grocery bags. There are many points in the production process where no sewing skills are needed, thus a reliable helper can step in and save you valuable time and energy.

- **Ironing the raw yard goods.** Anyone who can handle an iron can do this.
- **Ironing the straps.** Whoever is ironing your yard goods can do this, too.
- **Measuring and cutting webbing, grosgrain ribbon, or twill tape for straps.** This is an easy task for anyone who can pay attention and use a pair of scissors safely. I routinely outsource this step to one of my kids to save my back.
- **Marking the start location of the trimline.** All you need is the bag, the spacer, and a piece of chalk.
- **Pinning the straps.** Anyone who can handle pins, the straps, the bag insert, and the spacers can manage this.
- **Cutting 2-inch ribbon tags.** I sew this folded over piece of ribbon under the strap to identify my bags. This is a very easy task and your assistant can cut a bowlful while you're doing something more important.
- **Marking the notch point on the flanges and cutting out the notch.** If you've got only a few bags to sew, this doesn't take much time. If you are sewing several dozen bags, have someone else make that 2-inch tick mark on all those flanges and then cut out the notches.
- **Clipping thread ends and removing whiskers from seams.** Another job that someone competent with a pair of scissors can manage, freeing you for sewing-machine duty.
- **Flipping bags right-side-out or inside-out.** This happens a couple of times in the sewing process. As with notches, if you are sewing two or three bags, having to explain what to do to someone else won't save you any time. If you've got dozens of bags to sew, have someone handy to turn the bags as you pull them from the sewing machine.
- **Ironing the 2-inch foldover.** Whoever ironed your yardage can do this task too, especially if you've got dozens of bags lined up, waiting their turn.
- **Making bag inserts and spacers.** Provide the measurements and let someone else mark and cut that cardboard or hardboard.
- **Cutting the panels for boxed bags.** A careful assistant should be able to manage this as it involves drawing straight lines and then cutting exactly on those lines. You may be able to have your assistant lay out and cut the tailored bag panels as well, although these are more complicated to lay out. They also have to be more precise in their measurements because of the way the panels and gussets fit together.
- **Folding and rolling bags for storage.** It has to be done, but somebody else can do it.

OTHER PRODUCTIVITY TASKS

Here are some other things you should do to improve your productivity.

Wind several bobbins beforehand so you don't have to stop in the middle of sewing a bag.

Have a stack of boxed panels or panels and gussets ready to go when you're ready to sit at the sewing machine.

Cut and sew straps from stash fabric or webbing so you've got plenty on hand. You can sew a pile of straps, when the ribbon or twill tape has to be doubled-over for strength, without too much trouble. Fabric straps take longer, but if you've got a yard of fabric and an hour, you can make a set of straps. Remember that plain bags benefit from colorful, patterned straps, as that adds a design element justifying your price tag.

Selvage is the edge of the cloth that credits the designer. I keep it when measuring the fabric unless it distorts the cloth.

10. Cutting Layouts and Measurement Charts

Included in the appendix of "Sew Cloth Grocery Bags" are many cutting layouts and charts that you can refer to while making your boxed and tailored bags.

Let's start with a few words of explanation about those strange drawings.

Remember that I include the selvage in my measurements! I <u>only</u> remove the selvage when it distorts the cloth. The selvage doesn't show on tailored gussets. On panels of both the boxed and tailored bags, you may see no selvage showing ranging on up to a line of color ½-inch-wide or so.

Boxed bags, which are faster to sew, are also easier to plot on paper and then on fabric. They are easier to cut. Each boxed bag is constructed from a single, rectangular panel of 19-by-36-inch fabric.

I chose this size because the finished boxed bag is approximately the same size as a tailored bag using 13-by-15-inch panels. That let me use the same size straps and a similar length of trim for the trim-line. Two 19-by-36-inch rectangles also fit very nicely within a single yard of 45-inch-wide fabric — leaving a 7-inch-wide strip — or a single yard of 54-inch-wide fabric — leaving a 16-inch-wide strip. Best of all, three 19-by-36-inch rectangles fit within a single yard of 60-inch-wide fabric, leaving a 3-inch-wide strip.

This is not waste fabric. Both the 3-inch-wide strip and the 7-inch-wide strip can be repurposed into trim-lines. The 7-inch-wide strip can be made into a strap, although a short one.

If you are cutting your boxed bags from longer yardage, the 7-inch-wide strip can become gussets for tailored bags or pieced panels. If you have enough length, you can piece three 7-inch-wide strips to make another 19-by-36-inch rectangle, eking out another boxed Frankenstein bag from the cloth you paid for.

This excess cloth also allows you to trim off the selvages if they distort the fabric without having to cut narrower panels.

The 16-inch-wide strip is more interesting. It can be recut into tailored bag panels or, if you are using a longer length of yardage, panels and gussets for tailored bags. It can also be pieced to make more 19-by-36-inch rectangles for boxed bags.

Obviously, should you use a longer piece of yardage to cut out more 19-by-36-inch rectangles, you will get longer strips of leftover fabric.

CHANGING THE BAG'S SIZE

If you want to change the size of your boxed bag, keep the rectangle's proportions about the same. The width of a boxed panel should be one-half of the length, plus 1 inch. So, if you make a 40-inch-long rectangle, then it should be 21 inches wide. Otherwise, you get tall, skinny bags or short, extra-wide bags.

Before you change the size of the panel, make a muslin prototype out of that old Hannah Montana fabric and see how the finished bag looks. If the proportions don't suit you, change the rectangle's dimensions and make another prototype before you cut that expensive home-decor fabric.

Keep in mind that if you change the size of the rectangle, your fabric requirements will be different from my layouts. After you make your prototype in the size you want, sketch out the number of bags you want on paper, work out the yardage mathematically, and add a few inches for kerf losses (kerf is discussed in chapter 22). Ask yourself if your chosen rectangle uses the fabric in the most economical way. Does it work only for one width of fabric but not for the other widths? If it does, then when you purchase your fabric, you have to keep to the width that is most efficient.

If you are cutting boxed bags from stash or repurposed fabric, square the fabric edges, measure carefully, and sketch the rectangle on paper. Work out how many panels you get before you cut. You may discover that you can cut a whole series of panels that lay with the straight grain and one extra bag that is cross grain.

Or, you can use that leftover cloth for tailored bag parts or straps or trim-lines.

LAYING OUT TAILORED BAGS

Tailored bags are more challenging to lay out as you need three pieces of cloth for each finished bag: two nearly square rectangles for the side panels and one very long, much narrower rectangle for the gusset. Thus, my layouts for tailored bags are more complex. This is especially true with 54-inch-wide fabric as there is always waste with this odd width.

I provide layouts for both 13-by-15-inch panels and their 43-inch-long gussets and, if you want slightly larger grocery bags, 14-by-16-inch panels and their 46-inch-long gussets.

This requires making an important choice.

Decide before you start production which size of tailored bags you prefer. If you make dozens of bags, you will end up with spare panels and gussets. If they are all the same size, then you can sew the stray panels and gussets together as Frankenstein bags and not waste that fabric.

The difficulty with 14-by-16-inch panels is that their layout takes much more fabric. They don't fit neatly within 45-inch-wide, 54-inch-wide, or 60-inch-wide fabric nearly as well as the 13-by-15-inch panels. Their corresponding gussets, 46 inches long, have the same problem. In fact, you cannot lay out 46-inch gussets on the cross grain of 45-inch-wide fabric at all. You will require 1 1/3 yards of 45-inch-wide fabric to cut gussets, over and above what you need for the panels. They take up more fabric by themselves and result in more and larger waste strips.

This extra cloth adds up, and if you are making cloth grocery bags for sale, you need to account for this in your pricing. Keep in mind that very few customers will notice the size difference unless the bags are side by side.

On each tailored bag layout, I use a * symbol to indicate a pair of panels. Any panel without a * symbol is a stray extra, destined for the Frankenstein pile. Waste fabric is filled in with vertical lines, indicating how much excess you can expect.

Cutting Layouts and Measurement Charts

If you want to make a different number of bags from what I have shown, take a specific chart — such as the one that makes 12 bags using 5¾ yards of 45-inch-wide fabric — and double the amount of cloth. Thus, 11½ yards using 13-by-15-inch panels will give you 24 tailored bags.

If you're using repurposed or stash fabric, you'll have to do some math. The charts can help. It's easy to calculate 36-inch lengths for boxed bags; why, that is one yard! Multiples of 13, 14, 15, or 16 inches for tailored panels are harder to suss out. I did the math so you won't have to.

Chart 1 in the Appendix helps you calculate how many panels can be cut from a particular size of fabric for a tailored bag.

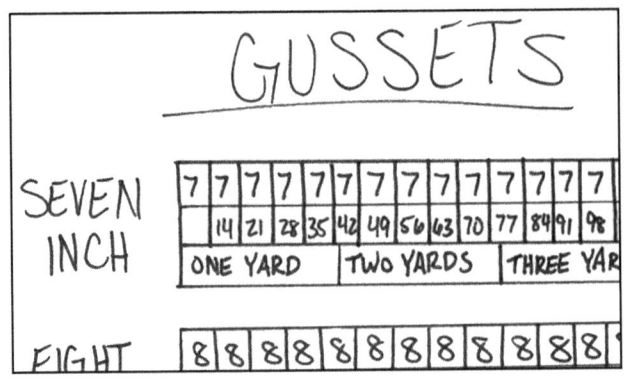

Chart 2 in the Appendix helps you calculate how many gussets can be cut from a particular size of fabric.

So, looking at our first panel chart (13 inches) you can see that if you run 13-inch panels down the length of your fabric, you'll need 39 inches to cut a row of three 13-inch panels. Your fabric width will determine how many panels you will get in each column. Forty-five-inch-wide fabric will give you three panels per column with zero waste; 54-inch-wide fabric will give you three panels per column with some waste; and 60-inch-wide fabric will give you four panels per column with zero waste.

The measurements for 14-inch panels, 15-inch panels (a 13-by-15-inch panel turned on its side), and 16-inch panels (a 14-by-16-inch panel turned on its side) are calculated the same way.

I've also made up charts for the gusset widths so you can see how many 7-, 8-, and 9-inch-wide gussets you can get.

Using these charts, you can estimate how many yards of fabric you need for a 'with nap' layout for forty-eight 13-by-15-inch panels (this is 16 columns of 13-inch panels, three panels high) using 45-inch-wide fabric. It is six yards. That gives you some overage for kerf. Forty-eight panels will make 24 tailored bags as each bag needs two panels: a front and a back.

Notice that for tailored bags this does not include the gussets! Those have to be calculated separately. Start by deciding on the width of the gussets and if you want them to lie on the cross-grain (which creates 2 inches of waste for each gusset) or on the straight grain (zero waste but each gusset will be approximately 7½ inches wide). Wider gussets on the cross grain will use more fabric. The most efficient layout for gussets is on the straight grain, evenly divided into six gussets, each 7½ inches wide.

If you choose this option, every 43 inches of fabric will net you six gussets. To make 24 gussets to match your 24 sets of panels you will need five more yards of fabric.

Thus, you need 11 yards of 45-inch-wide fabric to make 24 tailored bags using 13-by-15-inch panels.

Remember, if you run your gussets on the cross grain, as opposed to the straight grain, you will use more cloth and have waste. But using the cross grain gives you more flexibility in the width of your gussets. It is up to you.

PART II: BOXED BAGS

Boxed Bag Process
(not all steps are shown)

Key
R = Right side or facing fabric
Shade = Wrong side

11. Making Boxed Bags

While boxed bags are faster to make than tailored bags, there are two construction areas that are difficult or non-intuitive to learn.

1. Sewing the panels Right Sides Together. This seems strange to emphasize. Normally, everything is sewn Right Sides Together.

I'm stressing this because I conceal the raw edges using a French seam. A French seam is traditionally sewn Wrong Sides Together, thus putting the finished seam <u>inside</u> the garment. But my boxed bags end up with the French seam on the <u>outside</u> of the bag, forming a flange. I do this so that when I sew the foldover, I conceal the raw edge at the notch within the foldover.

If the boxed bag is initially sewn Wrong Sides Together, like a French seam would normally be sewn, the raw edge where the notch is cut out remains visible. There is a workaround I developed, but the cover-up stitching shows. If you sew your bag by accident this way, read the chapter on "Sewing Boxed Bags With an Inside Flange" so if you make this mistake, you don't have to rip apart the bag and start over. Never waste valuable time ripping bags apart when a patch will solve the problem.

I finish the French seam, which forms a flange on the <u>outside</u> of the boxed bag, by sewing it down. This keeps it from flapping and provides a bit of support to the sides. As with the tailored bags, the finished boxed bag will have no raw edges.

2. Boxing the bag. A boxed bag takes a simple two-dimensional sack and turns it into a three-dimensional box, with four sides and a bottom and an open top. This isn't hard to do as long as you're careful and pay attention. After you've made a few boxed bags, you'll zip right along when you box those corners.

Finishing a boxed bag, with foldover top, trim-line, and straps, is identical to sewing a tailored bag. As with the tailored bags, a walking foot can make the process easier. You'll also use your presser foot to measure by. I don't use pins other than to hold the triangular wings in place and to secure the straps for sewing. So, let's get started!

A note about needle positions. I can reposition my needle from left to center to right, allowing me to use my presser foot to easily measure my seam margins. If you can't adjust your needle position, you'll have to adapt the instructions to maintain the recommended seam margins.

Making Boxed Bags

THE FIRST PASS

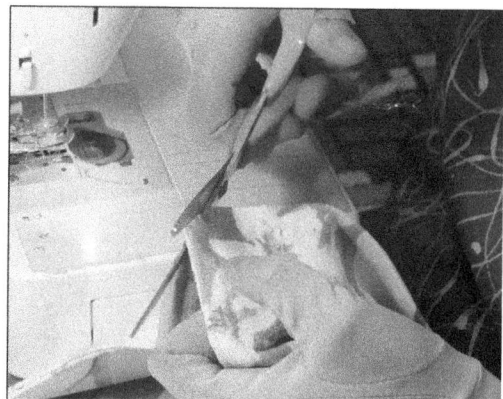

First Pass: Left: Fold the panel in half, bringing the two 19-inch sides Right Sides Together. Above: Snip off the corner seam margin at an angle.

Iron the fabric and cut the 19-by-36-inch rectangular panels. Each bag is made from a single panel.

Fold the panel in half, bringing the two 19-inch sides Right Sides Together. Sew a 3/8-inch seam. I use the presser foot edge as my guide. Sew from the raw edge down to the fold, pushing out any fullness as you go. When you reach the fold, shorten your stitch length to secure the seam or backtrack. Clip the bag free, then snip off the bottom corner seam margin at an angle, up to the stitch line.

Repeat for the other side of the panel, securing the seam and clipping the bottom corner seam margin.

Repeat for all your panels, turning them into sacks with clipped corners at the bottom fold.

THE SECOND PASS

Flip the bags right side out. Iron each bag flat, leaving a knife edge on the two side seams and *along the bottom fold*. The crease marks the centerline of the bag bottom for use later on.

Sew a ½-inch seam, using your presser foot as a measuring aid, down the side from the open top to the bottom fold, enclosing the raw edge. Cut the bag free and clip the bottom corner up to the stitch line. Flip the bag over and sew down the other side, clipping the bottom corner at the fold. Repeat for all the bags.

Second Pass: Iron each bag flat, leaving a knife-edge.

The Third Pass

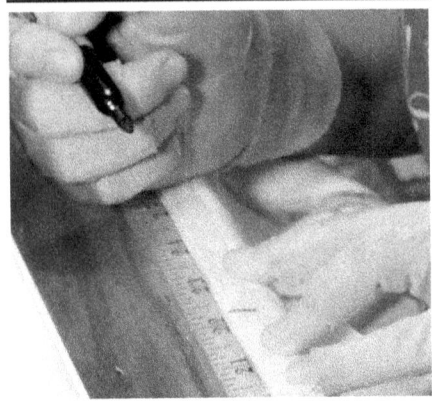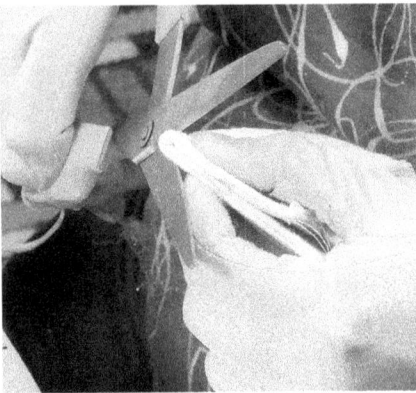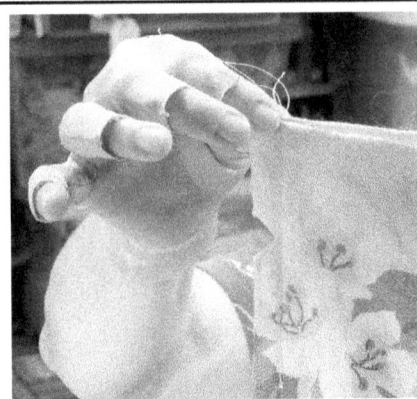

Third Pass: Measure 2 inches from the top of the flange and mark. Clip out a triangular notch on both sides.

You should now have a stack of sacks with a flange on each side (formed by the French Seam) and a pressed crease at the bottom of each sack.

Measure 2 inches down from the top of the right flange (at the bag opening) and mark. Flip the bag and measure down the left flange 2 inches and mark. Mark all the bags.

Clip out a triangular notch at the mark on both flanges, right and left. Repeat with all the bags on both sides. The triangular notch will let you fold over the top of the bag in a later step.

The easiest way to clip out the notch is to fold the flange at the mark and clip so the scissors are placed just a few threads past the seam line. Cutting from the outside in risks cutting the seam stitching.

Slide the bag over the nose of the ironing board with the right flange side on top. Press the flange, pushing the top portion of the flange above the notch towards the right ("R") and the longer portion of the flange towards the left ("L"). That is, iron the top of the flange towards you and press the longer, bottom portion of the flange away from you. Press the flange down and

Third Pass: Iron, pressing the short flange ("R") above the notch to the right and the longer flange ("L") to the left.

get as close as possible to the bottom fold.

Slide the bag around the nose of the ironing board so the second flange is face up and repeat; pressing the short section of the flange above the notch towards the right and the longer portion of the flange towards the left side.

Press all the bags in turn.

THE FOURTH PASS

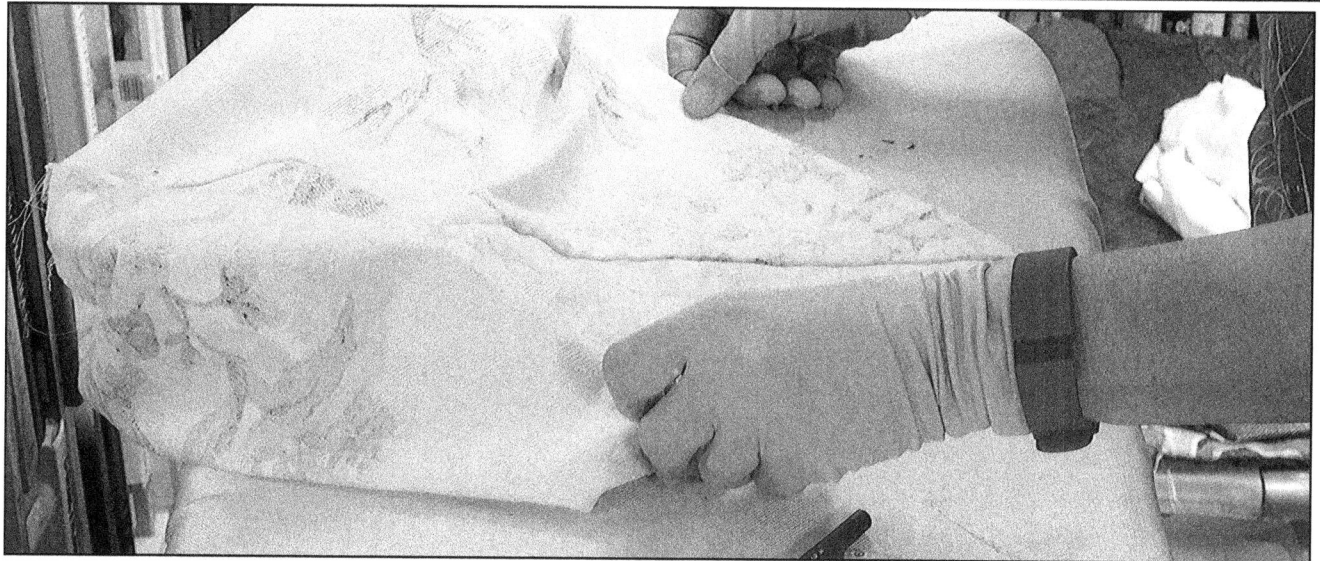

Fourth Pass: Lay the bag on the ironing board with the open top pointing away from you. The FLANGE side should be down and the pressed-in foldline side facing up. Iron the entire square corner down, up to 4 or 5 inches from the point.

Next, box the bags; that is, turn the two-dimensional sack into a three-dimensional bag with four sides, a bottom, and an open top.

The process is not intuitive and it looks odd when you are pressing, pinning the triangular wings, and sewing them down. Suddenly, the flat bag will become a box.

Turn the sacks inside out (Right Sides Together), making sure the corners are completely pushed out. A point turner or knitting needle makes quick work of this step.

Lay the bag <u>flange</u> side down with the pressed-in bottom crease on the top. The bag opening will be pointing away from you.

Remember the bag is inside-out at this stage. The flange will be sewn down later.

Line up the ironed-in crease with the seam line of the flange. You can feel the change in thickness with your fingers. The bag will form a 90° angle, like the corner of a square. Peek inside the bag to check that the seam line on the flange lines up with the crease on the bottom. The flange will lie to the <u>left</u> of the crease with its seam directly underneath the crease.

Press the entire square corner down, up to 4 to 5 inches from the point. The width of your iron, not the length, should be sufficient so use that to measure by.

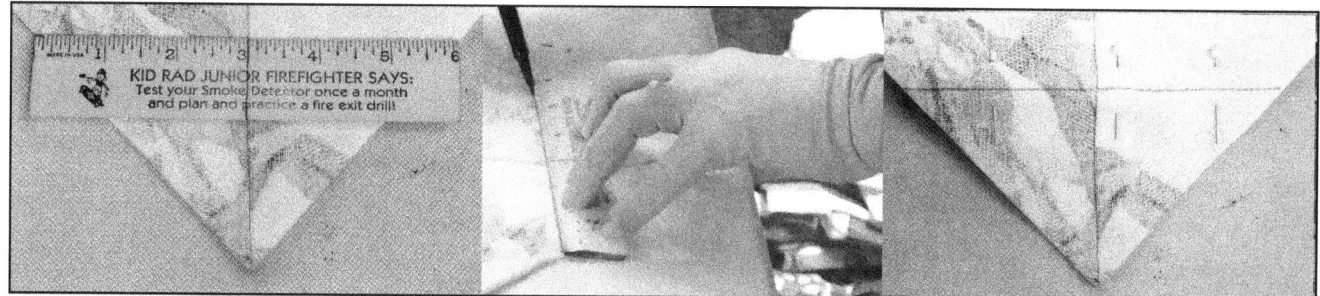

Fourth Pass: Mark the sewing line with your spacer. The sewing line is 6 inches long and is perpendicular to the fold line. Pin the triangular wing, keeping one pin in the flange to hold it in place. Repeat the boxing for the other side.

Making Boxed Bags

Mark the sewing line with your spacer. The sewing line is 6 inches long and is perpendicular to the foldline. Do not measure the sides of the square corner. Instead, line up your spacer so it stretches from side to side, while the black centerline aligns with the crease. Your 6-inch spacer will touch — but not go past or run short — both sides of the square corner you ironed.

Draw a 6-inch line from side to side keeping the spacer perpendicular to the crease. A fine-tip black Sharpie works perfectly. The line will be concealed in the finished bag, so whatever makes a thin, easy-to-see line will work.

Pin the triangular wing, keeping one pin in the flange to hold it in place. Three pins should be all you need.

Turn the bag over and repeat the boxing for the other side.

Repeat with all the bags.

At the sewing machine, sew the triangular wings down along the line you drew, first one side and then the other. As always, secure the stitch line with very short stitches at the start and end of each seam.

THE FIFTH PASS

Flip the bags right side out, pushing out the corners. They now have a three-dimensional shape. The next two steps will force that shape to stay in place.

First, you'll be working <u>inside</u> the bag. Arrange the bag under the presser foot so the triangular wing is lying flat and pulled smoothly away from its forming seam. Sew all around the wing, 1/8-inch inside the edge, onto the bottom of the bag. Rotate the bag and sew down the other triangular wing. Keep the point of each wing aimed at the ironed crease across the bottom of the bag. I use the toe of the presser foot to measure my seam margin. Sewing down the wings reinforces the bottom of the bag, helping it keep its shape. The wings are pulled away from the side of the bag so the outside corner you are shaping is sharp, without tucked or folded fabric.

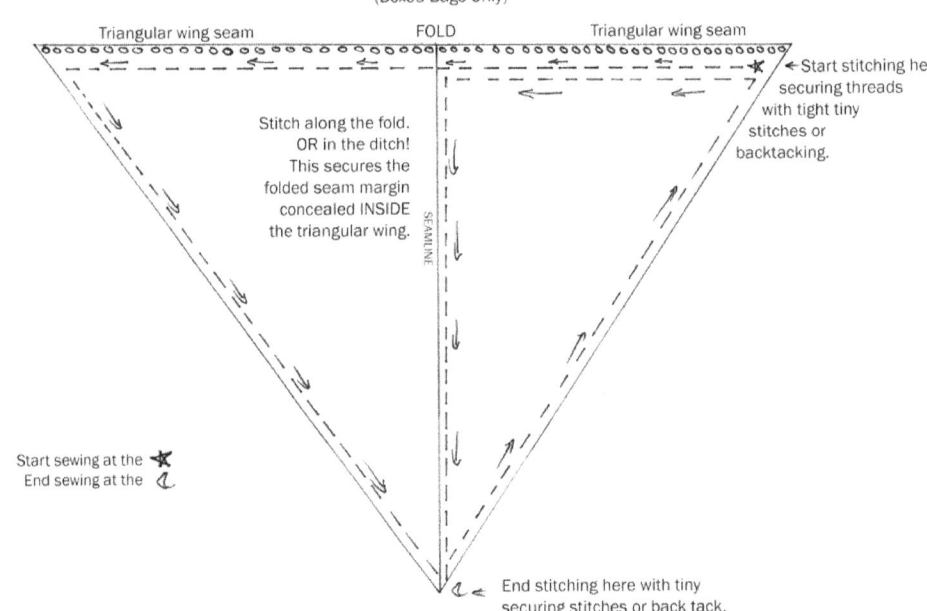

Refer to the stitch diagram above for the recommended sewing order. A larger, more readable version can be found on page 102.

Repeat for every bag, sewing all the triangular wings down, working inside each bag. A regular presser foot is easier to maneuver in this tight space than a walking foot.

(I find it easier to sew the triangular wings down inside the bag, rather than working with the bag inside-out, sewing the wings down, and then flipping the bag right-sides out. See what works better for you.)

Making Boxed Bags

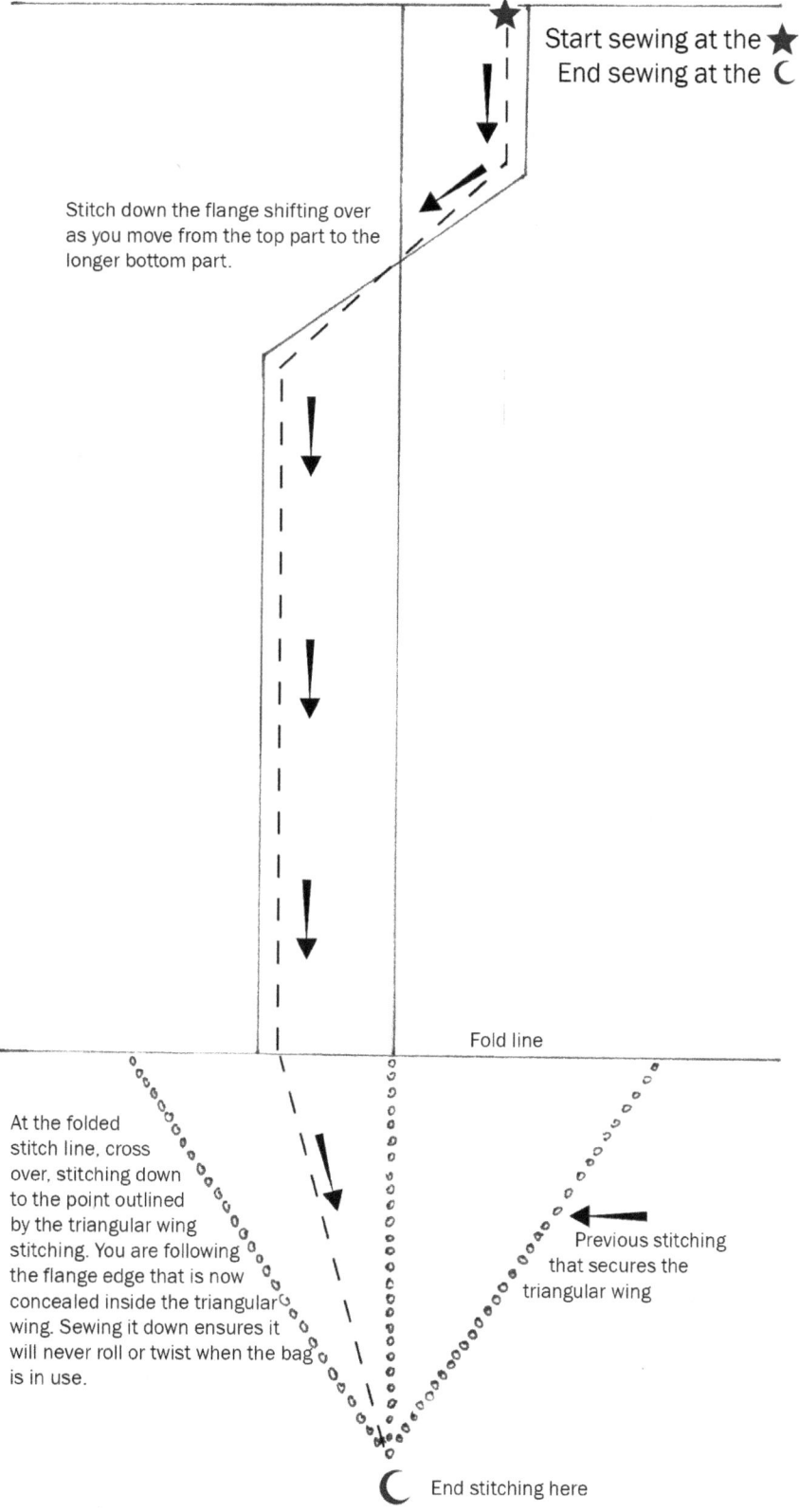

Flange Stitch Diagram
(Boxed Bags Only)

Start sewing at the ★
End sewing at the ☾

Stitch down the flange shifting over as you move from the top part to the longer bottom part.

Fold line

At the folded stitch line, cross over, stitching down to the point outlined by the triangular wing stitching. You are following the flange edge that is now concealed inside the triangular wing. Sewing it down ensures it will never roll or twist when the bag is in use.

Previous stitching that secures the triangular wing

End stitching here

Second, on the *outside* of the bag, edgestitch down the flange. The upper portion of the flange (2 inches long) should be pressed to the right and the lower, longer portion of the flange should be pressed to the left. Starting at the top of the bag, sew down. Pivot at the notch, following the raw edge over to the lower side of the flange and pivot again. Follow down the outside edge of the flange, over the triangular wing seam and down into the point of the stitched triangle. The presser foot will align nicely with the lower, longer portion of the flange.

Sew all the way, following the thickness of the flange when it disappears into the triangular wing and stopping at the seam line that secures the triangular wing. This secures the flange, ensuring it won't roll, distort, or twist, when the bag is used.

Flip the bag over and edgestitch the second flange the same way, continuing down to the side of the triangular point. Secure your seam with a ¼ inch of very short stitches.

Repeat these steps for all the bags.

The Sixth Pass

The next steps — making the foldover, sewing the trim-line, and adding the straps — are identical to what you do when constructing tailored bags.

The bag is kept right-side out.

At the ironing board, fold over the top 2 inches using the triangular notches as a guide. The wrong side of the bag's fabric will show as a decorative edge. Press the foldover down, making sure the flange seams lie alongside each other without overlapping. The triangular notch you cut out will allow the foldover to lie flat, with no bulk at the foldline.

Press both sides of the bag top edges flat, then press out any other wrinkles in the bags.

Iron the foldovers on all the bags.

At the sewing machine, sew down the center of the flange, stitching in the ditch. Rotate the bag and sew down the center of the remaining flange. Then sew a seam 3/8 inch from the foldline all around the bag top to secure the foldover.

It is faster to handle each bag once, rather than sewing all the flanges on all the bags, and then sewing the 3/8-inch seam along the foldline.

Sew each bag in turn.

The trim-line comes next. This strip of trim wraps horizontally around the bag, covering the raw edge of the foldover. We want to hide where the two ends of the trim meet, so let's figure out where the bag's straps will be sewn down, and hide it under that.

Lay the bag flat on the ironing board. Use the boxed strap spacer and mark the bag (left front side only) with where the left side of the strap lies. When you sew the straps on later, you will conceal the butt joint in your trim-line.

The trim-line encloses the raw edges and stiffens the opening of the bag. Your trim should be ½ to 2 inches wide as described in Chapter 7.

Folding over the top 2 inches will reveal the wrong side of the bag's fabric as a decorative edge.

Notes On Sewing On The Trim

- I do not measure trim in advance. I sew it down and cut it short as needed to minimize waste.
- I don't pin down the trim-line, but sew it down by eye.
- The trim-line's bottom edge should be placed just below the raw edge of the foldover.
- The narrowest trim, ½ inch wide, will just cover the raw edge. There won't be much margin of error. I normally choose wider trim so that the bottom edge of the trim lies just below the raw edge of the foldover and the upper edge of the trim falls where it falls.
- Place very wide trim (2 inches) so that the bottom edge lies further down the bag and less of the foldover is covered up. The exact arrangement depends on the width of the trim and what you think looks best.
- I match my top thread to blend in with the trim, just as I match my bobbin thread to the bag fabric.

How To Sew Down The Trim

Sew down the trim, starting at the top edge [Point 1 on the diagram at right]. Adjust the stitch to whatever length the trim wants. Allow the trim to unspool as you sew all around the bag [2].

As you close in on your starting position, clip the trim to the exact length so the ends butt together. Thin, flat trim like ribbon can overlap.

When you reach your starting point [3], cross back onto the original stitch line, pivot, and sew down the width of the trim to its lower edge [4]. Pivot and sew around the bag in the same direction [5]. If any fullness accrues in the trim, trim it short or push the excess under the strap. When you reach the end, secure the stitch. [6]

You are sewing the trim down in one continuous motion, all the way around twice, rather than starting and stopping a stitch line.

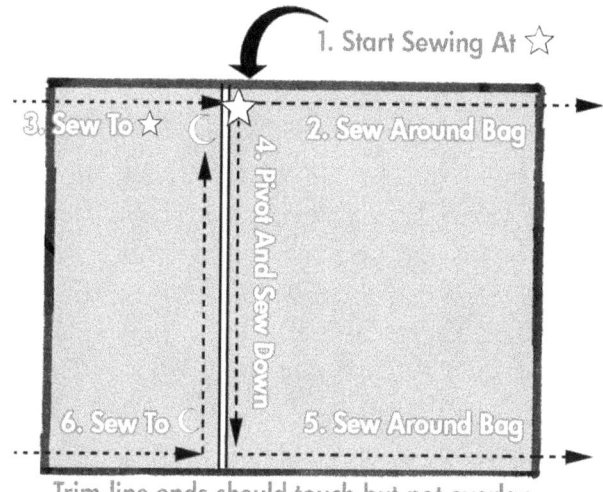

Trim-line ends should touch but not overlap.

This method is faster when you have dozens of bags to sew.

Sew the trim-line on all the bags before proceeding.

The Seventh Pass

If you haven't done so, make your straps as described in Chapter 8. You need two for each bag.

The Eighth Pass

Pin the straps on the bag. The procedure is identical to what you do with a tailored bag, but it uses a different set of cardboard spacers.

Boxed bags get a pair of rectangular spacers, each 4½ inches wide and 10 inches long. They do not need a bottom spacer.

I use different strap spacers for the boxed bags since they do not have a convenient, highly visible seam going all around the bag with which to measure. The only landmarks for measuring on a boxed bag are the sides of the bag, when it is laid flat on the work surface. These side seams need to be at opposite ends of the flat bag, and as far apart as they'll go.

Lay the bag on the ironing board, face up and lying flat with the side seams at each side. Slide the cardboard insert into the bag. The insert is vital because it keeps you from pinning the straps to both the front and the back of the

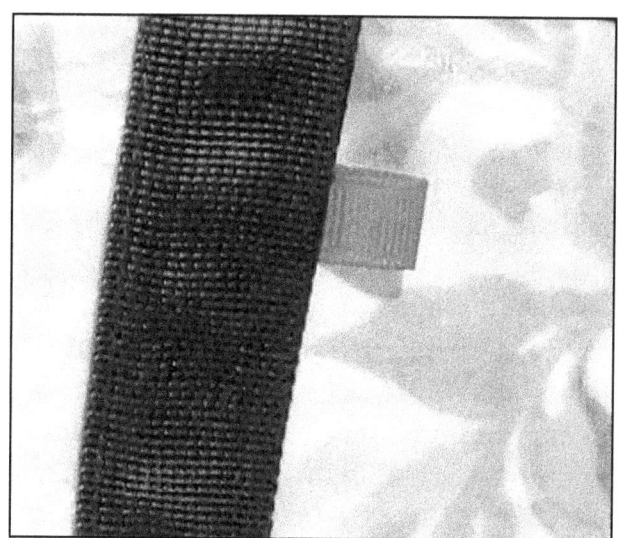

I add a red ribbon tag under the strap. It adds a pop of color and provides a finished look.

bag! It's impossible to pin the straps correctly without the insert keeping the pins away from the other side.

Making Boxed Bags

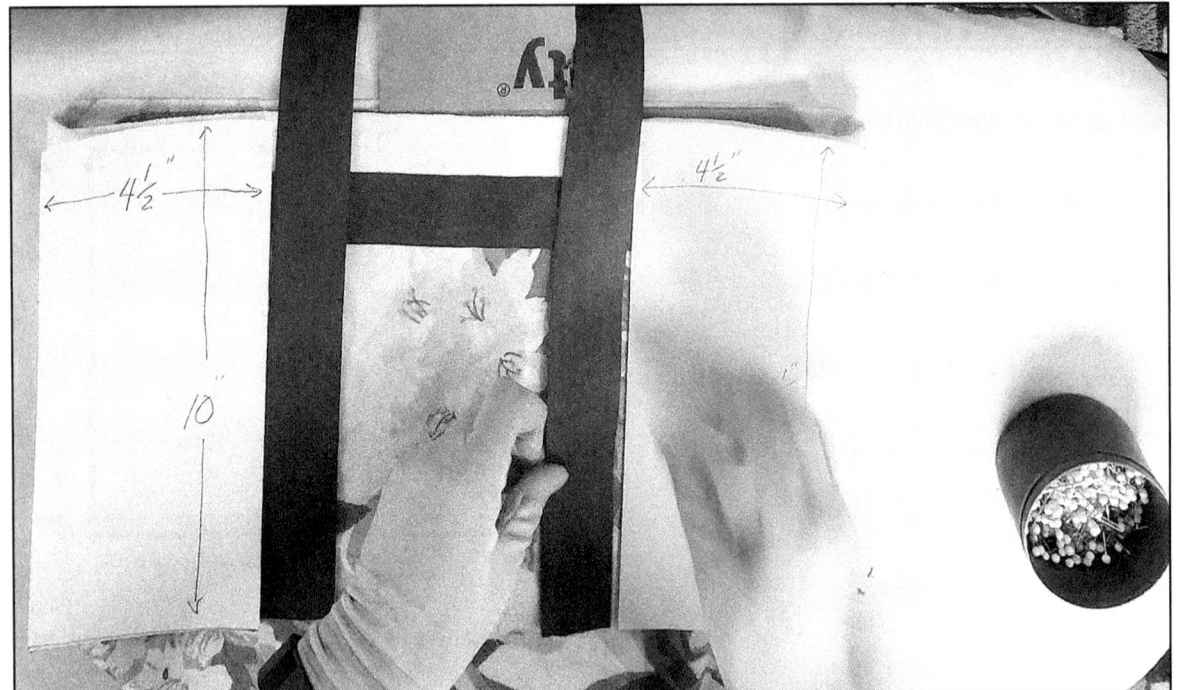

With the trimline sewn down, put the cardboard insert in the bag. Place a cardboard spacer over each end of the bag. Position a strap in an upside-down U shape on one side of the bag and pin in place.

Lay your spacers on each side of the bag, aligning the top of the spacers with the top of the bag and the sides of the spacers with the sides of the bag. Arrange a strap alongside the spacers, with the bottom of the strap aligning with the bottom of the spacers.

Remember that the strap's two legs will be sewn on the same side of the bag; they do not straddle the flange seam.

Pin the strap in place.

Flip the bag over, adjust the bag insert, replace both strap spacers and pin down the legs of the second strap as before.

If you have one, add your ribbon tag under the left leg of the strap where it looks best. A ribbon tag isn't necessary; I like the pop of color and it provides a finished look. If you sew bags for sale, you may want to purchase labels with your company logo. Sew your company label here (in place of the ribbon) so your bag can be easily identified by potential customers. Repeat for each bag.

At the sewing machine, sew down the straps, finishing one bag before moving onto the next. Be careful to keep the front and back of the bag apart as you sew the straps down. It's all too easy and hugely irritating to catch the back of the bag or a part of a strap in your seam and then have to rip out the bad stitching. Edgestitch all around each strap with a second line of stitching just inside the first line. Cover the raw end of the strap leg with a zigzag stitch, completely enclosing the edge. Sew the folded-over strap end with a regular line of stitching.

The stitching diagrams for the straps are found on pages 45 to 47.

I do a lot of backing and forthing when sewing, so that each strap leg is sewn down with a continuous line of stitching, adjusting the needle and stitch as necessary. Continuous stitching means less thread cutting, fewer readjustments of the bag in the machine, and a stronger set of stitch lines holding the straps in place.

Repeat the procedure for each bag.

After each bag is sewn, check for and remove any stray hanging threads or whiskers.

Store them flat or roll them and place in a bag. Both ways keep the bags neat and wrinkle-free.

Making Boxed Bags

Strap Stitching Diagram
(Boxed and Tailored Bags)

This is one continuous line of stitching giving an outer line that follows the left edge of the strap edge, encloses the raw bottom end with zigzagging, goes back up the right strap, goes across the width of the strap, back tracks a few stitches, then back down the left side of the strap 1/8 inch inside the 1st row of stitching.

At the bottom of the strap, switch back over to zigzagging, sew over and just above the previous set of zigzag to further cover and contain the strap's raw edge.

Then, sew a straight stitch back up the right side of the strap 1/8-inch inside the outer line. Go up to the top, back track down 1/2-inch, then stitch to the right edge, then across the strap to the left edge, then back across again to the right edge, securing your stitch.

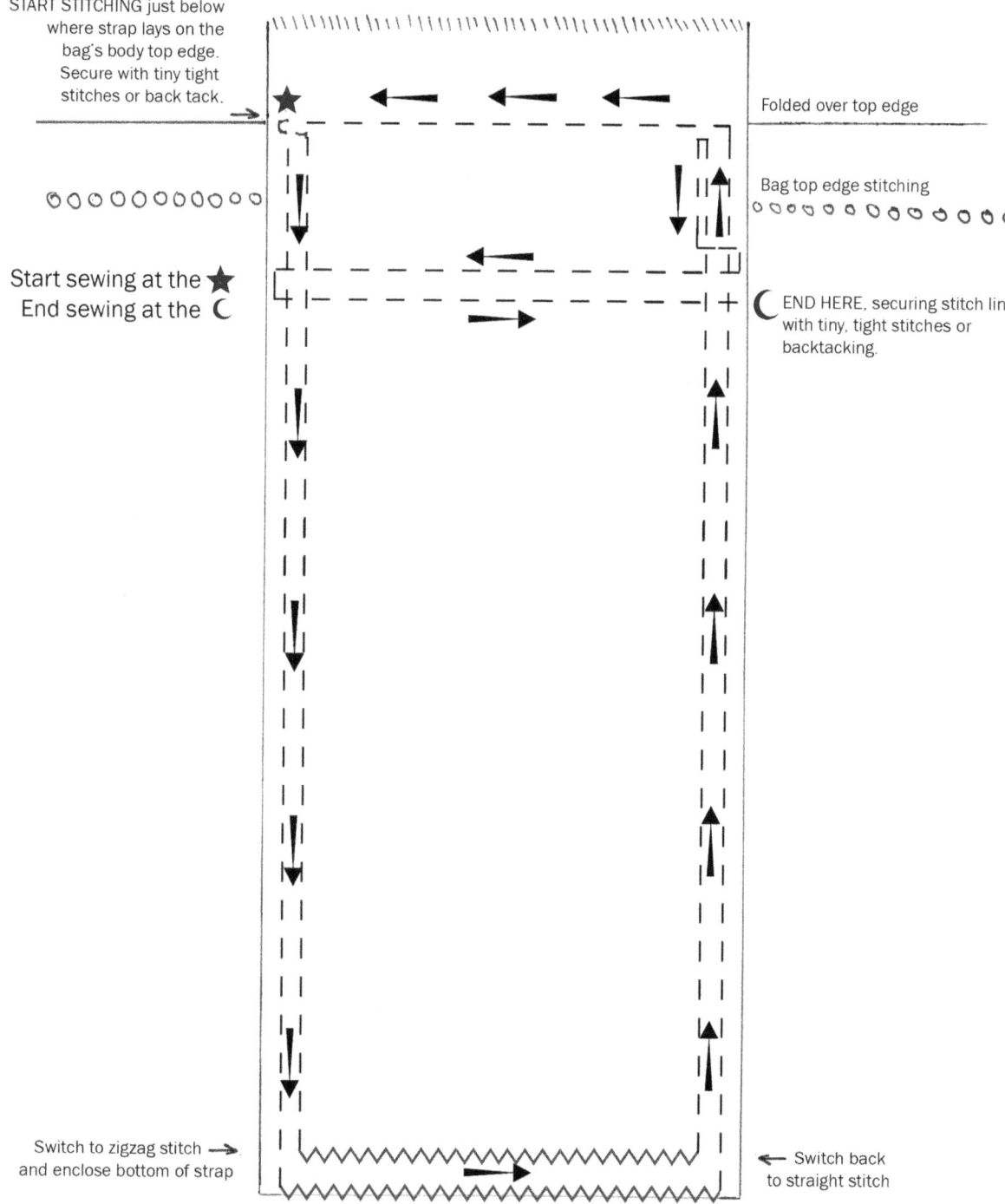

Top edge of bag strap stitching
(Boxed and Tailored Bags)

Do a lot of back tracking at the top. It's faster, stronger and neater than starting and stopping separate lines of stitching.

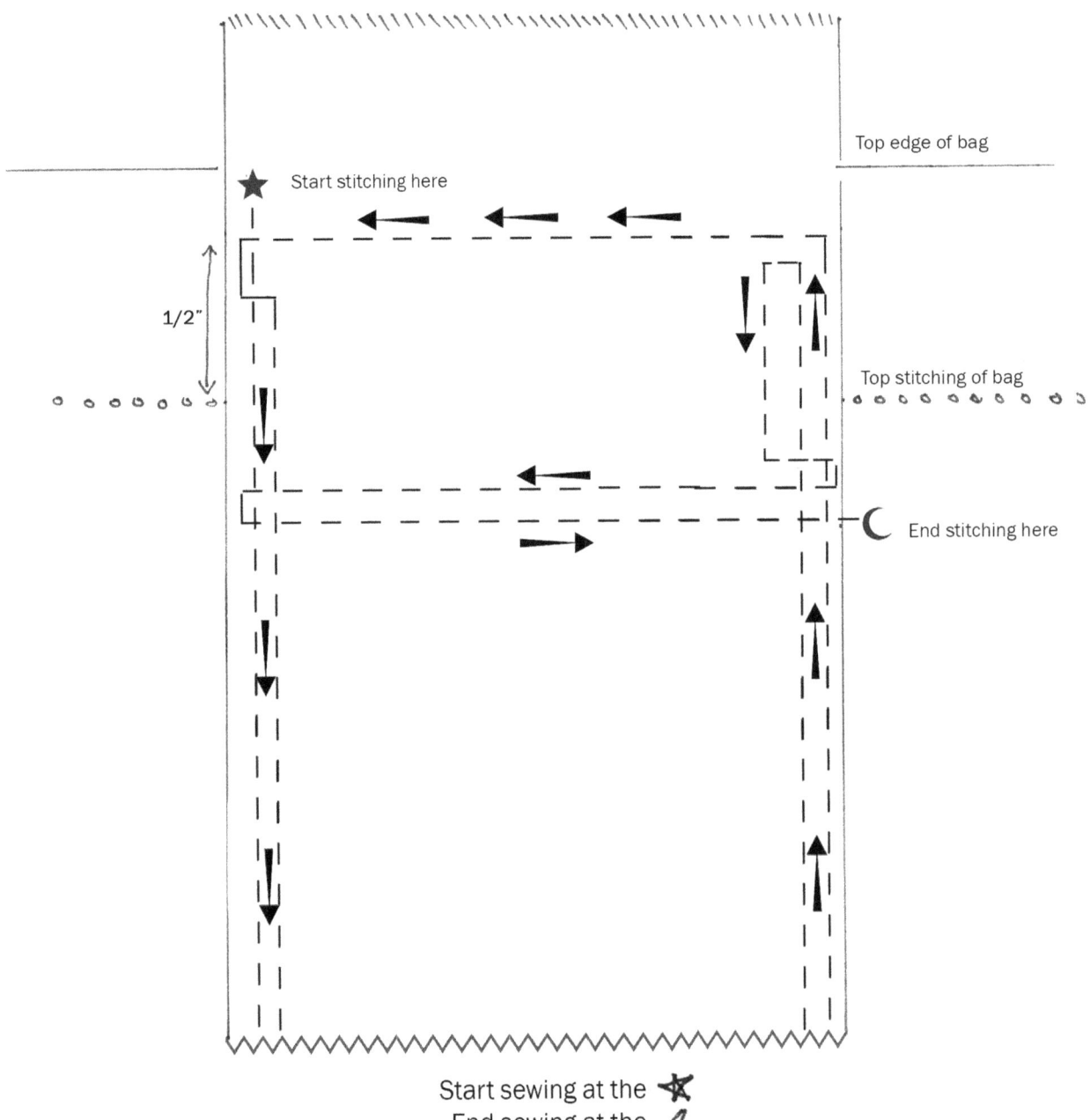

Start sewing at the ★
End sewing at the ☾

Bottom edge of bag strap stitching
(Boxed and Tailored Bags)

The second set of zigzagging is slightly offset and higher than the first row. This better contains the raw edge AND spreads the stitching out so you don't get a huge lump of thread that catches the presser foot. Sew the second inner row of stitches (1/8-inch from the outer edge) keeping 1/8-inch distance until you near the bottom. At that point, my inner stitch line merges with my outer stitch line so I cover MORE of the bottom strap edge with zigzagging.

You don't HAVE to do this BUT the corners of the webbing are where it is MOST likely to fail. MORE zigzagging secures and covers the corners best.

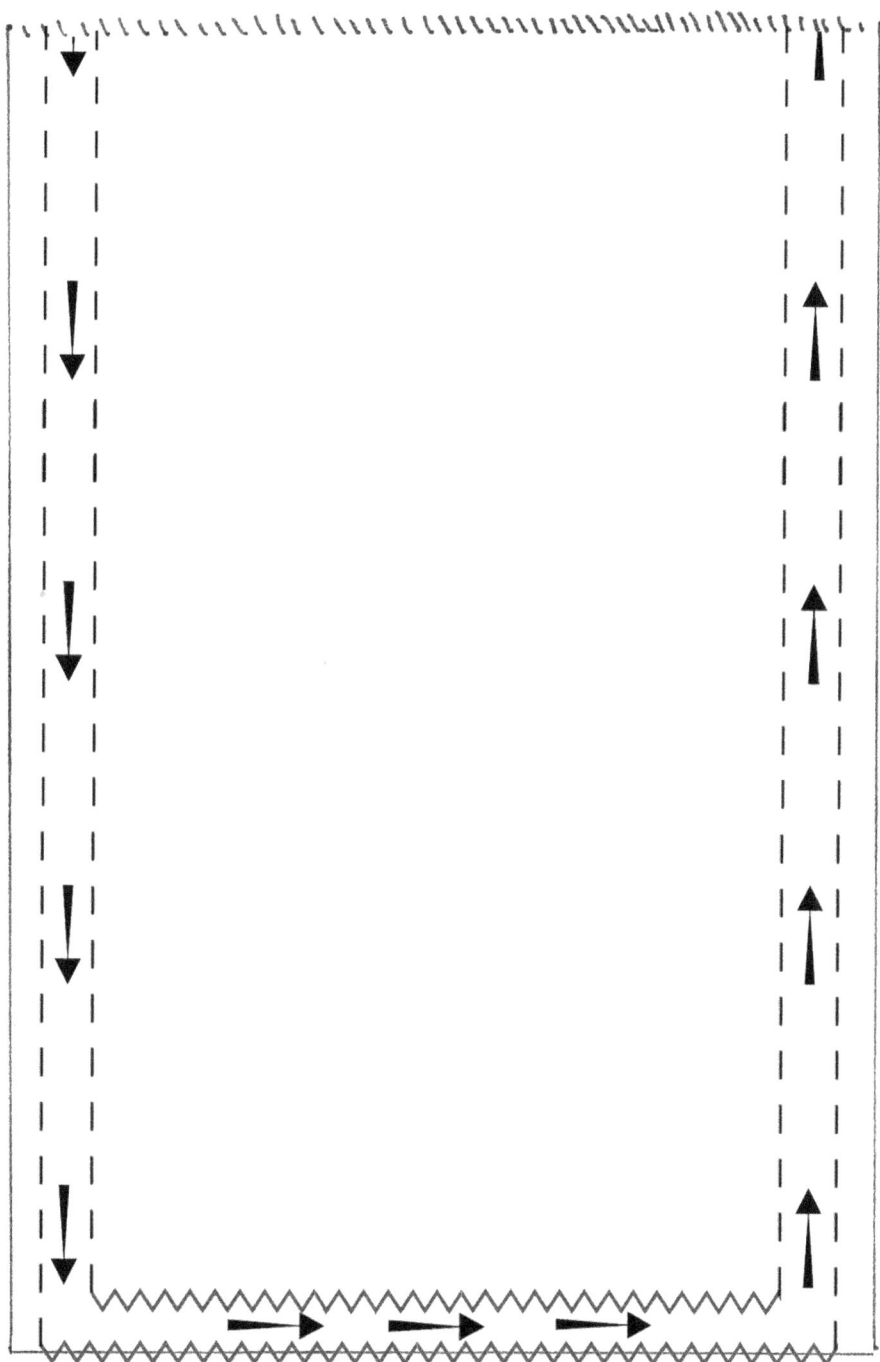

12. Boxed Bags With the Flange On the Inside

I normally sew my boxed bags with the flange on the outside of the finished bag. That means the French seam shows, but there are no raw edges anywhere on the finished bag. Constructing the bag so the flange is on the inside leaves an exposed raw edge that must be zigzagged over. This will show, but you may prefer the way the finished bag looks otherwise.

If you want the flange on the inside of the bag — or you sewed the first pass with the fabric the wrong way — here's how to deal with it. The procedure is similar to boxed bags with the flange on the outside, but with a few critical differences.

THE PROCESS

1. Fold over the 19-by-36-inch panel, short sides touching, with the Wrong Sides Together.

2. Starting at the top opening, sew down both sides with a 3/8-inch seam, finishing at the bottom fold.

3. Clip both bottom corners at an angle.

4. Flip the bag inside out, so the fabric is right sides together, and poke out the corners.

5. Press a knife-edge crease at each seam and press a crease at the bottom of the bag. This bottom crease will mark the centerline of the bag's bottom.

6. Starting at the bag opening, sew down each side with a ½-inch seam, ending at the bottom fold. DO <u>NOT</u> CLIP THE CORNERS! You now have a flange on each side.

7. Make a tick mark 2 inches down from the top on each flange. Clip a triangular notch at each mark.

8. Pull the bag over the nose of your ironing board, flange side up. Press the flange so the top section, above the triangular notch, faces towards you, to the right, and the long section below the triangular notch faces away from you towards the left. Press down the length of the flange as close as possible to the bottom crease.

Use plenty of steam and pressure so the flange remains in place until it is sewn down a few steps from now.

9. Rotate the bag and press the second flange the same way.

10. Lay the bag, with its wrong sides out, on the ironing board, flange side down. Line up the bottom crease with the <u>seam</u> of the flange. You can feel the change in thickness with your fingers. Peek inside the top of the bag to double-check. The bag should lie on the ironing board like a square with the corner towards you and the opening in the opposite direction. Press out the triangular corner, using the width of your iron as your measuring device.

11. Mark the sewing line with your spacer. The line is 6 inches long and is perpendicular to the foldline. As with regular, outside flange boxed bags, line up the spacer so it stretches from side to side, while the black centerline aligns with the crease. Your 6-inch spacer will touch — but not go past or run short — both sides of the square corner you ironed. The black line at the 3-inch mark (center) of the spacer should line up with the crease.

12. Draw a 6-inch line from side to side. Keep the spacer perpendicular to the crease. A fine-tip black Sharpie works perfectly, but anything that makes a thin, easy-to-see line will do. The line will be concealed in the finished bag.

Boxed Bags With the Flange On the Inside

13. Pin the triangular wing, keeping one pin in the flange to hold it in place. Three pins should be all you need.

14. Turn the bag over and repeat the boxing for the other side.

15. Sew down the triangular wing on both sides. The only difference from the outside-flange boxed bag is the location of the flange.

16. Flip the bag right side out, putting the triangular wings and the flanges <u>inside</u> the bag. Working inside the bag, edgestitch down the triangular wing starting along the side. Pull the wing out so the wing lies flat and the point of the wing aligns with the ironed-in crease. When you reach the point of the triangle, ignore the square edge of the flange and sew the point as if the square edge didn't exist.

17. Rotate the bag and sew down the second triangular wing, again ignoring the square corner of the flange as if it weren't there.

18. Still working <u>inside</u> the bag, secure the flanges and cover the raw edge of the triangular notch. See this page for the stitching diagram. (A larger version is on page 103.)

19. Begin edge-stitching at the top of the flange. When you reach the triangular notch, lift the presser foot and pivot the bag. Change the stitch to a tight, wide zigzag stitch. Center the zigzag over the raw edge and zigzag from one side of the notch to the other, completely enclosing the raw edge. At the bottom of the raw edge in the notch, change the back to a straight stitch and continue to edgestitch down the length of the flange. Sew to the bottom of the flange, crossing over the triangular wing seam. Pivot at the bottom square corner of the flange and sew across the width of the flange. Secure your stitching.

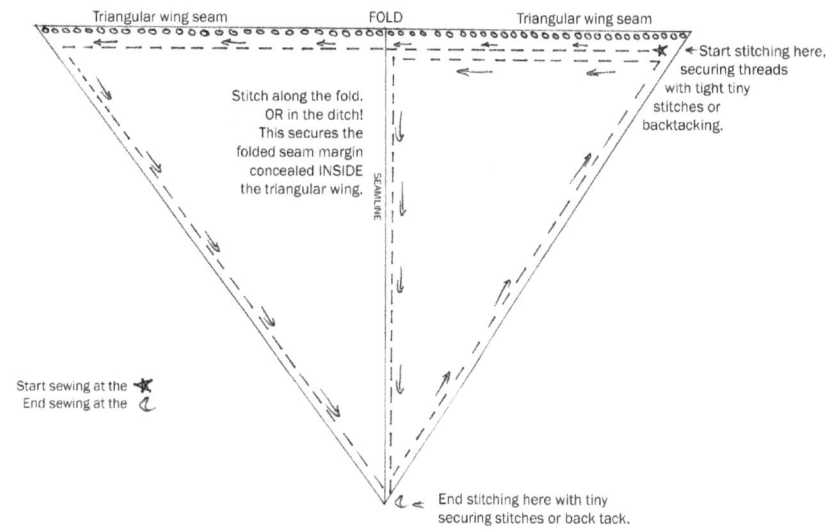

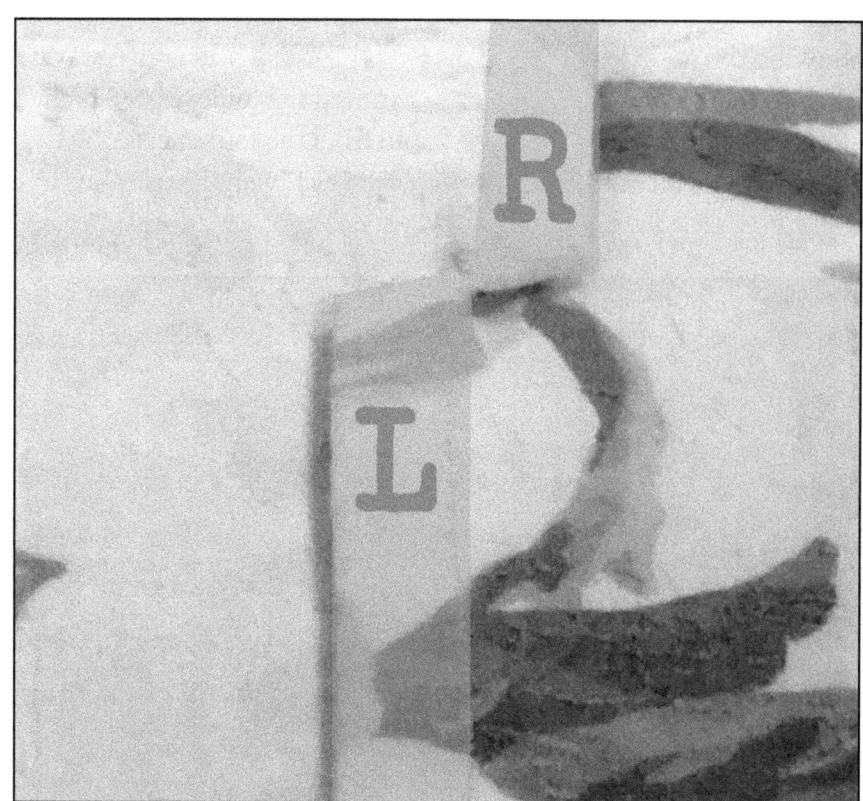

#19: Begin edge-stitching at the top of the flange.

49

Boxed Bags With the Flange On the Inside

This section of the flange is why you did not clip the corner when you sewed the second step on the bag using a ½-inch seam margin. Clipping the corner would have left you with an exposed, raw edge that would have to be finished. Leaving the corner unclipped stops this problem.

20. Rotate the bag and repeat the above steps and edgestitch the other flange, zigzagging over the raw edge at the triangular notch and following the outside of the flange to the end.

21. Examine the zigzagged area on both flanges. Trim whiskers and decide if you need to go over the raw edge at the triangular notch with another set of zigzag stitches.

22. Iron a 2-inch foldover around the bag top. Line up the flange so the seam stays centered at the foldover. Keep the flanges from overlapping to avoid bulk where the seams meet.

23. Sew down the foldover at the flanges, stitching in the ditch.

24. Top-stitch all the way around the foldover, 3/8 inch in from the fold line.

25. Finish the trim-line and the straps as usual and the "inside flange" bag is done.

To sum up, there are a few differences to constructing a boxed bag if the flanges are on the inside:

- Start with the Wrong Sides Together.
- Don't clip the corners when sewing the second set of side seams.
- Enclose the raw edge of the notches on the flanges with zigzagging.
- Sew both the triangular wings and the flanges down while working inside the bag.

Otherwise, the procedure is similar.

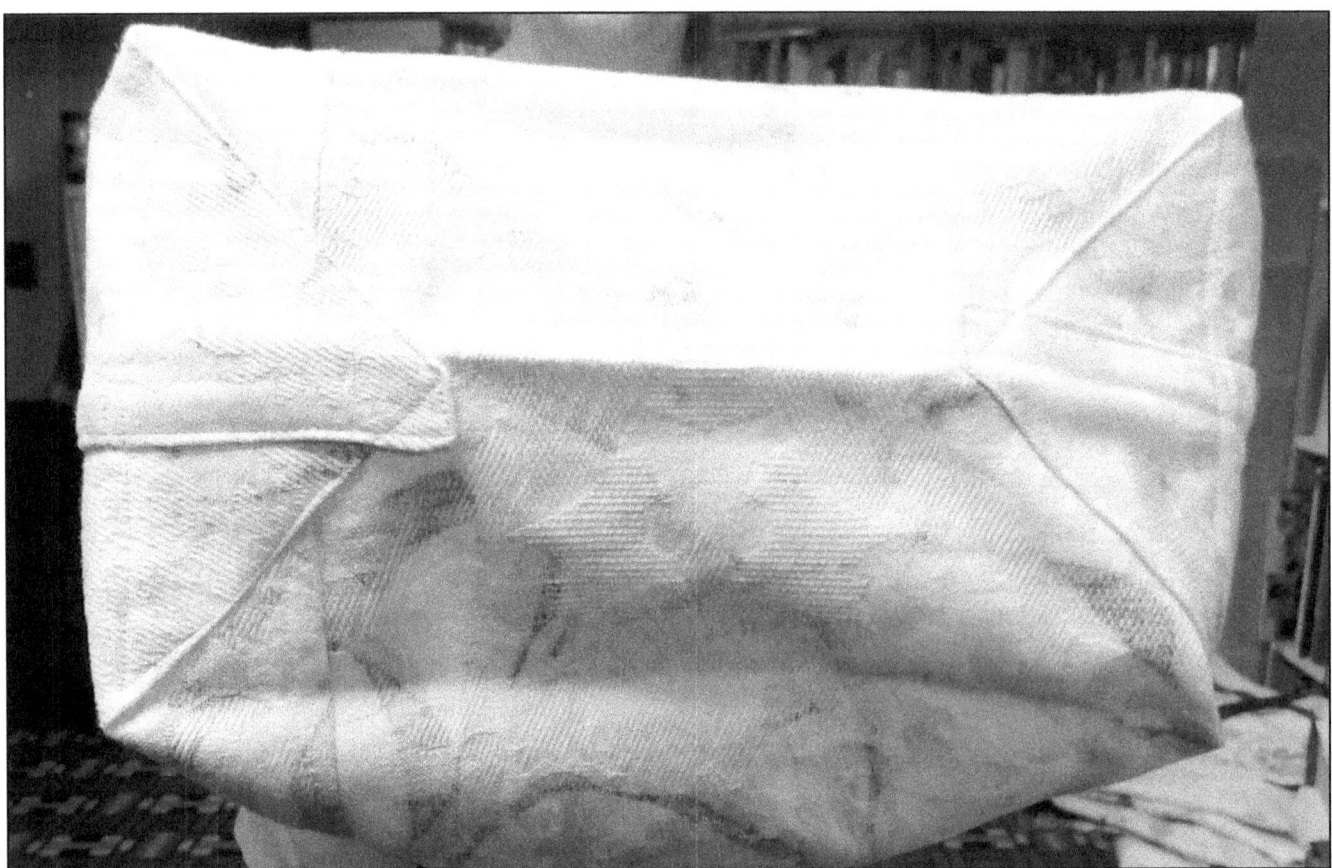

This is what you should see inside the bag, with the flanges sewn down and the square edges left alone.

13. Boxed Frankenstein Bags

When I make a Frankenstein bag, either boxed or tailored, my first consideration is where I locate the joining seams on my pieced fabric. Boxed bags use one large panel and are put together differently from tailored bags, so the locations of bad joins are also different.

In a boxed bag, the worst location for a lengthwise joining seam is within five inches of the long side of the panel. The seam overlaps stack up under the triangular wing, making it much more difficult to sew. A seam running crosswise at the halfway point, turning two squares into a single 19-by-36-inch panel, has the same issue.

Joining seams may cause a problem if they run directly under and parallel to where the straps go. This depends on the thickness of the fabric; a very heavyweight upholstery versus a drapery weight fabric. It's a judgment call, and you may even have to sew the bag to find out if it works.

How you finish the seam will affect the bulkiness. A serger allows you to overcast the joining seam and that thread won't add to the bulk.

Trimming the seam margin on one side, folding it and ironing it under its partner (a flat-fell seam) is fiddly work that adds plenty of bulk.

Since I do not own a serger, I often finish my seams with twill tape. Years ago, I got lucky at the fabric closeout store and bought a cone containing thousands of yards of ½-inch-wide white twill tape. Sadly, unlike my immense roll of construction crew yellow ribbon, this is not a lifetime supply. When I eventually run out, I'll turn to single-fold bias tape or grosgrain ribbon. I have plenty of both on hand, and I'll use them up before I buy more twill tape. Avoid using rayon seam tape as it won't hold up in a grocery bag.

Taping the seams also reinforces them. A joining seam introduces a weak point into your bag, and you want to compensate for this. Finally, sew down the taped seams to keep them from curling. Taping seams works well with thinner fabric.

I also use my overcasting foot to enclose the raw edge, since this stitch is available on a regular sewing machine. This is a two-step process. First, reset your overcast stitch so the wrapping stitches are closer together. Sew the seam, enclosing the raw edge.

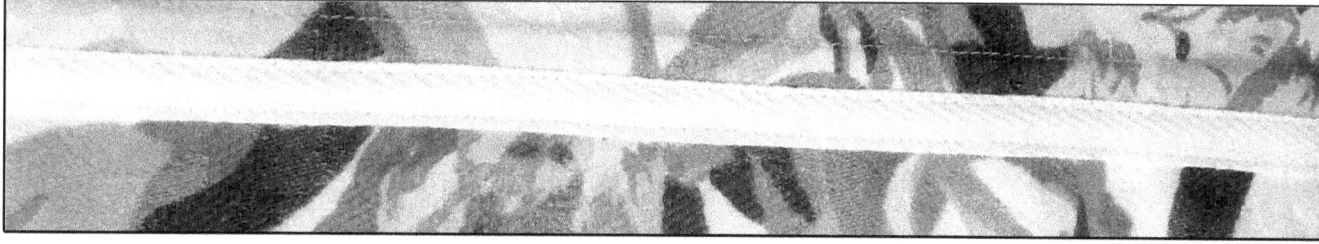

Above: Since I do not own a serger, I often finish my seams with twill tape.

Below: An example of an overcasting seam.

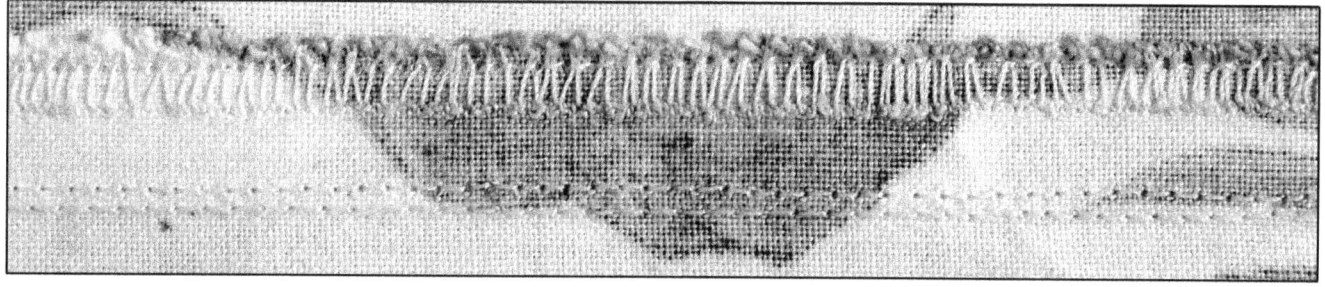

Boxed Frankenstein Bags

Second, sew a second line of regular stitching ½ inch inside the overcast edge, simulating what a serger would do in a single pass. As with a serger, an overcast seam doesn't add bulk the way a taped seam would.

How To Sew Down Seams

First, decide which type of seam you want and stick to it! If you are taping your seams, decide if you want to see the tape. If you are piecing together scraps of the same fabric, especially if it's a solid color or a tiny print, arranging the seams so they show on the outside will shout that you had to piece the fabric. Inside seams will just look like lines of stitching.

If you are using different scraps, it will be obvious that you pieced the fabric. Lines of white twill tape will highlight those joins and add a coordinating design element. The more pieces of fabric you use, the better the twill tape will look. Think of the twill working like the black lines of leading in a stained-glass window.

You do not have to use white, by the way. White twill tape is what I have so that is what I use. Use whatever you like and have on hand in your stash. See what looks best with the fabric you are using.

If you are overcasting your seams, decide if you want to match the thread or use the same, contrasting color (such as black) throughout. Once you've decided if the seams will show, then it's time to piece your fabric.

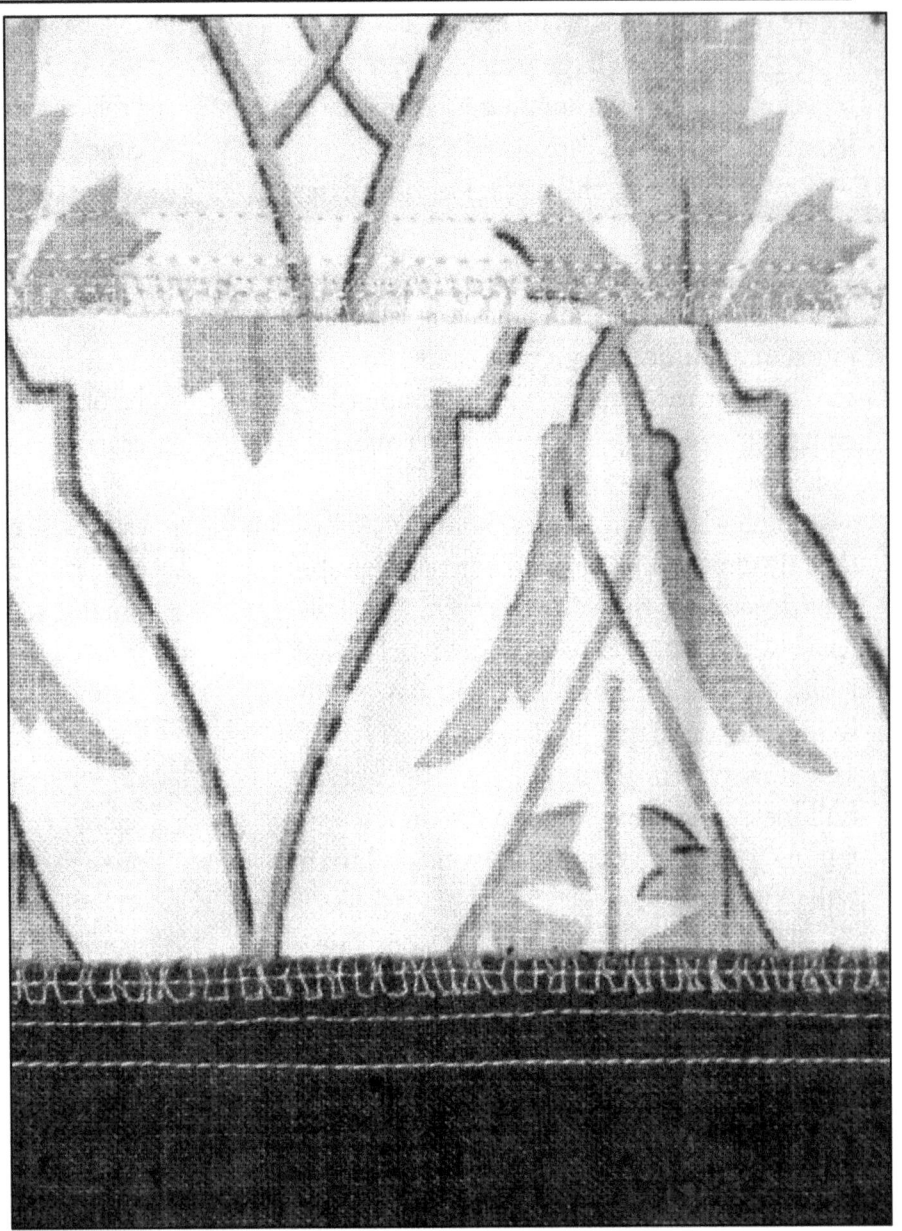

Examples of a Frankenstein seam.

- If you want the seams to show, sew your scraps Wrong Sides together.
- If you don't want the seams to show, sew the scraps Right Sides together.

The larger the pieces, the fewer seam joins you will

have. As much as possible, square up your scraps so they are on the true grain. If you have to sew fabric cut on the bias, the taping will help control the stretch, but it may not be perfect.

Avoid curved seams! Save those for your quilting projects.

To piece your scraps with tape, sew two sections together with a 5/8-inch seam. Decide which side you want the tape to end up on, keeping the taped layer further away from straps or other seams. Trim that side of the seam to ¼ inch to reduce bulk. Then, press the other seam margin over top of the trimmed margin, so the wider seam margin lies on top of the trimmed seam margin. Do <u>not</u> press the seams open. This seam has to support the weight of two gallons of milk and a line of thread isn't going to perform well.

Back at the sewing machine, sew a line of tape over the raw edge, just covering the raw edge on one side. The other side of the tape should be, depending on its width, close to the original stitching line. Sew down the second side of the tape. The

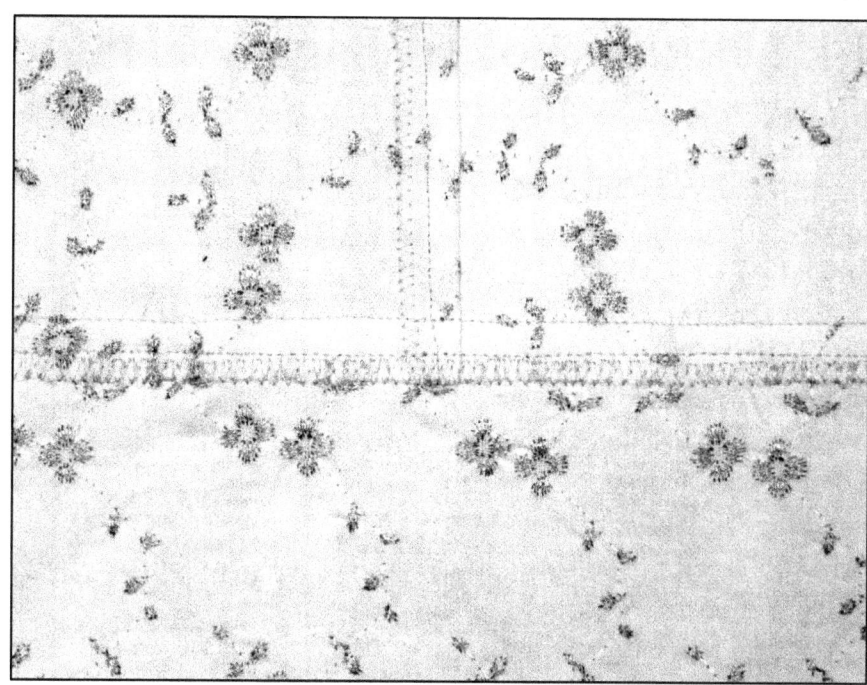

When Frankenstein seams intersect, press them so that they do not overlap and create an unsightly bump.

two lines of stitching will enclose the raw edge and reinforce the joining seam.

If you are blessed with a serger, you may want to serge the two raw edges together and sew them down with two lines of stitching, forcing the seam to lay flat and reinforcing the join.

If you decided to overcast the joining seams – pretending you own a serger – press the finished seam to one side and sew it down with two lines of stitching, forcing the seam flap to lay flat and reinforcing the join.

When you have pieced together a large enough rectangle, measure and trim it to 19 by 36 inches. Cut the pieced panel as close to the true grain as you can manage. More joining seams may mean some twist or distortion in your finished panel. The sewing process, followed by adding the foldover, trim-line, and straps should subdue this tendency.

After you have pieced as many panels as you need, sew them together in the usual, boxed bag manner.

Voila! Functional bags from leftover fabric.

14. Making Boxed Bags With One-Way Cloth

A boxed bag is made of a single rectangle, so any design motif on the cloth will wrap around the bag. One side will display the cloth right-side-up and the other side will display it upside-down. If you are using a solid color, a tiny, non-directional print, or anything without an obvious orientation, your boxed bag will look fine from both sides.

If your fabric <u>does</u> have an obvious direction, then you have three options:

• Use the fabric and ignore the mismatch;

• Make tailored bags instead and orient the panels the right way up. Half the gusset will still go the wrong way, but that won't be as noticeable as a misoriented side panel;

• Or make a modified Frankenstein boxed bag.

To construct one, you need to start with a longer rectangle that will later be cut down to 19 by 36 inches. This allows you to offset the seam from the 18-inch mark (the halfway point).

1. Measure and cut a panel 40 inches long and 19 inches wide.

2. Make a tick mark at the *17-inch mark* on each of the panel's long sides. Cut the panel in half, leaving two

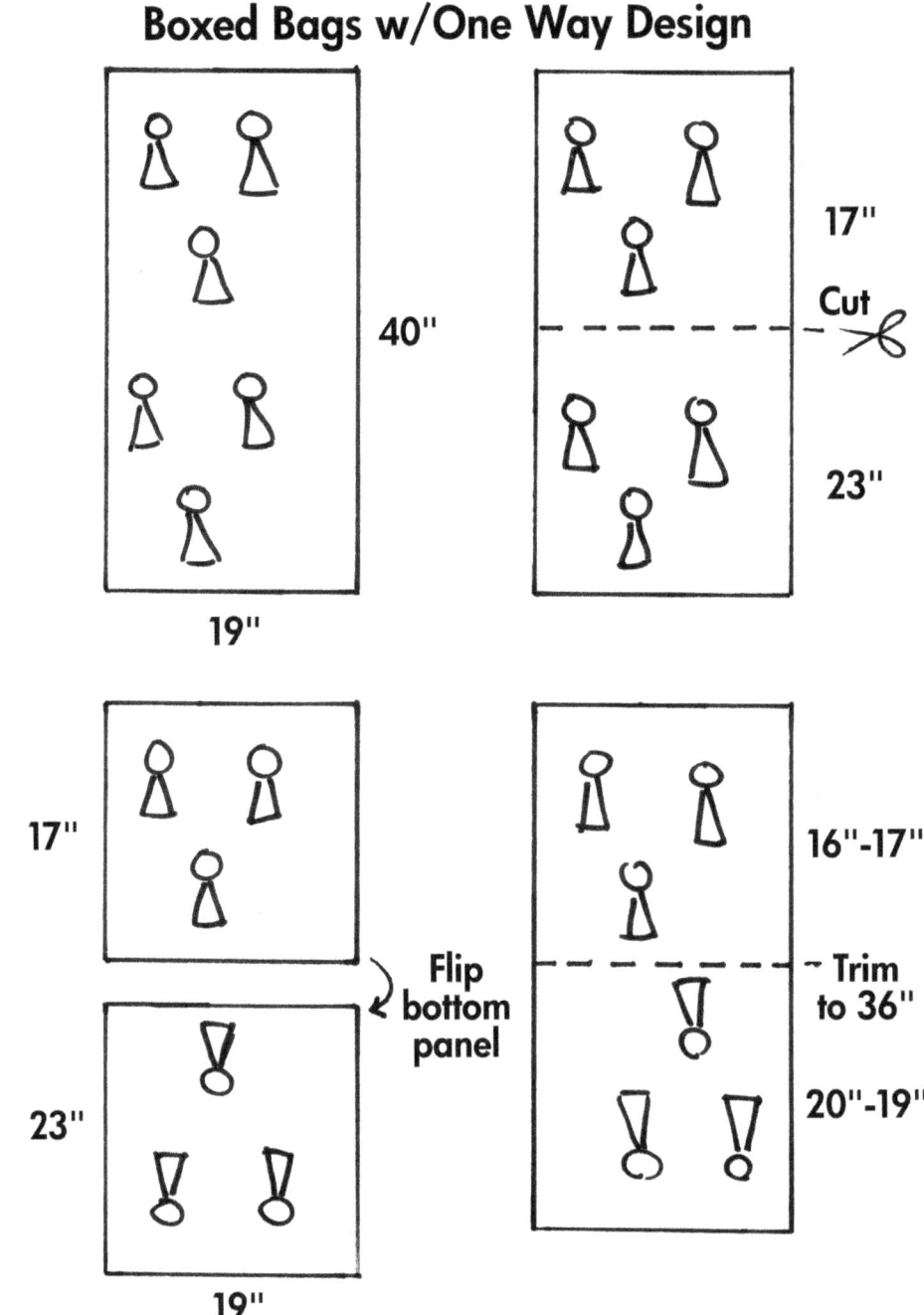

sections each 19 inches wide. One rectangle is 17 x 19, the other 23 x 19.

3. Turn the shorter rectangle around so that <u>both</u> sides of the cloth are going right side up; i.e., the design meets in the middle with both sides going in opposite directions. Line up the 19-inch-long sides and sew the two sections right sides together.

4. As with a taped Frankenstein-bag-joining

seam, trim one side of the seam margin, press it over, and sew over the raw edge with twill tape.

The twill tape will remain unseen, concealed with in the bag. It will be strong, but bulky.

Or, enclose both raw edges in a close overcasting stitch, press and sew down.

Or make a French seam, starting wrong sides together, then right sides together, press to one side and sew the seam down, just like making the flange seams that form the sides of a boxed bag. Very strong, very bulky.

All of these methods work as the seam remains hidden at the bottom of the bag, visible only when you peek inside.

The key to all of these seams is to press the finished seam to one side and sew it down again. This extra row of stitching reinforces a weak point where the bag needs the most strength: on the bottom where it supports the groceries. A single line of thread won't hold up under the weight of two gallons of milk.

5. Remeasure the rectangle. The 19-inch width will remain unchanged.

6. Press and trim the length of the rectangle to 36 inches. The key is to keep your new joining seam at the 16-inch mark or so. The section above this seam is shorter. This section will become the back of the boxed bag and the joining seam will be concealed in the bottom of the bag.

The longer section, the one you will trim, will become the front of your boxed bag.

Do NOT place the joining seam at the halfway point. The layers of cloth making up the reinforced seam will interfere with boxing the bag and sewing down the triangular wings. Placing the joining seam at or near the 16-inch mark keeps it out of the way, while still hiding it from casual view.

7. Your panel is now ready to be sewn into a boxed bag like any other 19-by-36-inch rectangle. All finishing, including trim-lines and straps, remains the same.

Remember that the <u>longer</u> panel will be the front of the finished bag, so place any ribbon tag on this side, underneath the straps.

Forty inches is longer than you need to make a "both sides right-side-up" boxed bag, but it is much easier to trim the finished rectangle so that the joining seam is off-center, than coming up short and having to add a piece of cloth.

When you have made a few bags, you may want to try with 39-inch long rectangular panels. If your fabric has a large repeat, you can cut panels to showcase the motif but understand that this can mean a lot of wasted fabric and more time spent cutting and sewing them.

PART III: TAILORED BAGS

Tailored Bag Process
(not all steps are shown)

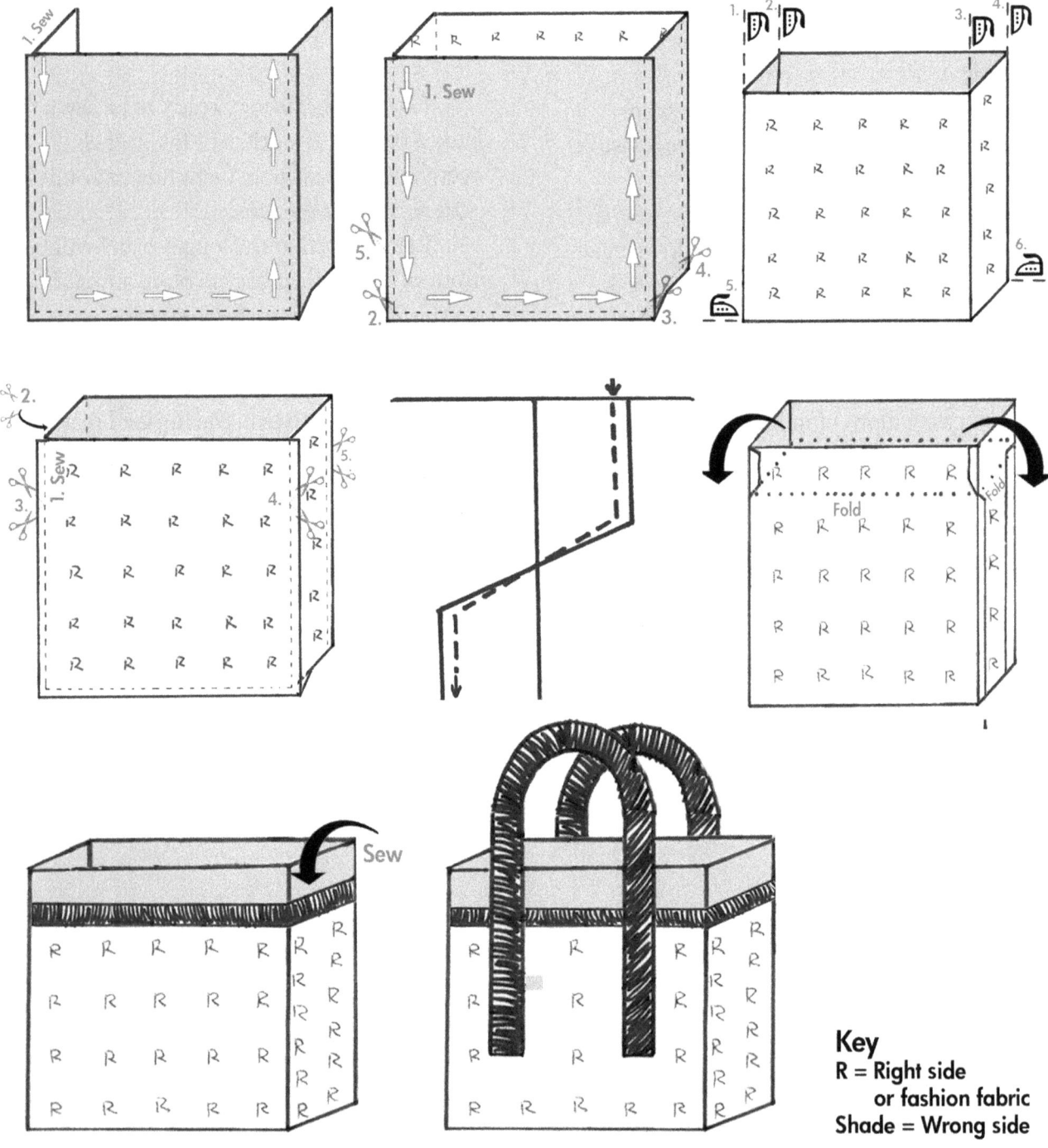

Key
R = Right side or fashion fabric
Shade = Wrong side

15. The First Pass

The cloth has been purchased. You've washed it if needed, unpicked any seams if it's repurposed fabric, and ironed it. You've measured the fabric, worked out the most economical layout of panels and gussets on paper, and cut out the fabric.

It's time to start sewing the Cadillac of grocery bags: the tailored bag.

But before you begin, here are a few notes and best practices.

- These instruction assume that your side panels are 13-by-15 inches. The top and bottom edges will be 13 inches wide, and the right and left edges are 15 inches tall. That means the bag will be taller than it is wide. The gusset should be 43 inches long and between 7 and 9 inches wide.

- The first pass is the hardest, most time-consuming step. I sew tailored bags <u>without</u> pinning the panels and gussets together. I mark my pivot points by eye as I come to them. I finish sewing one complete tailored bag — two panels and a gusset — to the end of the first pass before sewing the next bag. I sew each bag in turn until I have matched all my side panels and gussets. Any leftover panels or gussets are dropped on the Frankenstein pile for reuse later on.

- I strongly recommend sewing tailored bags with a walking foot. It isn't required — I sewed many bags without one — but it makes the process much, much easier and with smoother results. No matter what you do, the fabric tends to creep and bunch, and the walking foot slows this process down. If you sew without a walking foot, you <u>must</u> sew very slowly to avoid stretching the upper layer of fabric under the presser foot.

- When you reach the end of sewing the gusset to the first panel, you will have some overage on the gusset. This is by design. It's far easier to trim the gusset than to have it come up short and have to insert a patch. Do not trim the excess off now! You'll do that later.

- When you sew the other edge of the gusset to the second panel, you may get more creep in the gusset fabric, ending up with a trapezoid to trim off instead of a rectangle. Without the walking foot, the second side of the gusset excess may be two or three inches longer than the first edge. This looks strange and your fabric stretching this much makes for a twisted bag. You can force the bag into submission via the trim-line, the side corner seams, and the straps — I've done this — but it is easier to avoid the issue by using a walking foot and sewing slowly.

- I don't use a pattern, just chalk outlines, and I don't mark my pivot points in advance and pin carefully, matching edges, so there is no way around this potential problem, other than hand-basting or using a walking foot. Get the walking foot. If you're like me, you will wonder why you waited so long.

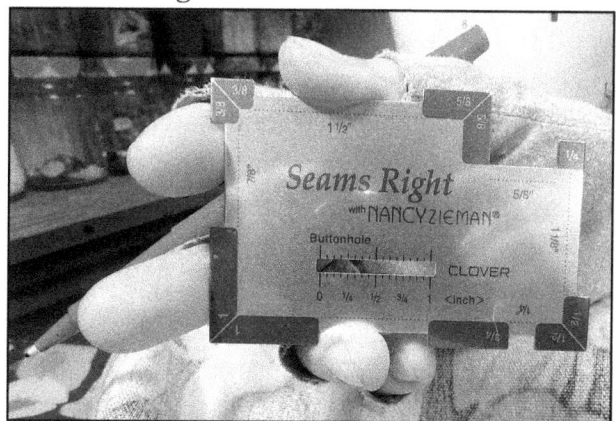

- The other tool I recommend is a "Seams Right with Nancy Zieman." This little metal gadget is made by Clover and is found in the sewing notions area in most fabric shops or online. It's perfect for accurately marking the pivot point. I made hundreds of tailored bags before acquiring this little gem so you don't need it — certainly not as much as the walking foot

The First Pass

— but it sure is handy.

- The directions look complicated, but it gets easier quickly. In essence, you are performing the same motion six times for each bag. That is, you do the same thing for the left-side seam, bottom seam, and right-side seam when securing the front panel to the gusset, and then repeat the steps for the left-side seam, bottom seam, and right-side seam attaching the back panel to the gusset.

The result is a five-sided bag (side, side, side, side, and bottom), open at the top, which is inside out.

- You will be changing your stitch length frequently. This is because you cannot backtrack with a walking foot. Switching to a tight stitch at the beginning and end of a seam helps secure the stitching. You will also shorten your stitch length when you near a pivot point, sew the pivot and go around the corner. This ensures a tighter seam that does not come undone later on. The long stretches of stitching should be done with whatever length works best for the fabric. You may have to adjust to a longer stitch for thicker fabric. Trial and error is the only way to determine what works for a specific fabric.

Now that I have thoroughly confused you, let's get started.

SEWING THE GUSSET TO THE FIRST SIDE PANEL

Tip: It's easy to confuse the 13-inch-long top and bottom edges with the 15-inch-long left and right edges. Mark the top edge of each side panel with chalk or a pin so you don't mis-sew it when you grab it from the pile.

1. Set your needle in the center position to sew a 3/8-inch seam, using the edge of the walking foot as a measuring device and aligning the cut edges of the cloth.

If you can't adjust your needle position, you'll have to make your own adjustments to keep to the recommended seam margin.

2. Lay the gusset on a flat surface, right-side-up. Lay the front panel, right-side-down, on top of the gusset, aligning the top edges and the side edges. You will be sewing the right-side seam, starting at the top of the bag.

3. Set your machine (since you cannot backstitch with a walking foot) to .4mm and sew down ± ¼-inch to secure the seam.

Lengthen the stitch setting to what the fabric prefers and sew the **right-side seam**, the panel to the gusset, stopping when you are within 2 inches of the bottom of the panel.

4. Mark the pivot point on the wrong side of the front panel. The "Seams Right" gauge is perfect for an accurate measurement, although I

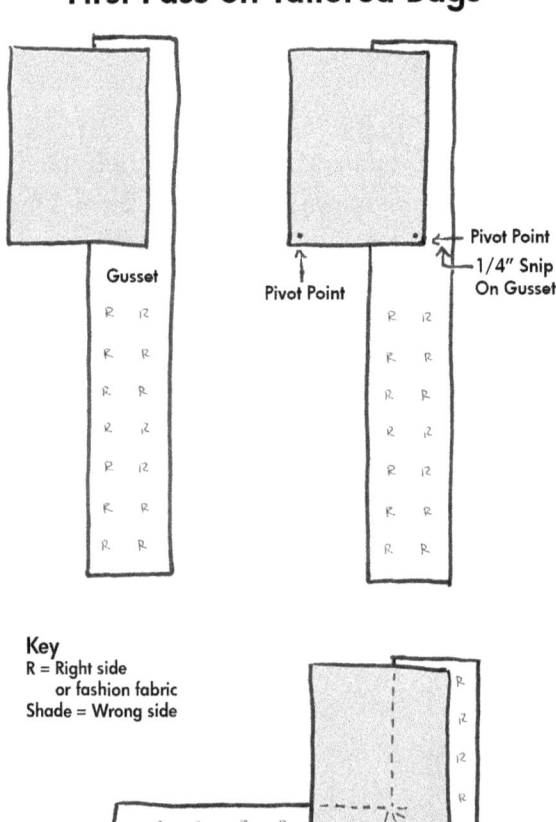

First Pass on Tailored Bags

This is an exploded view of the layout, drawn not to scale, to show the relationship between the side panel and the gusset.

did it by eye for years. Using the ¼-inch

projection, align the "Seams Right" gauge with the bottom corner of the front panel. Make two crossing lines, each one ¼ inch in from the two sides. I use a fine-point black felt-tip pen. The marks don't show in the finished bag as they end up inside a seam.

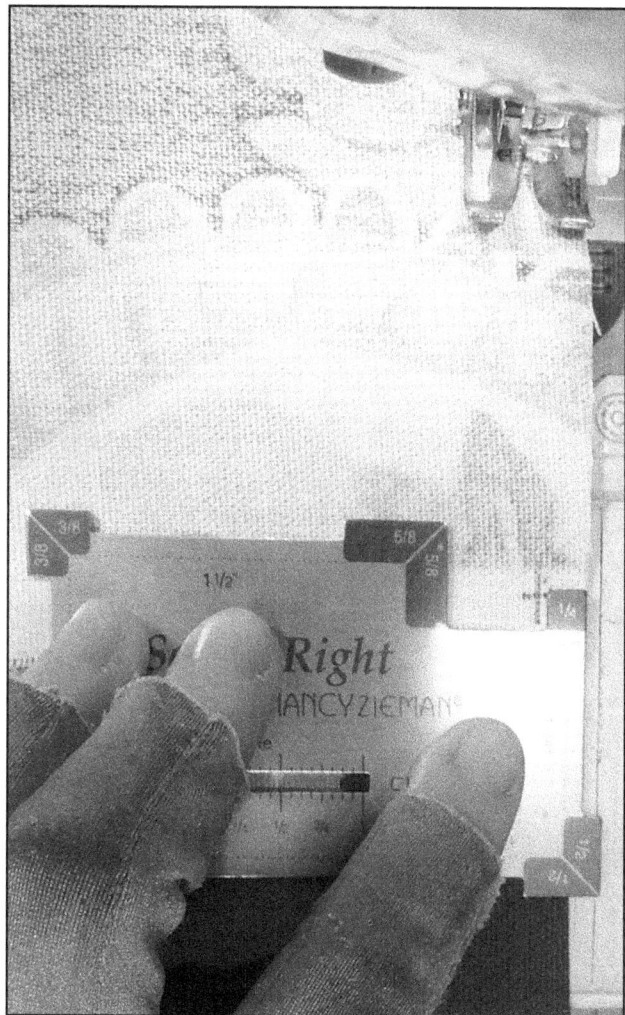

Step 4: Marking the pivot point on the wrong side of the front panel.

5. Here's a tricky part. You have marked the pivot point on the front panel. With the front panel lying smooth and even atop the gusset, line up your scissors with the horizontal line and make a ¼-inch snip in the <u>gusset</u> underneath. The pivot marking on the front panel tells you <u>where</u> to turn. Snipping the gusset allows <u>that</u> piece of fabric to turn, when you pivot the front panel to sew the bottom seam.

6. Continue sewing until you are about 1 inch away from the pivot point. Shorten your stitch (to strengthen the corner). Sew up to the pivot point.

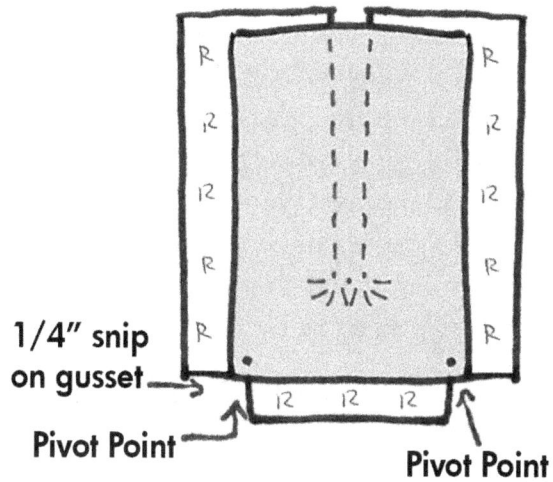

7. At the pivot point, lift the presser foot and turn the front panel so you will be sewing the **bottom seam**. Align the gusset with the bottom edge of the front panel. Sew about an inch with the machine stitch length still set a short, tight stitch (to strengthen the corner).

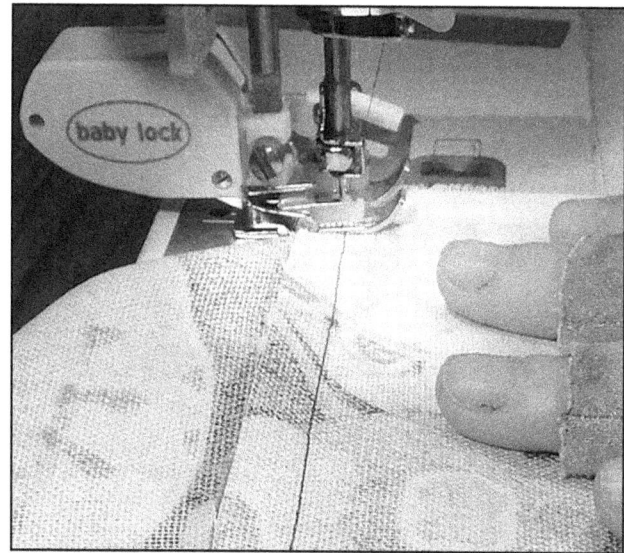

Step 7: Sewing the bottom seam starting with the pivot point.

8. When you are 1 inch away from the pivot point, lengthen the stitch proceed along the bottom seam, keeping to your 3/8-inch seam margin.

9. When you are within 2 inches of the corner of the front panel, it's time to mark the

The First Pass

pivot point again. As before, mark a set of crossing lines ¼ inch inside the corner of the front panel, using your "Seams Right" gauge if you have one. Snip a ¼-inch slit in the gusset underneath. Sew down towards the corner.

10. When you are 1 inch away, shorten your stitch length again (to strengthen the corner) and sew up to the pivot point.

11. At the pivot point, lift the presser foot and turn the front panel so you are sewing the left side seam. Align the front panel left side with the gusset and sew another inch using the shorter stitch length.

12. When you are 1 inch away from the pivot point, lengthen your stitch and , keeping your 3/8-inch seam margin, sew to the end.

The gusset strip will be longer than the front panel. Don't trim it off! We'll do that after the back panel is sewn on.

Congratulations! You have finished attaching the front panel to the gusset and the bag is taking shape.

SEWING THE GUSSET TO THE BACK PANEL

Attach the back panel to the gusset in exactly the same way, adjusting the stitch length to reinforce seam starts and endings and the corners. As before, sew your 3/8-inch seams slowly so that the gusset doesn't stretch too much. And as before, mark the pivot points as we get near them. The difference is that this time, the gusset side is up and the back panel is down.

So, let's get started.

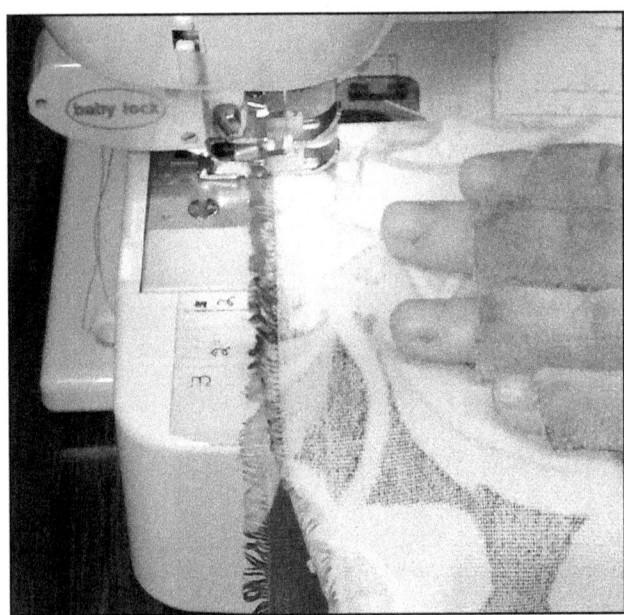

Step 1: Place the free, long edge of the gusset – the one lined up with the panel it is sewn to, not the uneven end – right sides together, on the back panel.

1. Place the free, long edge of the gusset — the one lined up with the panel it is sewn to, not the uneven end — right sides together, on the back panel. Line up the top edge of the gusset with the back panel top. At the same time, align the free, right side of the gusset with the right-side edge of the back panel, right sides together.

2. Using a short stitch length, secure the right-side seam. Lengthen your stitch length and sew to 2 inches from the bottom edge of the back panel. Watch carefully; you don't want to get too close to the bottom edge of the panel. Remember, the back panel is underneath the gusset so you cannot see it.

3. Slide your "Seams Right" between the gusset and the back panel. Line up the ¼-inch tab of the "Seams Right" with the bottom panel corner. This is underneath the gusset and on top of the bottom panel corner. From the top of the gusset, you should be able to feel the change in thickness. Mark the pivot point on the gusset, using the same crisscrossing lines.

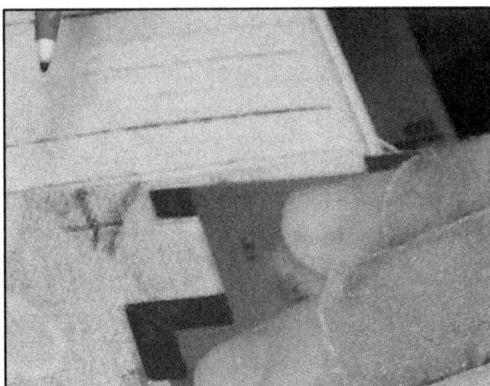

Step 3: Slide your "Seams Right" between the gusset and the back panel.

4. Snip a ¼-inch cut on the gusset to the pivot point. This time you can see exactly where you are making your snip but you are estimating where it is in relationship to the back panel. This is the opposite of how you marked and snipped the pivot point when sewing the gusset to the front panel.

5. Sew closer to the pivot point and when you are an inch away, tighten your stitch length to reinforce the corner. Sew up to the pivot point.

6. At the pivot point, lift the presser foot and swing the back panel around under the gusset, aligning the bottom edge of the back panel with the gusset. The gusset will turn with the snip cut.

7. Sew ± 1 inch using the short stitch length, securing the corner. Then adjust your stitch length back to normal and proceed, with your 3/8-inch seam margin down the bottom edge of the bag.

8. When you are 2 inches away from the corner on the back panel, stop and mark the pivot point again on the gusset.

9. As before, snip a ¼-inch cut at the pivot point on the gusset. Adjust your stitch length when you are within 1 inch from the marked pivot point.

10. At the pivot point, lift the presser foot, pivot the back panel, aligning the edges, and sew for an inch using your short stitch length to secure the corner.

11. Readjust your stitch length to normal and proceed along the left side seam to the top of the bag. When you are within ½ inch of the end of the back panel, shorten your stitch length to secure the stitch line. Cut the bag free from the machine and set it aside.

CLEAN UP THE BAGS

Before starting the second sewing pass, do a little clean-up first.

1. With the bags still inside out, look over the six seam margins and remove any loose threads, clipping them off or pulling them free. This seam margin will be captured within the next pass. Cleaning up the loose bits now will mean not having to remove whiskers sticking out of the seam later.

2. Clip across each of the four outside corners, coming within a few threads of the pivot point. Clipping close to the point will make enclosing this corner seam easier and less bulky.

3. With the bag still inside out, lay it down flat. The too-long part of the gusset should be down and the panel side up. The bag is inside-out, with right-sides together. Straighten the bag so the edges of the two panels and the other edge of the gusset make a straight line. Trim off the excess gusset fabric. If you sewed slowly, using a walking foot, it should be a rectangle about 1 to 2 inches long and the width of the gusset. If you did not use a walking foot or you went too fast, it may be a trapezoid, with one side longer than

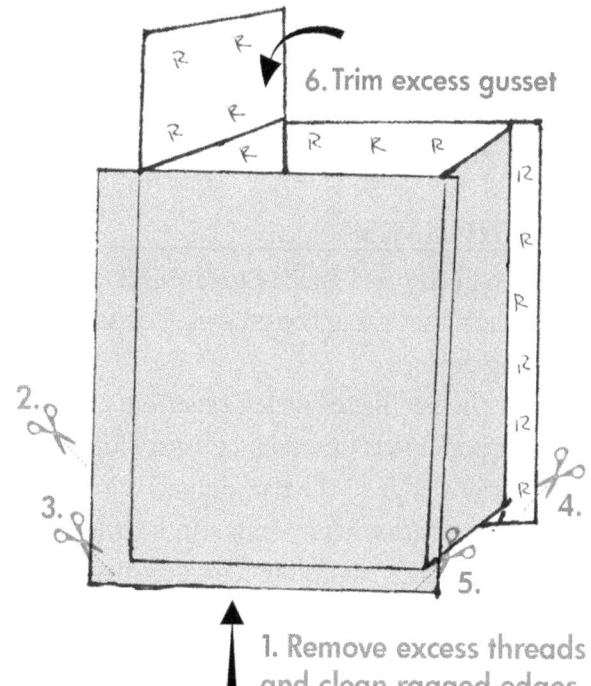

the other. The finished bag will have a little twist to it, but it will be perfectly functional.

4. Flip the bags right-side out, laying them flat with the bottom of the gusset folded inside to discourage wrinkles. You are ready for the second pass.

16. The Second Pass

In this step, you will iron a crisp knife-edge on each of the six seams. Then you will sew a ½-inch seam all the way around, front and back, producing a flange, identical to a French seam, that will enclose the raw edges. The flange will be sewn down in a later pass, reinforcing the corners and providing a skeletal structure for the bags.

IRON THE BAGS

1. Lay the bag on the ironing board with a panel side down and the gusset exposed. Pull the gusset to your left so that it lays flat on the panel, giving you a knife-edge on the right side, with the bag opening up and away from you. Iron the right-side hem to a crisp knife-edge.

Keep the seam line right at the outside edge of the flange you are making.

2. When you reach the corner, pivot the bag, again pulling the gusset away from the panel. Iron the bottom seam flange flat. When you reach the next corner, pivot the bag again, and iron the left side seam flat.

3. Flip over the bag and repeat the above steps, starting with the right-hand seam.

When you have finished, each of the six seams — right side, bottom, left side on the front panel and right side, bottom, left side on the back panel — should be pressed flat.

Your bag should have the shape of a paper grocery sack.

To keep those nice edges, lay each bag flat in a stack, with the gusset folded into the bag's front and back panels.

Continue to use your walking foot. You will be changing stitch lengths to secure a seam line at its beginning and end, and to reinforce the corners.

To be most efficient, iron the bags first and then sew down the flanges.

SEW THE BAGS

You will sew a ½-inch seam around the six sides of each bag, using the presser foot as a measuring device.

1. Set the needle to the left position. Lay the bag, front panel side down and gusset side up, with the right edge of the bag aligned with the presser foot. Start with a .4mm stitch to secure the seam line, then switch to a longer stitch length to accommodate your fabric. Sew down the right-side seam, keeping that ½-inch margin.

2. When you near the corner, pull the gusset fabric into a pleat, stacking the fabric as neatly as you can. Shorten the stitch length and sew to within ½ inch of the bottom. You will be sewing over the gusset fabric, pleating it up as smoothly as you can manage. Don't catch more fabric in the pleat than you have to.

Step 2: When you near a corner, pull the gusset fabric into a pleat. Don't catch more fabric in the bleat than you have to!

The flatter the pleat, the neater the final seam will be.

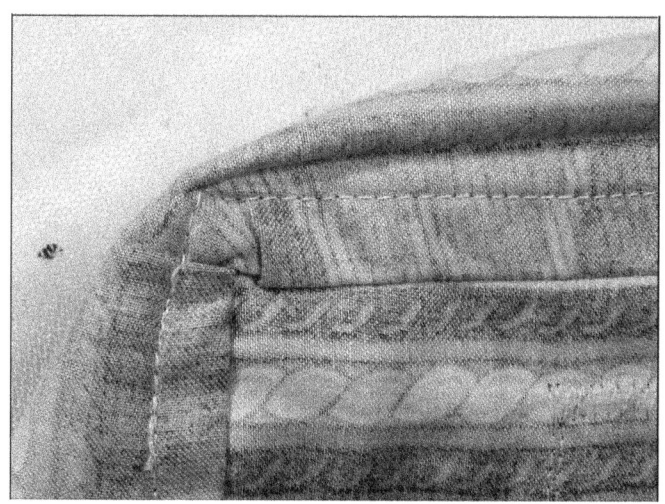 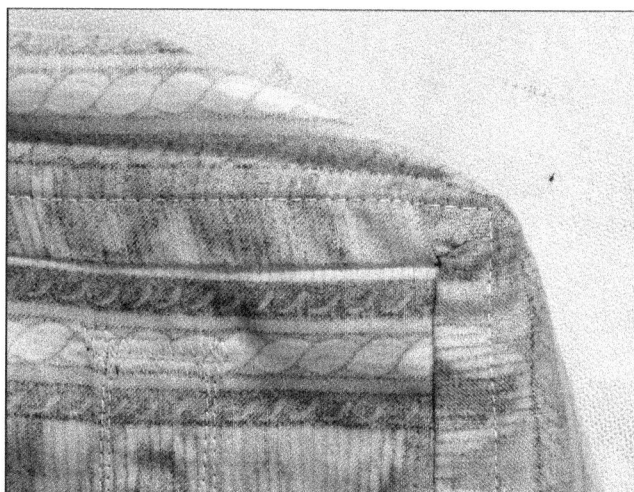

Examples of what the finished seam should look like on the inside of the bag.

3. When you are ½ inch from the knife-edge at the bottom of the bag — I measure this using my presser foot and by eye — lift the presser foot and pivot the bag.

Sew another inch using the shorter stitch to finish securing the corner.

4. Lengthen your stitch and sew the bottom flange.

5. When you're within an inch of the left corner, set your stitch length back to the shorter length. Pleat the gusset fabric again, so you catch as little of it as you can manage and, as before, sew up to ½ inch of the knife-edge.

6. Lift the presser foot and pivot the bag. Finish securing the corner with the shorter stitch.

7. Finish sewing the left-side seam with your ½-inch seam margin. When you near the end, shorten your stitch length to secure the line of stitching.

8. Flip the bag over, with the back panel side down, and repeat the process, sewing the right-side seam flange, pivoting at the corner, the bottom seam flange, pivoting at the corner, and then the left-side seam flange.

As you finish each bag, lay them flat with the gusset folded within the front and back panels, to discourage wrinkles. You are ready for the third pass.

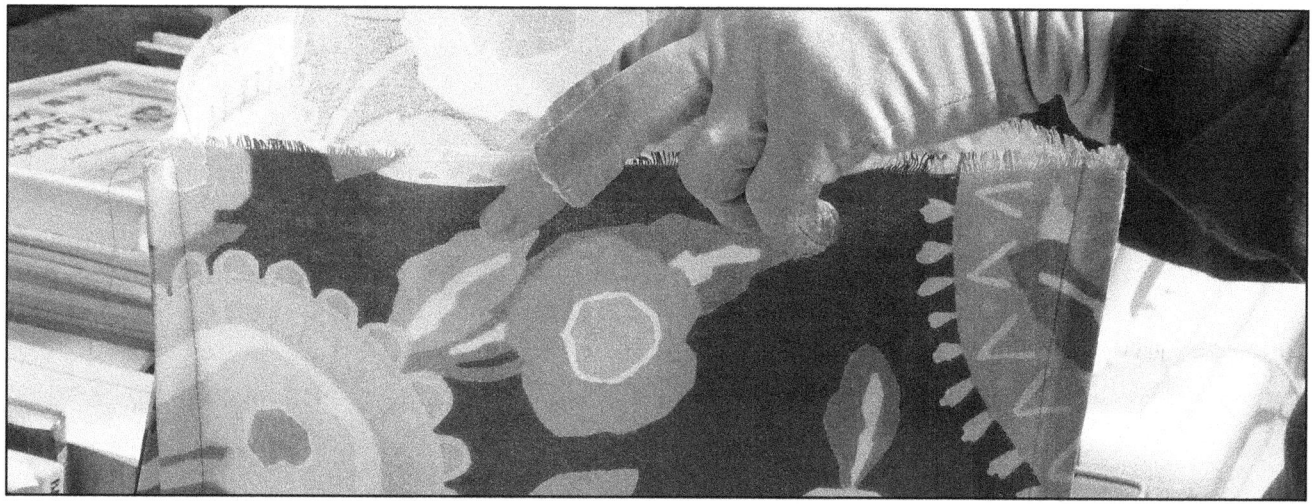

At the end of the second pass, the flanges have been sewn with ½-inch seam margin.

17. The Third Pass

In this step, the bag's flange is turned into a skeleton, supporting the tailored bag.

We'll be measuring and snipping a triangular notch on each of the flanges to make it easier to fold over the material at the open end of the bag. This procedure is identical to the boxed bag, other than tailored bags have four flanges and boxed bags have two.

1. Measure down 2 inches from the top edge and draw a line on each of the four flanges, perpendicular from the stitch line to the outer edge. This measurement is the same whether you cut 13-by-15-inch panels or 14-by-16-inch panels.

2. Snip out a triangle of cloth on each of the four flanges, coming within a few threads of the stitch line.

Tip: It takes fewer hand motions to draw the notch tick mark on all of your tailored bags and then drop the pen and pick up the scissors to make all the triangular cuts rather than marking and snipping each flange in turn.

The easiest way to cut the notch is to fold over the flange with the marked line facing up and then cut a wedge from the stitch line to the outer edge. This way you don't accidentally cut through the stitch line.

Work your way through all the bags.

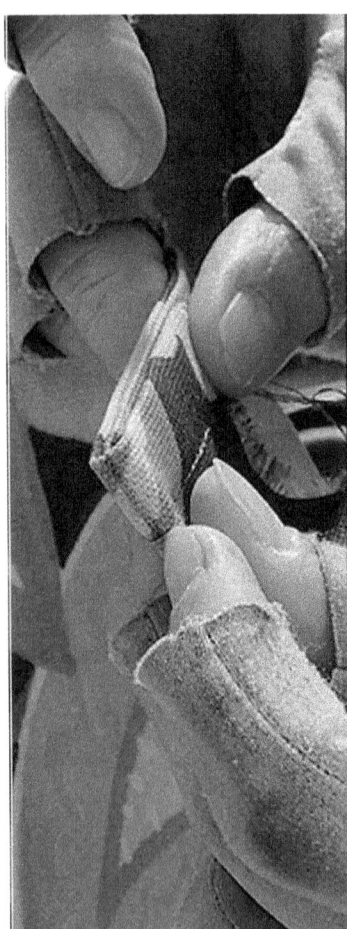
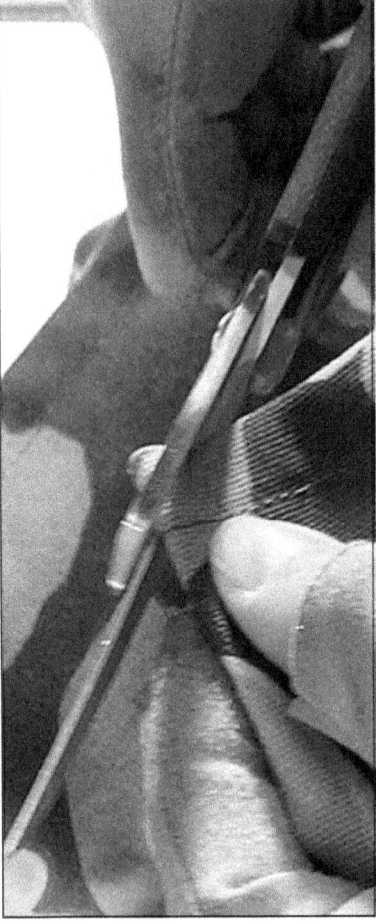

Folding the flange and cutting the notch. If you're working on more than one bag, it's faster to draw the notch tick mark on all the bags, then make the cuts instead of marking and snipping each flange in turn.

SEW DOWN THE FLANGES

This step reinforces the bags bottom four corners and six edges (the front panel's left side, bottom, and right side, and the back panel's left side, bottom, and right side).

The notch you cut from the flange will let you fold down the top of the bag, while minimizing bulky seams.

Here's a tricky bit: The flange is sewn down so the upper part (above the cutout) is sewn to the PANEL. The lower part of the flange (from cutout to cutout) is sewn to the GUSSET. When you sew all the way around and reach the second cutout, the upper portion is again sewn to the panel.

It works best to align the flange-to-gusset seam so that the stitch line is at the far side of the presser foot. That is, you want the presser foot resting entirely upon the flange when sewing it to the gusset. This won't happen when sewing the small upper portions to the panels.

You may find it easier to iron the flanges in place before sewing them. I don't. I press them in place with my fingers as I go. Either way works.

Here's the procedure:

1. Shorten your stitch length to secure the seam. Position the bag with the gusset to the left of the needle and the panel to the right.

Press the upper portion of the flange, above the notch, down on the panel. Stitch down the flange about ¼-inch to secure the seam, then adjust your stitch length to normal.

2. At the notch, lift the presser foot and pivot the bag to stitch down the cut edge, crossing across the seam line, sewing the second part of the cut edge onto the gusset, and pressing down the flange onto the gusset. Pivot the needle again at the end of the raw edge and sew the flange to the gusset, following the shape of the bag.

Keep the fabric taut as you stitch down the flange along the side seam.

3. When you're an inch from the corner,

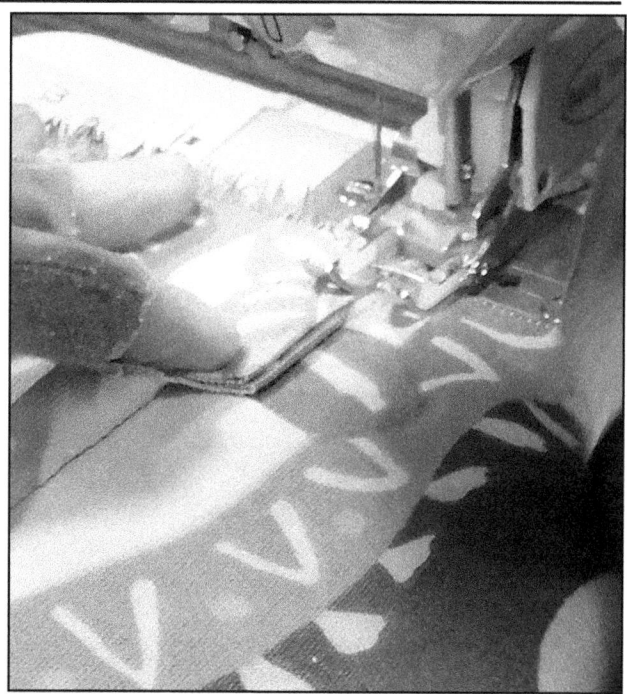

Keep the fabric taut as you stitch the upper part of the flange to the panel, and the lower part to the gusset..

shorten the stitch length to reinforce the corner Sew the flange to the gusset up to the corner, adjusting to keep both flange and gusset smooth and wrinkle-free.

4. Pivot at the corner and sew another inch with a shorter stitch length. Lengthen your stitch back to normal, continue to the next corner, and repeat the corner sewing procedure.

5. Continue sewing down the flange to the gusset. When you reach the notch, sew across the seam line, and continue up the panel side. At the bag's top, shorten your stitch to to secure the seam line.

6. Flip the bag and repeat the procedure on the back panel side. Secure the flange to the panel above the notch, to the gusset for the remainder of the flange — side, corner, bottom, corner, side — and above the notch, secure the flange to the panel.

7. Repeat for all the bags. As you finish each bag, lay it flat with the gusset bottom folded between the front and back panel.

The Third Pass

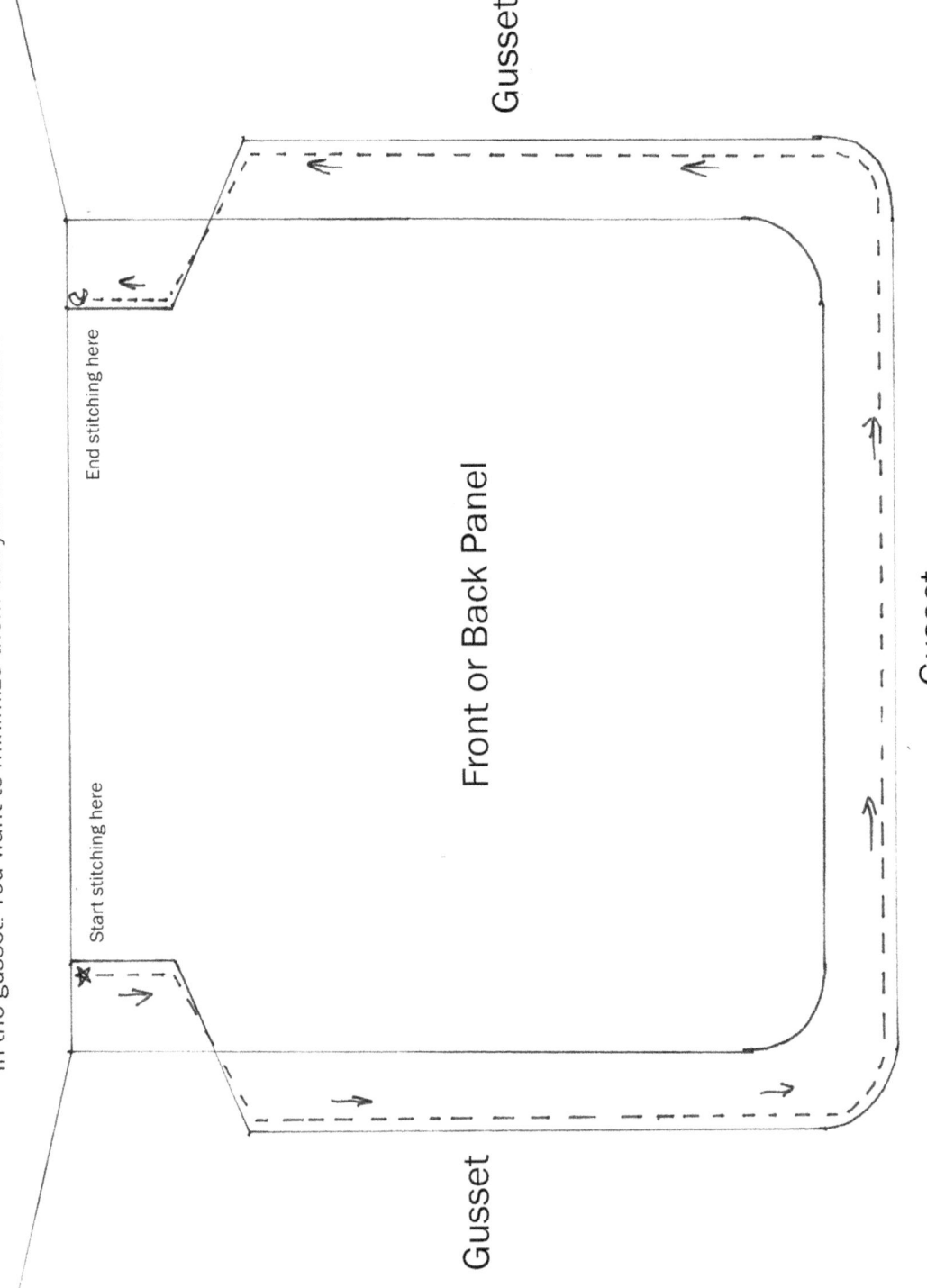

Flange Stitching
(Tailored Bags Only)

Follow the flange all the way around sewing it to the gusset. The corners of the panels are the most difficult part of the process. Pull the gusset flat and smooth out the flange as much as you can. You will get tiny tucks in the gusset. You want to minimize them but you cannot eliminate them.

18. The Fourth Pass

In this step, you will prepare the fold-down top, iron the bag, sew down the fold-down top, and then trim it out. Other than having four flanges instead of two, the sewing procedure for tailored bags is identical to boxed bags.

1. At the ironing board, fold over the top 2 inches of the bag to the outside and press. The notches will allow the foldover to lay flat, with no bulk at the foldline. Align the flanges so that they lie alongside each other, rather than overlapping. The folded over section shows the wrong side of the fabric, contrasting with the right-side of the fabric forming the body of the bag.

Press all four top edges flat, then press out any wrinkles.

If the foldover won't lie flat because the fabric stretched when going through the sewing machine, align the flanges carefully, then steam out any extra fullness between them. Some fabric is more amenable to this than others, but you won't know until after you start pressing. Use plenty of steam. If the fabric refuses to behave, iron a tuck as needed to make it fit; this will not affect how the bag functions. You are most likely to see this issue in the gusset end that had to be trimmed off. The trim-line will cover up most of the tuck.

Iron all the bags before moving to the next step.

2. At the sewing machine, shorten your stitch to secure the stitch line. Place the foldover corner seam at the needle, aligning the seam margins underneath and stitch in the ditch from the top of the foldover to the raw edge, securing the foldover to the bag. Sew all four corners down before proceeding to the next bag.

Sewing the corners down forces the bag to hold its shape and keeps the flange seams in place.

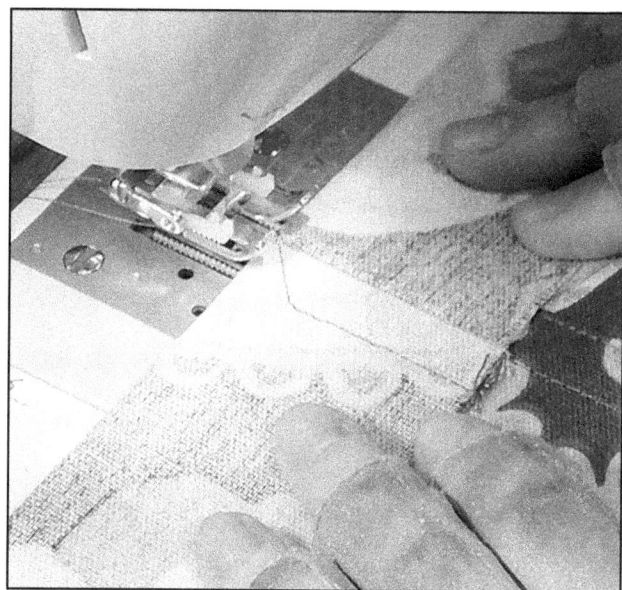

Step 2: With the top 2 inches of the bag folded over, sew all four corners in place. This will help the bag hold its shape.

You can swap these two steps: sewing the corners down in the ditch before pressing the foldover down. I've done it both ways. See what works for you.

If you ironed first and then sewed the corners, you may need to stop and steam out any unwanted fullness in the foldover on the gusset. Remember, much of this fullness will be concealed beneath the trim-line. A wider trim-line will cover more sin so no one will ever know of this flaw but you.

Step 3: Secure the foldover by sewing around the top edge of the bag.

The Fourth Pass

3. Finish securing the foldover. Sew a line 3/8 inch from the folded top edge of the bag all the way around. This keeps the pressed edge in place.

Do this step to the top edge of all the bags before proceeding to the trim-line.

4. The trim-line encloses the raw edges and stiffens the opening of the bag. Your trim should be ½ to 2 inches wide as described in Chapter 7.

As you'll see below, the trim is sewed down in one continuous motion, all the way around twice, rather than starting and stopping a stitch line. It's a faster method to use when you're making dozens of bags.

Some tips on sewing the trim:

- I do not measure trim in advance. I sew it down and cut it where needed to minimize waste. I hide the trim joint under where the straps will go. That means I have to mark their location <u>before</u> adding the trim-line.

- I also don't pin down the trim-line, but sew it down by eye.

- The trim-line's bottom edge is placed just below the raw edge of the foldover. The narrowest trim, ½-inch wide, will cover the raw edge, but there won't be much margin of error. I prefer wider trim so that the bottom edge is just

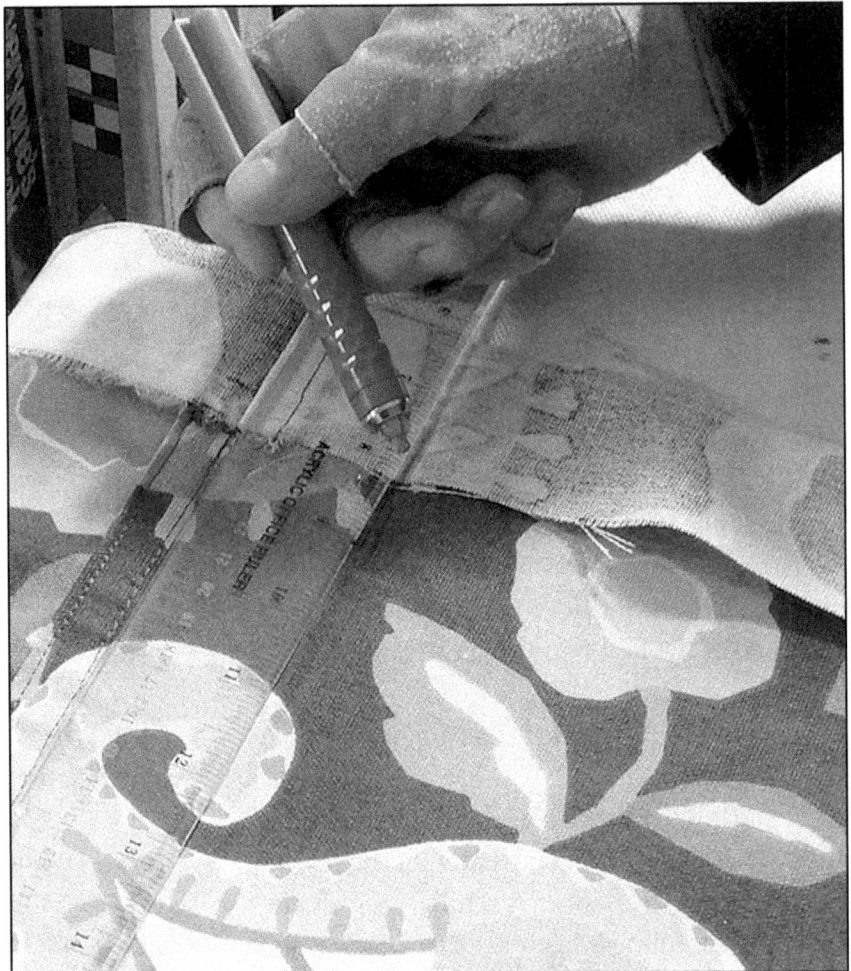

Step 4: If you don't have a cardboard strap spacer, a ruler can also work. The measurement depends on whether you're using 14-inch-by-16-inch panels or 13-inch-by-15-inch panels.

below the raw edge and the upper edge of the trim falls where it falls. Very wide trim (2 inches) is placed so that the bottom edge lies further down the bag and less of the foldover is covered up.

- I match my top thread to blend in with the trim, just as I match my bobbin thread to the bag fabric.

Here is the procedure: First, decide which side of the bag is the front panel. Mark where the left-side strap will go. This is the only mark you

make at this time. This will ensure that the join in the trim will be concealed.

5. Lay the bag flat, front panel side up. Slide in the cardboard insert that allows you to pin straps down without pinning both panels together. Lay the cardboard strap spacer on the left side of the panel, aligning it with the inner stitch line rather than the far edge of the sewn-down flange. Make a tick mark across the raw edge of the foldover; this indicates the

Step 6: Place the trim ½-inch away from the tick mark, ensuring the trim join lays beneath the future strap.

far side of the strap.

Mark all of the bags with one mark for the front panel of each bag. There is no need to mark the remaining strap locations.

6. At the sewing machine, place the start of the trim ½ inch to the right of the tick mark. This ensures that the trim's join will be covered by the future strap.

Arrange the trim so the bottom edge completely covers the raw edge and the top overlaps the foldover by a comfortable margin. The arrangement depends on the width of the trim and what you think looks best.

Beginning with a shortened stitch, sew down the trim, starting at the <u>top</u> edge. Adjust the stitch to whatever length the trim wants. Allow the trim to unspool as you sew all around the bag. As you close in on your starting position, clip the trim so that the two ends butt together.

7. When you reach your starting point, cross back onto the original stitch line, pivot, and sew down the raw trim edge (the <u>right</u> side) to the bottom edge. Pivot and sew around the bag in the same direction. If any fullness accrues, trim it or push the excess under the strap. At the end, secure the stitch with a few short stitches.

Sew the trim-line on all the bags before proceeding to the next step.

19. The Fifth Pass

It's time to pin the straps onto the tailored bags. You will need the stack of bags, your collection of straps, pins, your spacers and the bag insert. This process is identical to the boxed bags, other than the different spacer.

If you want to insert a horizontal fabric tag indicating you made the grocery bag, you'll need them too. I place mine under a strap on the front panel where it can be seen, and when the strap is sewn down, the label is sewn down as well. I don't buy pre-made labels. I use red rayon seam tape (½-inch-wide) or ribbon (3/8- or ½-inch wide). I cut 2-inch-long pieces, fold them over wrong sides together, and insert them when I pin the straps down. I put them in every bag I sew as my marker. It is a tiny pop of color and makes the bag look more professional. I like red, but any color will do. It is not necessary for functionality so you can skip this part.

If you haven't made your spacers and insert, now is the time to do so. The sizes and directions are in Chapter 5. Spacers make pinning the straps much faster as you won't have to measure their

Arrange the straps so each end rests against the bottom spacer and alongside the side spacers. Make sure the ends of the trim-line are covered.

location on every bag. The bag insert is vital for pinning down the straps without pinning them to the other side of the bag. You'll go crazy without the insert.

Lay a bag, front-panel-side up, on your work surface. Slide in the bag insert so that it lies directly behind the front panel down to the bottom seam. The insert will be longer than it is wide and the excess will stick out of the bag. You can also used the boxed bag insert for tailored bags.

Arrange the spacers on the bag. Place one of the wider spacers on each side of the front panel, aligning its far edge with the inner line of stitching on the flange. Place the narrow spacer along the bottom, aligning the long edge with the inner line of stitching on the flange. Arrange the straps so each end rests against the bottom spacer and alongside the side spacers. Make sure the strap is not twisted. Pin both legs of the strap in place.

For ease of sewing, I pin with the points oriented toward the mouth of the bag so I can remove them easily as I sew down the strap.

If you are going to add a horizontal fabric tag, insert it underneath the inner side of the left strap about an inch or so below the trim-line. Adjust it until you like the way it looks and pin it in place.

Flip the bag over and

If you pin the straps with the points oriented toward the mouth of the bag, you can remove them easily as you sew down the strap.

readjust the insert so it again slides against the back panel down to the bottom flange.

Place your spacers, arrange the straps and pin them down.

Repeat this process with all of the bags.

20. The Sixth Pass

This is the last step. You will sew down the straps, first on the front panel and then the back panel. The procedure for a tailored bag is identical to a boxed bag.

Sew down each strap using a single, continuous stitch line, never removing the needle from the strap or cutting the thread until the strap is sewn down. Each strap is sewn down twice, with the second line of stitching immediately inside the line along the edge. This requires some back and forthing, but this method is faster and sturdier than making two separate lines of stitching. Refer to the stitch diagrams on pages 122-124.

Starting at the open end of the bag, sew down the side of the strap, alongside the edge, removing pins as you go.

As part of this process, I also zigzag over the raw, narrow, bottom edges of the straps twice, securing them from fraying.

The process is difficult and cumbersome to explain but not hard to do. All that stitching ensures those straps aren't ever going to come loose.

Remember, keep the panels apart as you feed the bag through the sewing machine. It is endlessly annoying to discover you sewed the back panel down to the front along with the straps and have to rip out all that stitching. See pages 120-122 for the stitching diagrams.

THE PROCESS

Place the bag front panel up and slide the top of the left side strap under the presser foot. Start at the very top, left side of the strap where it lays on top of the fabric panel. Set your stitch to a short length to secure the stitch line and then adjust to a longer length to suit the bag. Sew down the side of the strap, right alongside the edge, removing pins as you go.

The bottom of the strap determines what you do next.

If the bottom edge is a folded edge, pivot and sew alongside the edge with the usual straight stitch, pivot again at the other side and sew up to the top of the bag.

If the strap bottom is a raw edge, enclose it in a zigzag stitch. Sew down to the bottom edge, and pivot. Reset the sewing machine to a wide, close zigzag stitch and slowly sew across the bottom edge, completely enclosing it within the stitching. At the end, pivot and reset your machine to a straight stitch and sew up the other side of the strap. As you work around the corners, adjust the placement of the bag under the needle. A tiny skip won't weaken the sewing.

After navigating the bottom edge, proceed up the side of the strap toward the top of the bag. If you have a tag, sew it in here. Pivot at the top and go across the top of the strap, securing it to the lip of the bag.

When you are back where you started, stitch back down towards the bottom edge, this time keeping your stitch line 1/8 inch inside the first line of stitching. Sew all the way to the bottom and then either enclose the raw edge in a second line of zigzag stitching <u>or</u> if the edge is a fold, sew a second line 1/8-inch above the first line.

Proceed back up to the top. Sew across the top of the strap below the first line of stitching, securing the strap to the bag's lip. Secure the stitching with shorter stitches, cut the bag free, and you're done.

Repeat the process with the right-hand side of the strap on the front panel. Then flip the bag over and do the same thing to both legs of the strap on the back panel.

STORING YOUR BAGS

Put the finished bag on the stack, laying it flat with the side gussets out and the bottom of the bag folded towards the inside. Laying the bags this way — they want to do it on their own — keeps them flat and wrinkle-free.

Another way to store a lot of bags is to lay them flat, in the same position, and then roll them up from gusset side to gusset side, letting the straps hang free. Store them in a box or in another bag.

One way to store the bags is to roll them up from gusset side to gusset side, letting the straps hang free, and store them in another bag.

21. Tailored Frankenstein Bags

Frankenstein bags are what I call the grocery bags made from mismatched fabric. I make both kinds, tailored and boxed. We'll talk about tailored Frankenstein bags here. Boxed Frankenstein bags are back in Chapter 13.

Because I lay out panels and gussets so that I cut as many as I can from a piece of cloth, I often end up with a leftover panel or gusset. These extras go into a stack to be matched up later with other panels and gussets that look acceptable together.

I also make far more mismatched bags. I take scrap fabric that isn't big enough to cut a single panel or gusset and piece it together. Sometimes they're matched so that the seams don't show. Other times, well, let's say that these bags can look avant-garde. They function fine and since I am using up cloth that would otherwise be wasted, these Frankenstein bags cost only my time.

The Frankenstein bags are another reason why I stick strictly to cutting my panels the same size and my gussets the same length (sometimes with varying widths). I can turn these leftovers into bags and those pieces don't go to waste.

When matching panels to gussets, the most important criteria is weight. Are the panels and gussets of a similar thickness and hand? This is far more important than matching colors. Having a panel that is noticeably thinner or drapier than the other panel and gusset will result in a bag that doesn't sew up straight. This bag will also tend to be tippy in use.

PIECING PANELS

Panels and gussets can also be pieced. As you would expect, match for weight first and then for color and pattern. When you piece a panel or gusset, the location of the piecing seam matters when you sew the bag.

Panel seams work best when they run horizontally across the width of the panel, staying 5 inches below the top and at least 2 inches above the bottom. This is so the seam does not interfere with the foldover at the top and its trim-line or the corner seams at the bottom. Vertical seams in the panel work, as long they aren't under the straps. The extra bulk can make the sewing harder. All the added thickness in a seam will make the flange sewing harder, but not impossible, as long as you avoid putting a seam near the corners.

Gusset seams that are parallel to the length of the gusset are fine. Gusset seams that are perpendicular to the length of the gusset are more problematic. They interfere with sewing the flanges (as do panel seams) and you must avoid putting a seam near where the gusset turns the corner.

If you piece both your gusset and your panels, then you have to be sure none of those seams intersect in the flange, as the added bulk will make the sewing machine balk and refuse to sew through all those layers. That means getting out a sturdy needle, the pliers and thimble, and hand-sewing those sections. Piece carefully to avoid the aggravation, laying the panel next to the gusset and seeing where the seams intersect before you sew the bag together.

When I piece a seam, I decide if I want it to show. Do I place the seam margins on the inside of the bag or the outside? I've done both. Seams on the outside get finished with a contrasting narrow twill tape, which strengthens the seam and adds a design element.

I sew all piecing seams with a 5/8-inch seam, then press both seam margins to one side. If I am going to sew a layer of ½-inch twill tape over the raw edge, I trim the underlaying seam margin before sewing down the twill tape. If I am not going to use twill tape to cover the raw edge, I enclose both raw edges with an overcasting stitch. If you have a serger, use that instead. Then I press and sew down the seam margin, along the edge, to force it to lay flat and reinforce the seam. On the outside of the bag, you can see the parallel lines: the ditch and the seam next to it. I do not use this seam finish if I'm putting the seam on the outside of the bag. I use twill tape for that.

Sometimes, I use twill tape to cover the inside seams instead of overcasting the raw edges. It depends largely on the fabric's thickness. If the cloth is very heavy and thick, the added layer of twill tape becomes a real concern when sewing the flanges. Overcasting adds less bulk and thread is cheaper than twill tape. Both methods are equally strong. The underlaying seam margin needs to be trimmed before sewing down the twill tape. The twill tape method leaves more lines of stitching showing on the bag's surface. It also adds a stiffening line, similar to a limp piece of boning.

Being willing to use up stray panels and gussets, along with piecing still more panels and gussets from odd-shaped scraps, will allow you to make more bags that are essentially free. Otherwise useless fabric gets used up and you didn't spend any extra money, just your time.

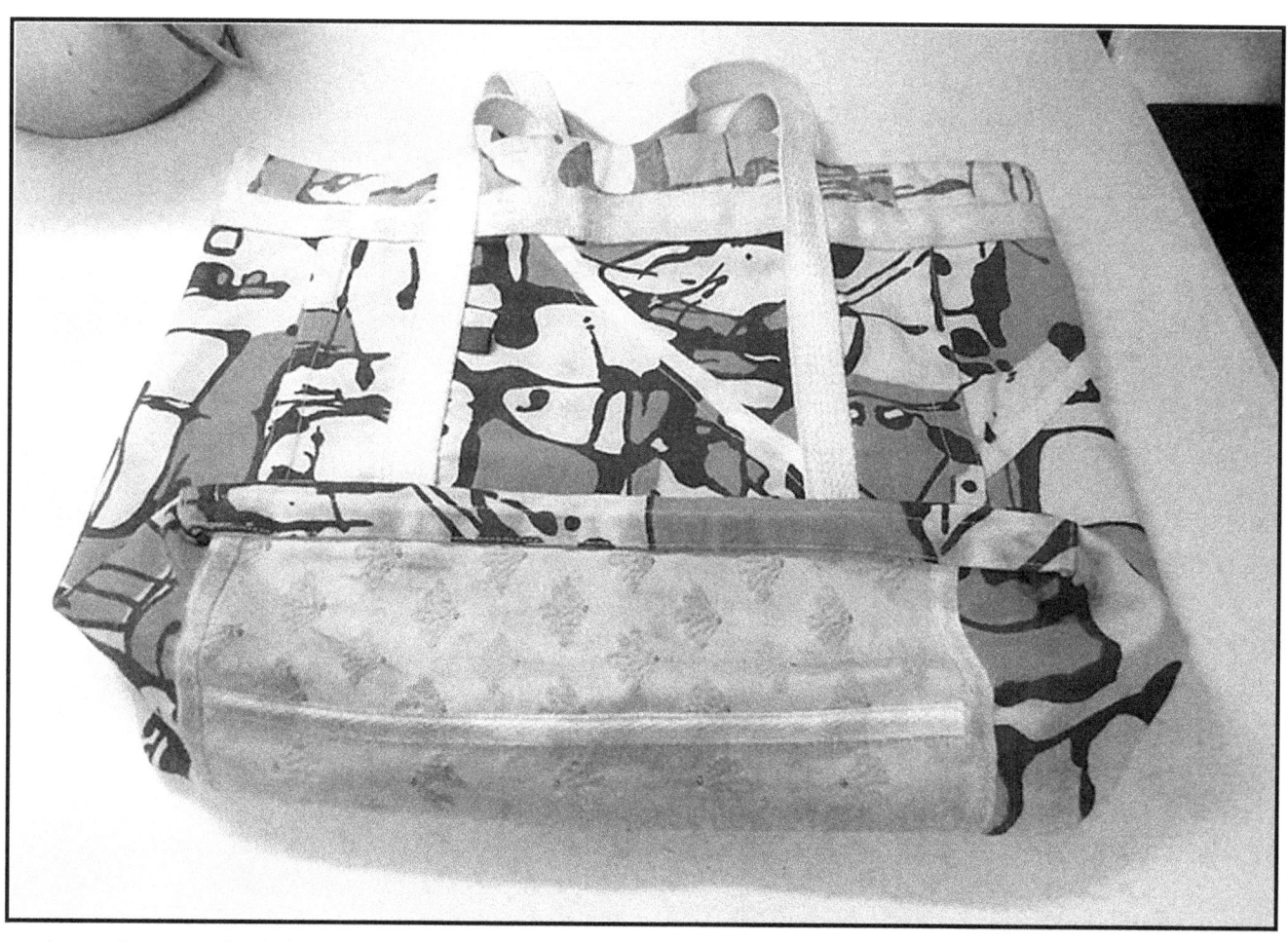

The outside seams get finished with a contrasting narrow twill tape, which strengthens the seam and adds a design element.

22. Layout Example #1: Brown Floral and Paisley Bags

As I've said before, repurposing fabric to make bags is a great use of saved or found material.

Shopping for fabric is fun, but it doesn't always get used up. Frequently, we end up with extra material that we don't want to throw away. So we put it in a box and feel virtuous because we didn't toss it. After all, we paid for it!

If you do this over the years like I have, a feeling of guilt begins to grow in you. You see the fabric and tell yourself, "I need to do something with that." But most of the time, nothing happens. And the stash grows and, as it does, it weighs on us, because we can't figure out what to do with it.

Making bags solves that problem. You make something functional and beautiful, use up those remnants you've been saving all those years, and feel *really great about it* at the same time. Win-win-win!

So, in this chapter and the next, I'll take you through the thinking and measuring process, where we'll take fabric from my stash and figure out how to make as many bags as possible, with little or no waste.

LAY OUT TWICE, CUT ONCE

This chapter is an example of how I cut out a set of tailored bags, using an odd-sized piece of fabric. Tailored bags are more challenging to lay out than boxed bags, hence these two chapters will clarify the procedure.

Layout is <u>critical</u> for getting maximum bags with zero waste. I always measure, calculate, and draw on paper how to cut out as many sets of gussets and panels as the yardage will let me. Panels don't vary in size. Gussets, however, while always the same length, can vary in width, depending on the available yardage.

I laid out the brown floral/paisley fabric on the floor to measure. I had 118 inches (about 3¼ yards) of 45-inch-wide fabric. That was enough for several bags, including side panels and gussets.

Before measuring, I took the trouble to pull threads from both raw edges, ensuring that I started with a straight edge on the grain. I was fortunate in that this piece of fabric had been cut straight to begin with. The cut edge of yardage can often be wavy, cut at an angle, or very uneven. That translates into less fabric that you can use, when every inch counts and all those inches have to be straight.

As explained above, a tailored bag consists of a front and back panel and a gusset that connects the panels in a sort of U shape. That's three pieces of fabric, plus a pair of straps made from webbing.

Each panel will be my standard size of 13-by-15 inches. My gussets will be 43 inches long and the width will be what the fabric wants to divide into, approximately 8 inches wide. Seven inches is getting narrow, so you never want to cut less than this. Nine inches is too wide, resulting in a square-bottomed grocery bag.

The length of the gusset is determined by the length of both sides plus the bottom. With side panels that are 13 inches wide and 15 inches tall, you will need a gusset that is 15 inches plus 15 inches (the two sides) plus 13 inches (the bottom measurement) for a total length of 43 inches. In reality, this gives you a margin for error as this measurement is a little too long; I learned through sad experience that you don't want to cut your gusset short in an effort to save expensive cloth. I end up having to sew in a patch, adding time and aggravation to the experience.

If you make your side panels larger, say 16 inches tall and 14 inches wide, you will need to make your gusset correspondingly longer: 16 plus 16 plus 14 or 46 inches long.

My handy charts show me that with a 45-inch-wide fabric, I can cut three panels 15 inches long if I stack them, one on top of the next. There will be zero waste, assuming that I include the selvages in my measurements. I nearly always do unless they are woven too tightly and they distort the sides of the cloth. Most of the selvage will be concealed within the hems where it won't show. At most, it will appear as a narrow line on one side of the panel. Selvages included as part of the gusset never show because of the way the bags are constructed.

During my panel and gusset calculation, I also keep track of **kerf**.

The word kerf is taken from carpentry and represents the thickness of the saw blade. When you cut wood, you have to measure and mark your line, cut the part off, and then measure and mark the next cut. You can never make all your measurements followed by all your cuts because the act of cutting with a saw blade eats a thin sliver of wood and throws off the measurements. Scissors and rotary cutters have a much smaller kerf than a saw blade does, but there is some and it accumulates over many parallel cuts in the length of a long piece of fabric. I allow for this by allotting a few inches over what my measurements suggest I need.

Pulling threads also uses up fabric. The width of two pulled threads doesn't seem like much, but again, when you pull threads, in parallel sets across the length of a piece of yardage, it adds up and that last set of panels will be smaller than you had calculated.

The brown paisley fabric does not have a definite direction so I can use the most economical layout for my panels and gussets. This is readily apparent in how 45-inch-wide fabric divides nicely into three 15-inch panels, each 13 inches wide. It doesn't divide nearly as well into 13-inch panels, leaving me with a 6-inch-wide strip that is too narrow to use for anything else.

(Here's the math: 13 times 3 is 39; 45 inches minus 39 inches equals a 6-inch-wide strip.)

THE LAYOUT PROCESS

I started by drawing my picture. This was a very rough sketch as you can see on the next page.

I drew my rectangle and then the gussets on the right and my panels on the left. Panels must always be in pairs.

I started with estimating the width of the gussets. Nine inches is too wide and it eats more fabric than 8-inch-wide gussets do. That is, six 9-inch gussets need a total of 54 inches, whereas six 8-inch gussets need only 48 inches in width, a difference of 6 inches.

Starting at the panel side, if I lay my panels one on top of another, I can get three 15-inch panels, each 13 inches wide. Two columns of panels will eat 26 inches, and give me three bags. Two more columns of panels will eat another 26 inches and give me three more bags, for a total of six bags (12 panels). Six columns need 52 total inches of fabric.

It looked like, from my sketch, that I would have about 12 inches left over, after cutting twelve panels (four columns worth) and six gussets, each nine inches wide. Twelve inches is awfully close to 13 inches in width.

If I cut my gussets narrower, I could get another full column of panels, giving me seven bags and one panel left over for the Frankenstein pile.

That is what I did. I started at the straightened edge and drew a chalk line 13 inches

Layout Example #1: Brown Floral and Paisley Bags

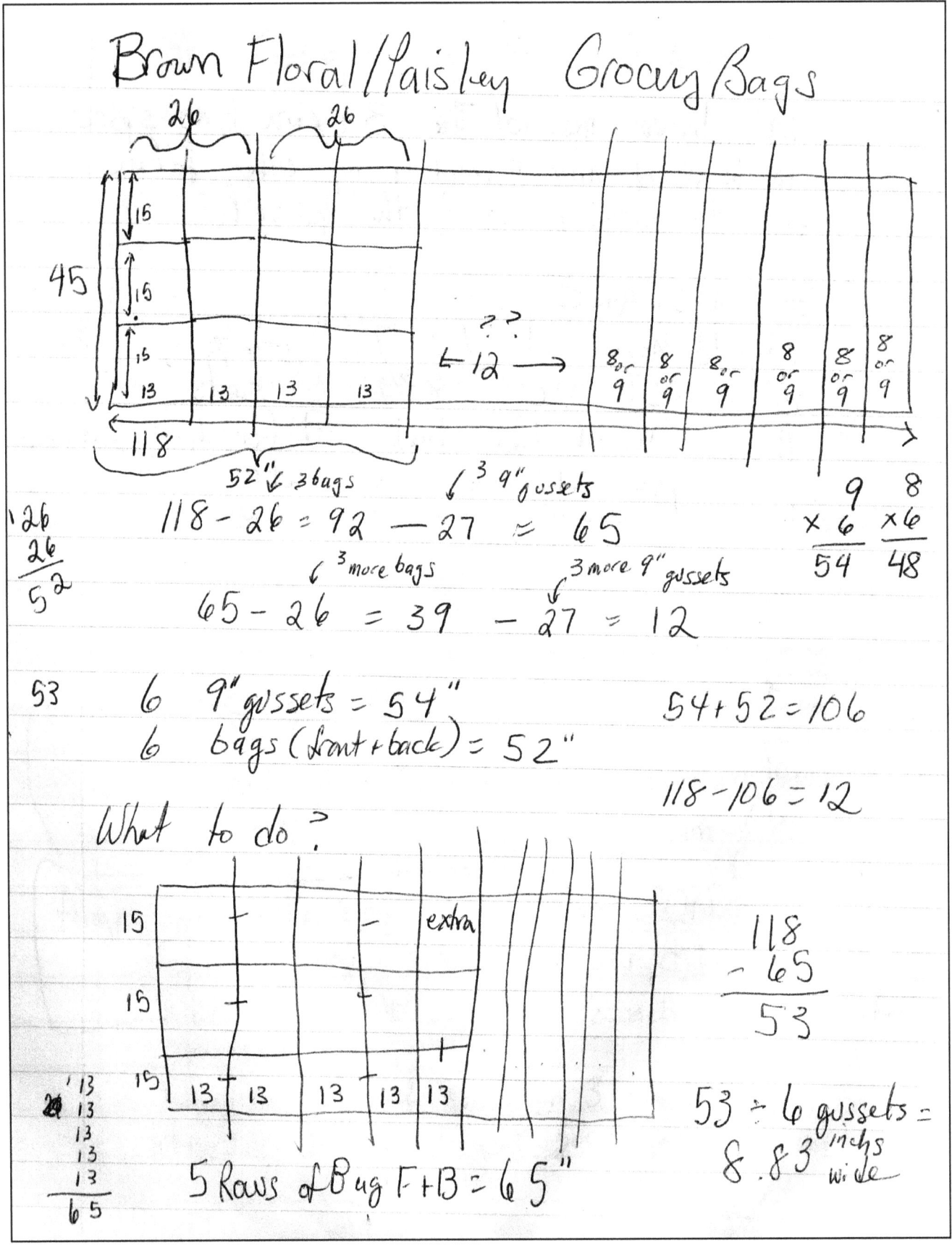

This page from my notebook shows I estimated what I could get out of the fabric.

in. I cut my fabric into a 13-inch-wide column stretching the width of the fabric. I cut this column into three panels, each 15 inches in height. I repeated this until I had cut five 13-inch-wide columns, cutting each column into thirds. This gave me seven pairs of panels with one left over.

The remaining fabric was ready to be turned into gussets. The gussets were oriented to run from selvage to selvage as they are 43 inches in length, fitting nicely within the 45-inch span of fabric. I went back and forth on how to do this. Subtracting 65 inches from 118 inches gives me 53 inches of cloth for the gussets. I can't cut them 9 inches wide. Dividing 53 inches by seven (that is, seven gussets) gives me 7.57 inches, a difficult measurement to make. Dividing 53 inches by six (that is, six gussets) gives me 8.83 inches each.

I chose to make six gussets, simply because it was easier to cut them. When cutting gussets, remember they don't have to be exactly the same width; length is what matters. I didn't have to measure 8.83 inches. Instead, I ironed the piece of fabric flat, folded it exactly in half, and then cut up the fold line. That gave me two identically sized pieces. I measured off 8 5/8 inches, drew my chalk line and cut that gusset. I then folded the remaining piece of cloth and cut along the fold line, giving me two more gussets, each about 8 5/8 inches wide.

I repeated this with the other piece of fabric. This gave me six gussets, each about 8 5/8 inches wide. This left me with an extra pair of panels, plus a spare panel to go into the Frankenstein pile. The alternative was to measure a gusset 7 5/8 inches wide, then iron the remaining fabric, fold it and cut along the fold line. That would have given me two pieces of fabric, that could have been cut into six more gussets, each about 7½ inches wide.

It felt too narrow, too close to seven inches, for my comfort, so I didn't do it. However, if I had done this, I would have gotten seven finished bags with only one unmatched panel for the Frankenstein pile versus the six bags I got with three stray panels left over. Seven bags, narrower ones to be sure, but seven bags instead of six.

This is the decision-making process that you will go through over and over when trying to squeeze out every gusset and panel possible from a piece of cloth. It can be time-consuming, but it results in greater savings and more productivity so it's worth it.

23. Layout Example #2: Blue and Gray Building Bags

Here is another example of how to lay out tailored grocery bags from a piece of fabric dug out of the stash. I bought this fabric a long, long time ago. I believe it came from the Walmart dollar bin, and it was, yes, a dollar a yard. I planned on sewing a coat or suit, but wiser heads prevailed, and it sank into the bottom of the stash.

The original length was about eight yards. When it came home all those years ago, I washed it and it shrank. It's now a few inches shy, but it's hard to tell how much because the edges are so uneven. The cloth also got narrower; it was 60 inches wide, and it is now, from selvage to selvage, 56¼ inches wide.

This fabric has plusses and minuses, as long forgotten stash fabric tends to. It's here, and it's free. I have a lot of it. The weight is heavy enough, but with a softer hand than I would have chosen. That won't stop this fabric from functioning as grocery bags but they won't stand up on their own either. That means the tailored bag style would be a better use for them than boxed bags.

This is also double-sided cloth. I can use either side as the right side. This is a real benefit as I can sew half of the bags with the lighter side out and half with the darker side out, giving me two color choices from one piece of cloth. With the foldover at the top, I get a contrasting, but perfectly matched border.

The drawback is that the fabric has a definite up-and-down image. It runs the length of the yardage as opposed to selvage-to-selvage.

DECIDING WHERE TO BEGIN

The best way to tackle a piece of fabric like this is to examine its orientation and measure it accurately. Decide if you want to include the selvages in your measurements. I nearly always do if the selvage isn't puckering or distorting the sides of the yardage. Every inch counts and most of the selvages will disappear into a seam. Measure the width, both with and without the selvages and see if including them will let you squeak out another set of panels or a gusset.

Then measure the length to see how much cloth you have to work with. Since you probably won't have a straight edge, start by choosing an end and straighten it by pulling threads until you have a perfectly straight, on-grain raw edge. All the panels and gussets have to be cut on the true, so start with a true edge.

Now that you have a true edge, measure the fabric again. You may have lost several inches after removing the raggedy end. It isn't necessary to go to the trouble of truing up the other end but when you remeasure, choose the shorter side of the uneven edge rather than the longer one if they are very different. It is immensely aggravating to discover when you cut that you mis-measured, and you won't get that full set of panels your diagram says you will.

This straight end is the one you will be cutting from.

This is another reason to subtract a few inches of your total working length. It gives you room for error.

MEASURING THE WIDTH

This fabric had been 60 inches wide. It would have cut very nicely into four panels, each 15 inches high, from selvage to selvage. That means zero waste.

But time took its toll, and it's 56 inches wide. That can't be divided into 13-inch or 15-inch increments evenly, so I used the cloth the way it wanted to go in the first place; each panel running alongside the selvage in 15-inch increments and stacking the 13-inch panels across the width of the cloth. By including the selvage in my measurements, I get four 13-inch panels using 52 inches of cloth in width, leaving a strip 4 inches wide. I can turn this strip into trim-lines or straps later.

The length of the fabric was 7 7/8 yards. To make my math easier, let's call it 7 yards and 32 inches, or 284 inches in all. This will give me a bit of margin.

This fabric's weave is open enough to let me to pull threads rather than mark the panels and gussets with chalk-lines. Pulled threads ensure perfectly square, on-grain panels and gussets. Pulling threads can be more troublesome than measuring and drawing chalk lines but it's much more accurate. Just remember this uses up a tiny bit more fabric with each set of panels and gussets measured, the threads pulled, and then cut apart. See my discussion of kerf in the previous chapter for details.

With my measurements set, I drew a rough rectangle.

At the right end, I drew seven horizontal gussets at my usual length of 43 inches long each. Fifty-six-inch-wide fabric divides into seven gussets, each 8 inches wide.

For these seven gussets, I needed fourteen panels; a pair for each. On the other side of the rectangle, I drew a grid indicating the panels. The fabric let me stack my panels four across the width, each 13 inches wide. The panels are 15 inches long. One column of panels (two bags) therefore used up fifteen inches of cloth. That led to marking out three more columns of bags, each using up a 15-inch-wide section.

In all, 60 inches of cloth divided into 16 panels. That's two more than I need, but I still have plenty of cloth left over.

Sixty inches of cloth for the panels and 43 inches of cloth for the gussets equals 103 inches. After subtracting 103 inches from my original length of 284 inches of cloth, I was left with 181 inches of cloth.

I already knew that 16 panels and seven gussets equals 103 inches so I can get that from the remaining 181 inches. I drew my picture to confirm this and, yes, I ended up with another set of sixteen panels (8 bags) and another set of seven gussets.

That meant I had 32 panels or 16 bags and 14 gussets. This did not match up evenly, but I still had 78 inches of cloth remaining.

I drew another picture. I started with the gussets, another set of seven as I knew that they would only take up 43 inches of cloth, leaving me with 35 inches of cloth left over (78 - 43 = 35). This gave me 21 gussets that needed matching up.

That final 35-inch width of cloth divides into two columns of bags (eight panels or four more bags) with 5 inches left over. My total count of bags then, was eight (round one) plus eight (round two) plus four (round three) for a final tally of 20 bags (40 panels).

My end result for 7 7/8 yards of 56-inch-wide cloth was 20 pairs of panels with 21 gussets. I had a stray gusset, but I will have that strip of fabric left over in the middle that's about 5 inches wide.

Remember that I underestimated by several inches how much yardage I actually have. That safety margin strip left over <u>may</u> be enough to piece another pair of panels to match my extra gusset. Or, I can add the extra gusset to my Frankenstein pile of tailored bag parts, along with whatever is left over. I won't know until <u>after</u> I'm finished cutting panels and gussets.

Pages 82-84: On the next three pages are my notes showing how I figured this out. I couldn't draw a piece of fabric this big, so I worked out the math in sections. Once you start cutting, you can't go back!

Blue & Gray

22 APR 2017

Buildings totebags

8yds? No! just shy of it (some shrinkage from washing) for overages & cutting waste better to use 7 7/8ths yards or **7 yds + 32 inches**

Width (including selvedge) 56 1/4
width (minus selvedge)

SELVEDGE is (USABLE) 55 1/4

Strong vertical pattern

```
 15
 15
 13
 ---
 43
```

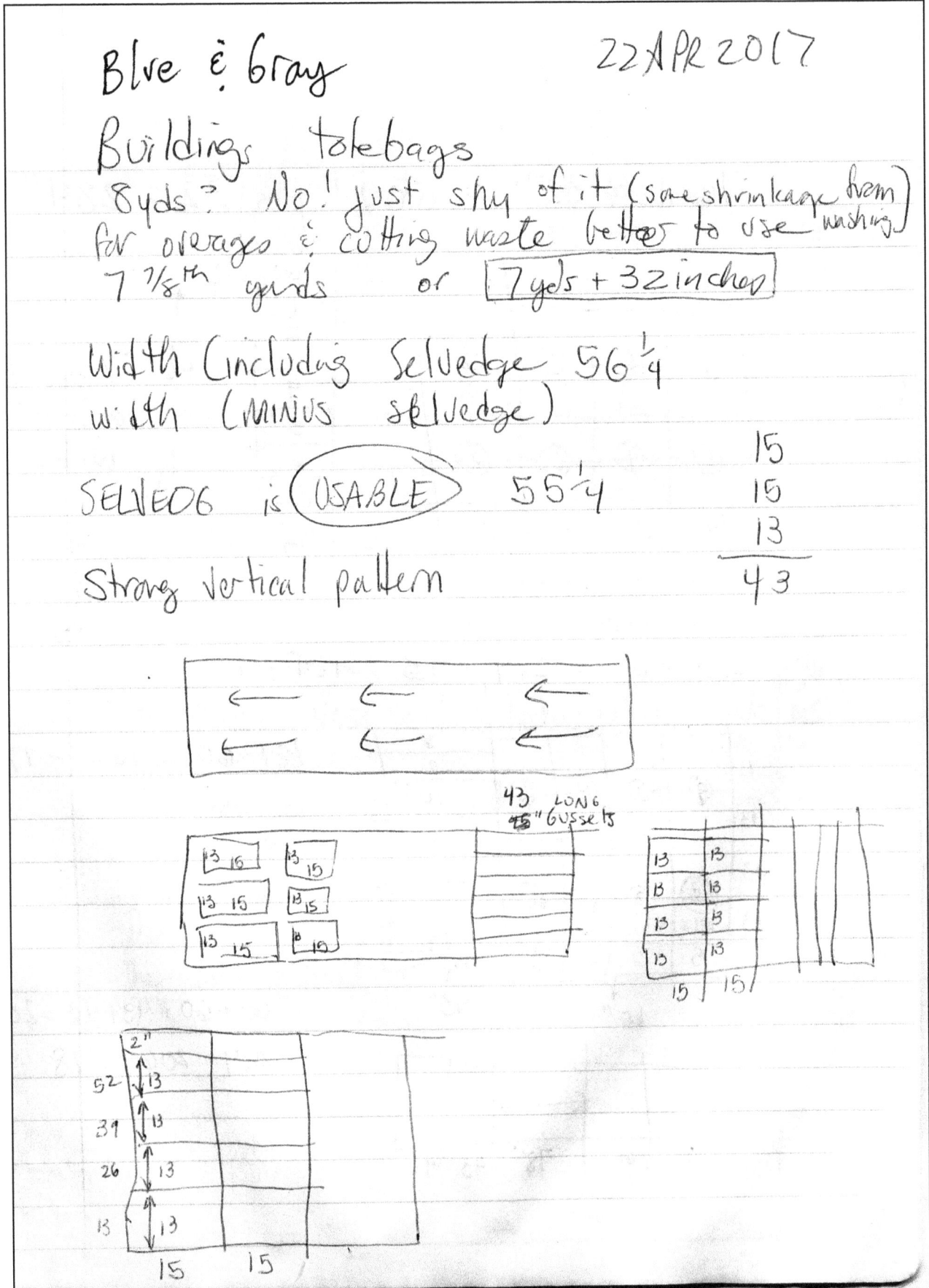

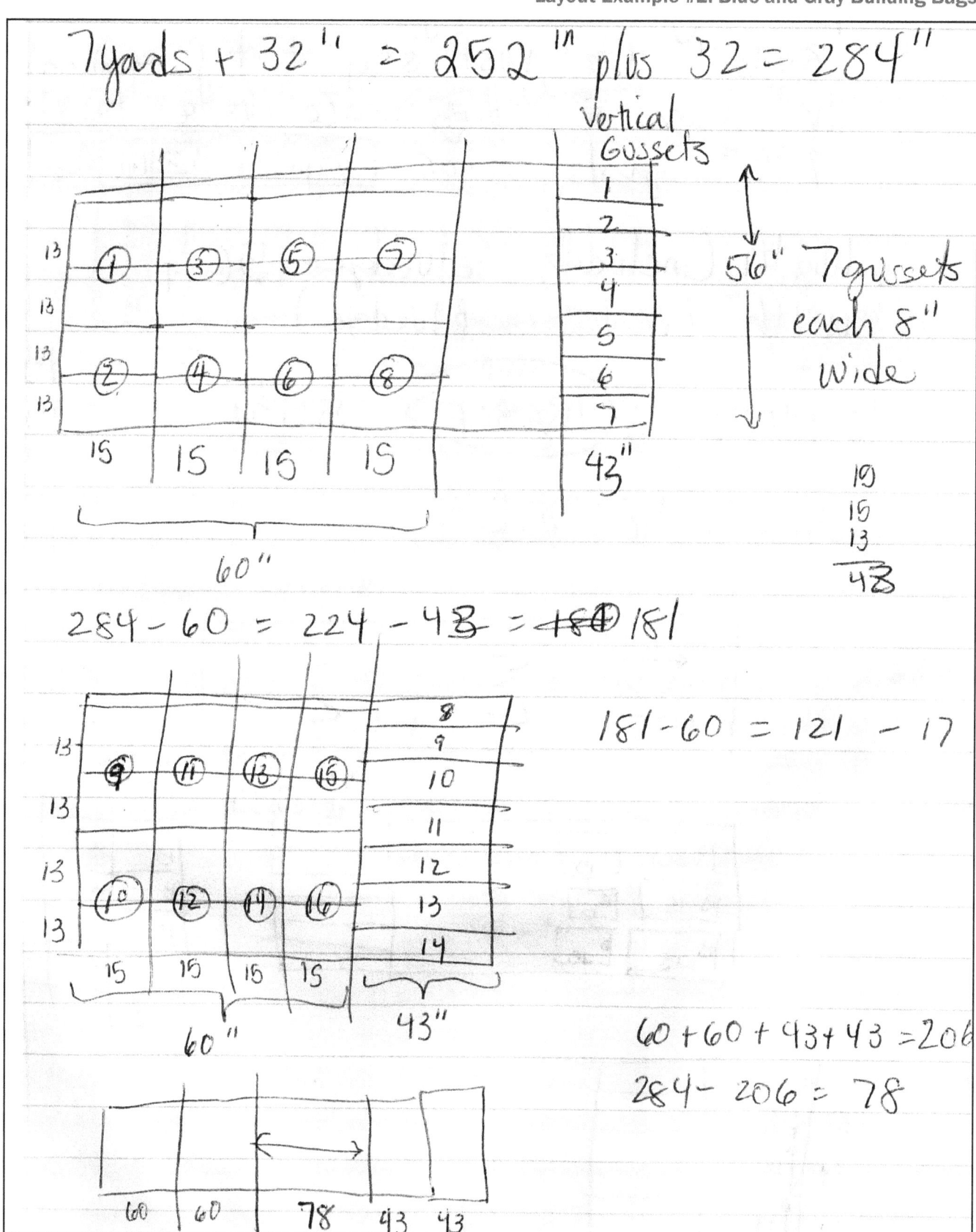

Layout Example #2: Blue and Gray Building Bags

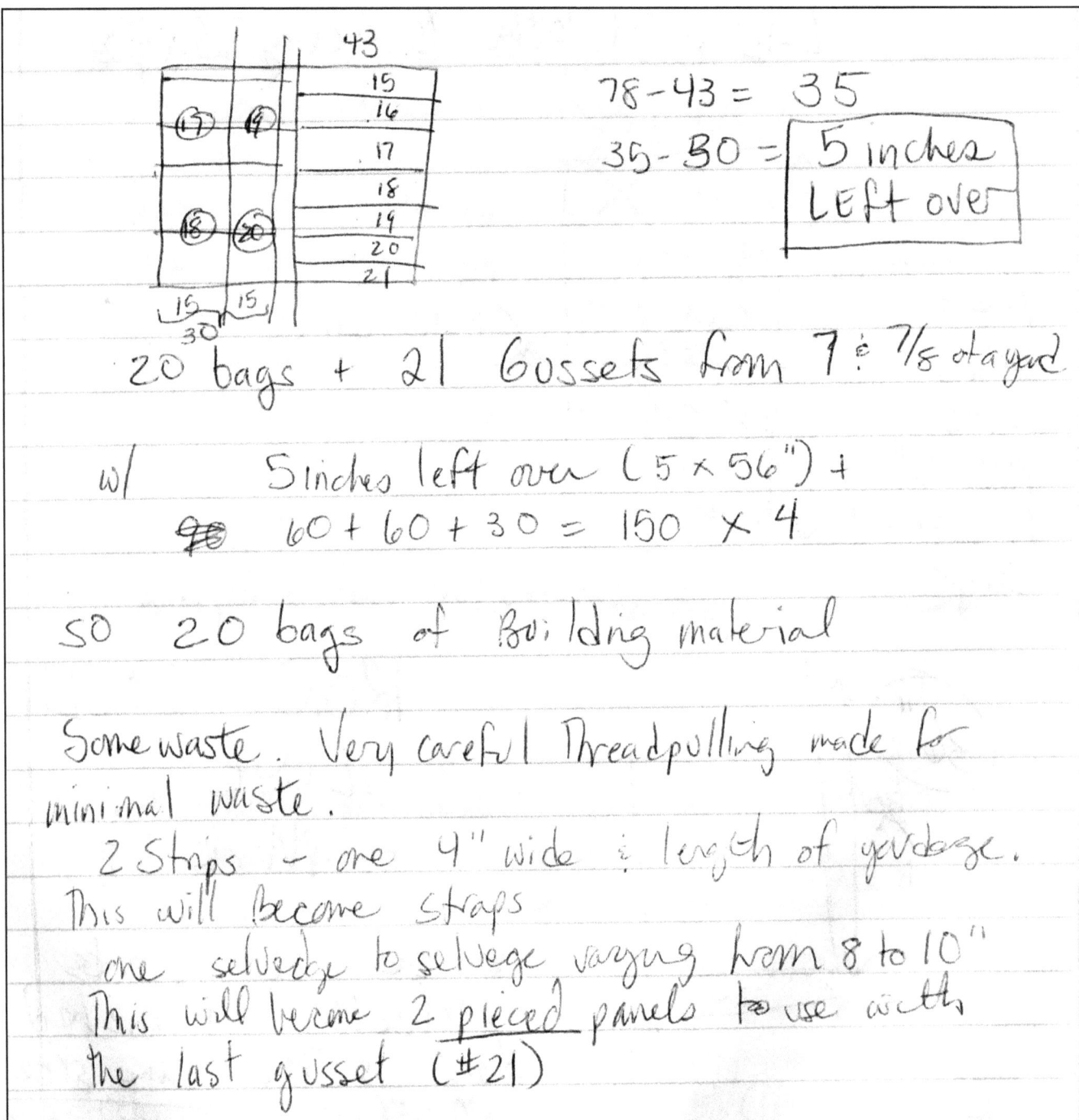

Cutting the Fabric

I started at the true edge, measured 43 inches, pulled my thread, cut the line, and divided that 43-inch piece into seven gussets. I did this two more times, ending up with 21 gussets. So far so good.

Then I measured, pulled threads, and cut apart my bag panels, column by column. When I finished, I had 40 panels, which makes 20 bags. I also had a strip left over that was 11 inches long at its widest and 8 inches at its narrowest and the full width of the fabric from selvage to selvage.

That's more than the five inches I expected, but that can't be helped now. The question was: What should I do with this? I considered my options:

1. Cut this strip into an 8-by-43-inch gusset, with the design orientation 180 degrees from the other gussets. It would go into the Frankenstein pile with the other extra gusset.

2. Cut four 13-inch-wide sections across the width of the fabric and piece another pair of panels, then trim them to 15 inches in length. Those two pieced panels would let use my stray gusset, giving me 21 bags from my 7 7/8-yard fabric. The pieced bag will be just as strong and functional as the whole cloth bags.

That's what I did. I had almost zero waste; several long narrow strips that could become trim-lines or straps, plus a few bits. I also had a mare's nest of pulled threads. That's it.

The biggest issue in sewing these bags was the fabric. It turned out that this cloth was a little too soft in its hand. These particular bags, even with the skeletal structure imposed on them by the flanges, would never be self-supporting. Moreover, the softness of the cloth didn't play as well as it could have with the doubled ribbon straps. I got puckering if I sewed the straps down too fast.

Fortunately, the bags look very nice and they should function just fine. You can see from the picture that both the light blue and dark blue sides look good. It's not perfect, but that is the

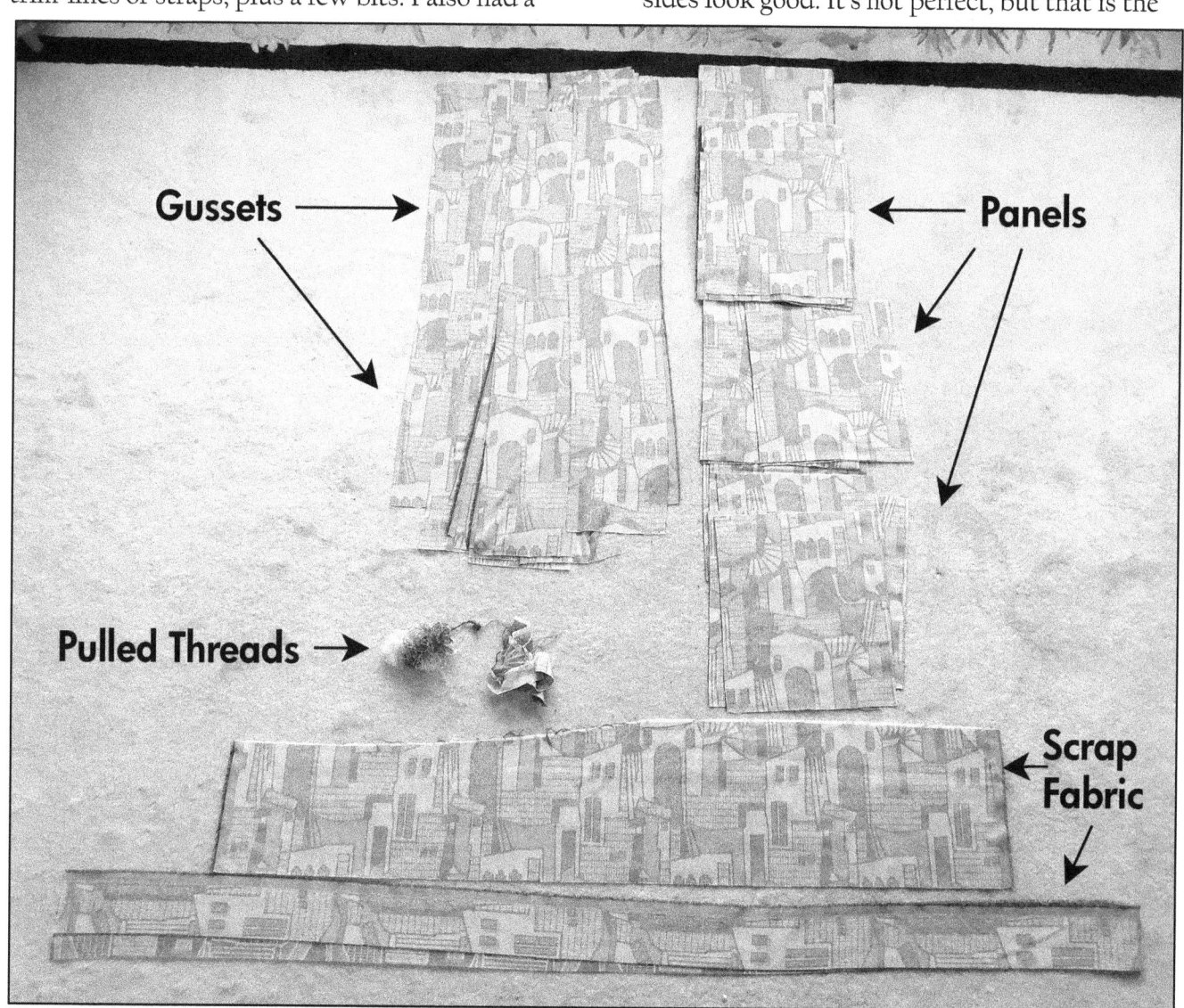

By laying out my panels and gussets on paper first, I was able to cut up this fabric with nearly zero waste.

Layout Example #2: Blue and Gray Building Bags

chance you take when using cloth out of the stash. It has to be used for <u>something</u>. Never forget: The cost of the fabric matters. Free fabric is worth taking the risk of the tension on the seam being not quite right, despite all the fiddling. And really, how noticeable will this be to anyone but me?

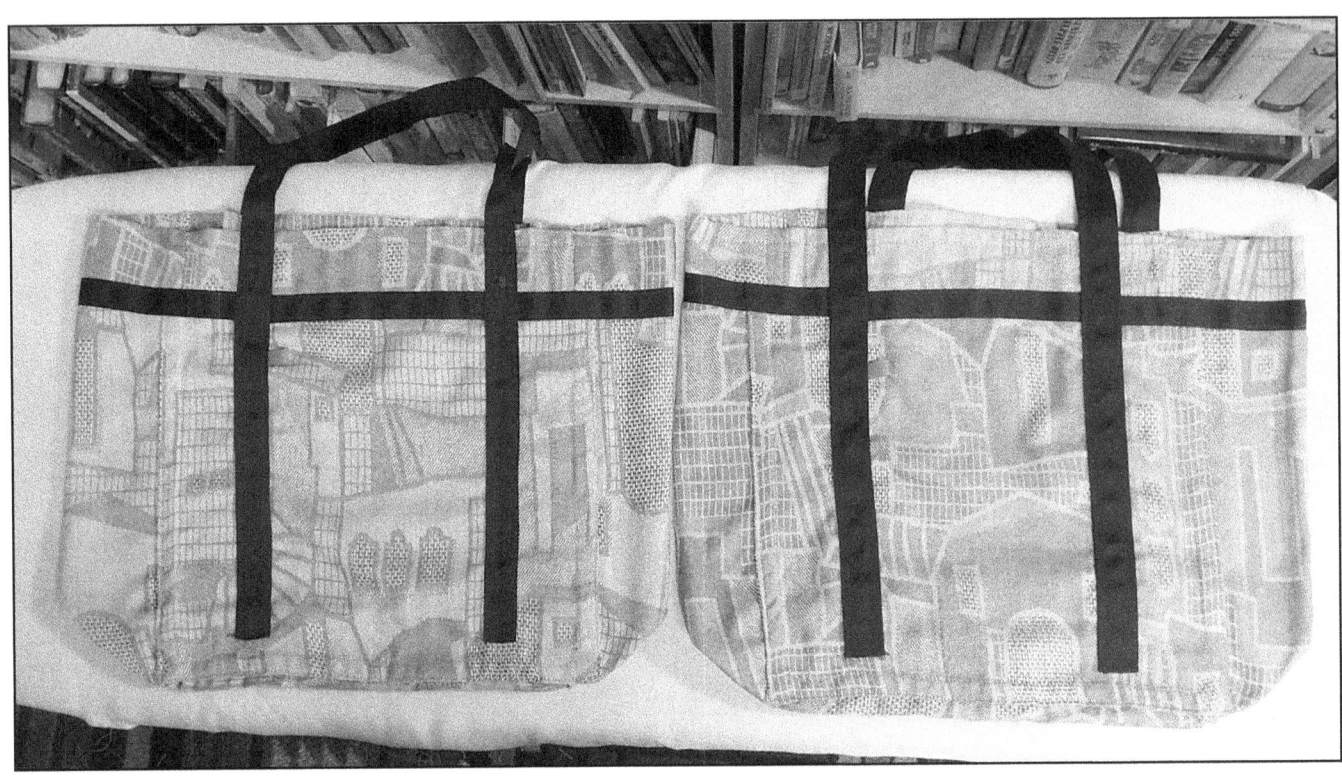

This fabric worked well with either side facing outward, giving customers more options to choose from.

Part IV: Production Sewing and Selling

24. Production Sewing

Production sewing is not the same as home sewing. You're not sewing as a hobby, to clothe your family, or to express yourself creatively. This is sewing as a business. It's a job, and like any job, you want to be productive, efficient, and professional. Your time is limited, and the less you spend at your job, the more time you can spend with your family or doing something you love.

This chapter will discuss what I've learned about production sewing and how it applies to sewing grocery bags in quantity. There isn't much information out there about sewing the same thing over and over, especially for the home seamstress. I taught myself how to do this, and I'll pass along to you what I learned.

Home Sewers And Patterns

There are differences between home sewing and production sewing. For example, look at the way home sewers treat patterns. The companies that sell them assume you'll make only one item and only one at a time. If you're making matching pajamas for the family for Christmas, figuring out the yardage needed is easy. You just add up all yardage the pattern says for the five sizes you need to make.

But is it that simple? You may realize you can lay smaller pattern pieces in the spaces between the larger ones and discover when you get to the end, that you've got enough yardage left over to make two more pairs of pjs. This translates into money you didn't need to spend.

When you cut the pajama pieces out, do you want to make only one cut between a pair of legs or two? If you cut out all those triangle marking points, then you cannot lay one pattern piece directly alongside another. If you aren't matching plaids, then do you need all those triangle points sticking out? Wouldn't it be nice if one cut gave you the raw edge on two separate pattern pieces? A closer layout would save fabric, too, enabling you to buy less.

When you sew the pajama pieces together, should you stay-stitch all those neck edges at once or do them as you come to them, one set of pjs at a time? Should you set in all the sleeves on all the tops at once? Or do them one set at a time? How about buttonholes? Once your machine is set up for buttonholes, you should sew all those buttonholes on all those plackets at the same time.

This is not the way home sewers operate. Certainly, everything I've sewed has been one-offs or I sewed multiples of a pattern one at a time spread out over years. Sometimes, what I sewed has been very complicated but each item was a stand-alone.

Learning Production Sewing

When I began sewing grocery bags, I had to work out my own methods— the methods you are reading about now. Fortunately, cloth grocery bags have straight sides and right angles, making it much easier to work out the process than multiple sets of pajamas in multiple sizes would have been. Writing this book drove me to think even harder about the best ways to make bags in quantity.

Here's what I learned about sewing as a

business:

- **Cost matters.** If you want to sell bags or any other products as a home-based business, then you have to keep a laser focus on cost. You won't earn any money if you can't sell each bag for enough money to pay for what you spent plus profit. This doesn't just include the cost of fabric. Cloth is not going to be your biggest expense. Your time is what costs you the most. You could source the fabric for less than $1 a yard, the webbing for pennies, and the thread from big cones you bought at the outlet. The time you invest in each bag, however, won't change until you become more efficient.

  How to do that? Outsource the easy jobs to helpful family members (see Chapter 9). They cannot operate a sewing machine, but they don't need to in order to turn bags right-side-out, iron, or clip thread tails. That's time you don't spend that you use for something nobody else can do.

- **Learn chain piecing.** If you make quilts and do machine piecing, then you're already familiar with chain piecing. Chain piecing saves you time and thread. Thread costs money, too, and those spools add up fast. If you're sewing dozens of bags, then consider where you could chain the sections to speed up the process. Have your assistant cut the chains apart and snip off the thread tails. Chaining the production process will change the order of operations a little, but if you want to make hundreds of bags, then look into it. Keep notes as you go for future reference.

- **Get a serger.** I have a horror of raw edges. They don't strengthen the seam, they unravel, they don't add any structure, and they look messy and unprofessional. With a serger, you can sew the seam and finish it at the same time. A serger would completely change the sewing process and make it faster.

I can't describe how to serge a grocery bag, either the boxed or the tailored version (although I have suggestions below). What I can suggest is make a bag (either kind) the regular way, then dig out that Hannah Montana fabric that nobody will accept even for free and serge a few bags, making mistakes and figuring out what you want to change. Again, keep detailed notes as you go.

I <u>think</u> you would only have to make one pass for the boxed bag, sewing it wrong sides together. The triangular wedge would be sewn with a regular stitch on your sewing machine and then sewn down with a regular stitch as would the flange. Or, sew the bag right sides together with the serged seam on the inside. Then, use your serger to sew the triangular wedge, trimming it short. Use a regular stitch to secure the serged flanges down. Or not. See what works.

The tailored bag should be similar. A serger would allow you to make many fewer passes through the sewing machine, saving you valuable time. You should end up with all your serged seams on the outside of the bag. If you sew them down to reinforce the sides, the bag will still function the same way; it will even look similar to a tailored bag sewn the usual way other than the thread edging the flanges. If you serge a tailored bag with the finished seams on the inside of the bag, sew the seams down as usual. The finished bag should look very neat, with all the stitching concealed inside.

One result I can forecast is that your finished bag (whichever type you make) will be slightly larger as you haven't used up as much cloth in seam margins. This is not a flaw so don't change the size of the pattern pieces. I chose those sizes to minimize cutting waste.

A serger won't help you with the straps or the foldover. It could help you with the trim-line, if you choose to serge the raw edge before doing the foldover. If you do this, the serged edge <u>becomes</u> the finished edge. A contrasting thread, with the stitches close together, could look very nice and completely enclose the raw edge. It would be faster and use cheaper thread as opposed to more expensive trim. The serged bottom edge of the foldover would still have to be sewn down to keep it in place.

- **Shorten the straps.** I make long straps, sewing them down almost to the bottom of the bag. They take more time to sew and use more costly webbing or fabric or twill tape. If you're sewing 1,000 bags for the craft show circuit, cutting each strap one foot shorter will save 667 yards of webbing. That's significant money, yet each bag will still look good and function as it should.

- **Carefully choose your fabric.** You are competing with 99¢ bags that every store sells nowadays. Worse, some stores are now selling very cheap, stamped design canvas bags for $3.99

You probably can't get a customer at the craft show to pony up $10 for a plain canvas bag. Those are everywhere, and your careful sewing won't matter.

However, you can get $10 for a unique bag made of floral upholstery, denim, or striped drapery fabric. Those bags are special. A customer couldn't get the same design anywhere else. That matters to many people.

Going down this route means you shouldn't make too many of any given fabric. Uniqueness is your selling point. You also have to choose a wide range of fabrics (from the clearance rack) since your taste won't necessarily be the same as the customers. I've made plenty of bags that I thought would sell nicely, and I've been wrong. Other bags that I made — to use up the ugly, free fabric I had — I thought would never sell. I was wrong there, too. The customers determine what sells, and they won't think like you or like each other.

- **Don't take my methods as gospel.** If you come up with an idea that contradicts what I wrote, try it out. Feel free to alter my designs to suit your own circumstances. Use the fabric you like and can afford and can easily find. Make the bags in the way that works best for you.

- **Keep careful records.** Write down what you spend on material and how much time it takes you to sew a set of bags. Checking your records will also show you if you're making a profit from the business, and how much.

- **Do your homework.** Before sewing hundreds of bags to sell, research running a small business. When you report your income to the IRS, you'll need records to show how many hours you're spending at this work, and what you spend on fabric, sewing supplies, and other things that you can deduct. There are many books on this subject so I won't repeat their information.

- **Decide how to reach customers.** Local boutiques? You have to ask and what they'll accept this month might not be accepted next month. You have to meet their delivery requirements and quality standards which may not be easy to do.

The craft show circuit, local or regional? I've done this and sales vary wildly from show to show. The shows vary, too, from the very small show at your annual church bazaar (low cost of entry and small customer base) to the large show (high entry fee and many more customers).

Online in your Etsy store? I've never tried this route.

All of these venues have their benefits and drawbacks and the only way to find out what works is to try.

A book that covers many of these issues is "The Entrepreneur's Guide to Sewn Product Manufacturing" by Kathleen Fasanella. Ms. Fasanella published her book in 1997 so it is out of date in some ways. It is still the only book I could find that discusses production sewing. Ms. Fasanella's book would be useful, too, if you're successful enough to start hiring people to sew bags for you while you manage the business. It is an expensive book, so get your copy via your library's interlibrary loan service and then decide if you want to buy your own reference copy to refer back to, use her handy worksheets, and make notes in. She is strong-minded and doesn't believe in sugar-coating her advice.

If cloth grocery bags work out for you, you may decide to expand into other cloth items. Again, keep detailed notes on your sewing processes and track all your costs. Revise your methods as needed. Try different ways and see what works best, just like you should keep track of what designs sell best.

Here's an example you can use. When you go to the grocery store, there is another kind of bag that can be very, very useful especially if you have to travel a long way to get your expensive groceries back home. This is the insulated bag.

I have not made any, but I can see how it should be done. Make your boxed bag out of your fashion fabric. Make another boxed bag out of wool or cotton quilt batting. Make a third, inner bag out of aluminized ironing board cloth. The quilt batting bag fits between the fashion fabric and the ironing board cloth bags. You'll have to make a few prototypes to get the sizing correct since you want a snug fit and the inner bag should be ever so slightly smaller in its original cutting dimensions than the outer fashion fabric bag. You'll have to decide what kind of top flap you need to close the bag. Skip the zippers and use Velcro tabs for your closures.

Naturally, you will charge a premium for your insulated grocery bags since they are far more complex to make. Your insulated bags should work much better for hot and cold foods than what the store sells for a few bucks and, unlike the store's bags, your much more expensive bag will never rip. Do not quilt your bags since every needle punch in the ironing board fabric and the batting will allow for heat exchange (as well as take too much time). Instead, handle the quilt batting as you would interlining.

Use ironing board fabric to reflect back the temperature of what's in the bag. Use wool or cotton batting rather than polyester: it will hold up better over use.

Your insulated bag can be marketed as something that can store either hot foods or cold foods for the journey home, thus making your customer's life a bit easier and less expensive in terms of wasted food. Frozen groceries won't thaw and takeout will still be hot and ready to eat. Moreover, these insulated bags can be hand-washed if they get dirty.

Never forget: If your business costs you money, it's not a business. It is a hobby. The IRS has strict rules on the subject so confirm the legality of what you're doing with your accountant. Save those receipts too. You'll need them come tax time.

You also need to use patterns where you can legally sell what you make. All the big pattern companies tell you on the pattern that it is for home use only. I seriously doubt that McCalls or Butterick send teams of lawyers trolling through the craft show circuit looking for people who've used their scrub patterns. The same thing is true of using that Disney themed cloth or 'Dr. Who' fabric for your kid's pjs or the 'Angry Birds' upholstery for grocery bags. I don't think Disney or anyone else keeps an eye on that market. They won't waste their time or money other than on big manufacturers.

Honestly, copyright law is complex and you should ask a lawyer. Or, draft your own patterns. Then you <u>own</u> them and you can do what you want.

In the case of my grocery bag patterns, I want them to be used. Philosophically, I am opposed to disposable bags. I want to see more people using cloth bags. I want to see more people making some money from small businesses within the United States (or whatever country you are reading this in) and cloth grocery bags are one way to do it.

I hope this book lets that happen. Make as many bags as you like and if you make some money doing so, that is even better.

Teresa selling our books and bags at Ashcombe Gardens outside Camp Hill, Penn.

25. Selling at Craft Shows

I came up with the idea to sew and sell cloth grocery bags because a few years ago, we needed to ensure that Peschel Press got a space at the Hershey Winter Arts show.

Although we write and self-publish our books, they aren't, technically, an arts and crafts item. I had been sewing tailored cloth grocery bags for years, giving them away to friends, family, and as teacher gifts. Everyone liked them and thought they were useful. The bags seemed like an easy way to fulfill the requirements for the Show. The organizers agreed and we've been doing the show ever since (in fact, 2019 will be our seventh show).

Since then, we've appeared at other shows, including Hershey ArtFest, CultureFest, the York Book Expo, and library shows. Check our website (peschelpress.com) for our schedule.

In my other life as a public-spirited citizen, I'm a member of a group which provides information at local farmers' markets and other events about composting and planting trees. Bill and I also attend craft shows and farmers' markets.

This means we've seen a lot of vendors and paid attention to what works and what doesn't. Owning a business and making fabulous products does not translate to being a fabulous seller. It's simply another skill you have to learn. This is important because if you aren't selling successfully, then you're wasting the time and money you spent on making great products.

I'm focusing on craft shows because I don't have an online store and don't know how they work. Learning how to do that well requires a lot of knowledge, starting with setting up a website with a secure commerce link. Worse, unless your products are truly unique, they have to compete with dozens, hundreds, even thousands of similar items, and the only distinguishing characteristics are price, written description, and tiny pictures.

I admit I'm suspicious of Etsy. It may have a million stores, but how many of them earn their owners more than walking-around money? When I type in cloth grocery bags on their site, I see thousands of results at every possible price point. I can't easily tell how many of those bags were handmade within the U.S. and how many were outsourced to China (not everything on Etsy is handmade by the store owner). I can't tell how well constructed those bags are, and I can't get the owners' compelling story.

Selling in person at a craft show solves those issues. You get to talk to potential customers and show them the features that allow you to charge $10 for a cloth grocery bag.

The biggest show we show at is Hershey ArtFest, which has about 130 vendors. Our competition for books is negligible, and my competition for bags is likewise minimal.

Do I sell a lot of bags? I don't, although I do sell some. Fortunately, bags are not our primary focus. They are a sideline to Peschel Press books, our main focus and concern. We use cloth grocery bags as a value-added line. After all, you have to put books in some kind of bag, and giving away a bag as a premium encourages customers to buy more books.

Learn How To Sell

If selling cloth grocery bags is your primary focus, then you need to go into the business knowing the lessons we learned the hard way.

First and foremost, selling is a business. The skill of selling is unrelated to your skill in sewing bags. Here's how to develop that skill:

- **You and your booth should present a professional image.** The next time you're at a craft show, look closely at the vendors. How many of them dress like they're cleaning their garage? Can you tell who is running the booth so you can give them money? If you don't know, are you encouraged to ask, or do you move on to the next booth? I'll bet you (like me) move on.

You shouldn't make it difficult to buy your product. It should be frictionless.

In our booth, we wear a uniform. My husband wears a shirt I made him covered with rows of letters — he is a writer — along with a distinctive leather hat. For winter shows, I wear a Peschel Press sweatshirt I made, with our logo on the back and a statement about novel writing on the front. For summer shows, I wear my robin's-egg blue T-shirt with our company logo appliqued onto it. When our kids assist, they also wear a similar shirt. We do not look like we are doing yard work, nor do we look like the rest of the customers.

Repeat visitors to our booth remember us from year to year.

Do something similar. Choose an outfit in a bright color that coordinates with your logo and always wear it. If you can, put your logo on your shirt. It's possible now to get a company online to do that for you if you don't want to sew them yourself. This uniform also puts you into the selling mindset.

Your uniform should reinforce what you are selling. If you're an artist, then look like one! If you sell something musical, wear a shirt with a music theme. If you're selling fancy dog leashes, have a picture of your dog wearing your fancy dog leash silk-screened on your shirt next to your company's logo. If you sell handmade goat cheese or goat's milk soap, there should be images of frolicking goats on your aprons.

- **Have at least two people at the show.** That lets one of you get something to eat, run to the bathroom, or deal with another customer. Even a small show can get busy at times, and you never want to leave your booth unattended. The minute you walk away is the minute a customer approaches your booth, sees nobody to take their money, and moves on.

Another reason to hang around is to make sure your merchandise doesn't walk off on its own. Arts and crafts shows are not immune to shoplifters.

Everyone who helps you should be dressed the same: matching polo shirts with your logo, matching aprons with your logo, or at least matching solid color T-shirts in a bright color with your logo painted on with fabric paints. Make sure the customer knows who gets the money. Your assistants need to know how to talk to customers, make change, smile, display your merchandise and demonstrate its special features.

The Peschel Press logo.

You may need more than two people to set up and break down the booth. We draft our children to provide unskilled labor at both ends of the day. Most craft shows have a limited time window to get set up so you need to get it done fast before the show opens. Breaking down the booth can take longer as you aren't under a deadline.

- **Be organized in packing and unpacking your vehicle.** Load your vehicle <u>last</u> with the things you want to set up in your booth space first. Also, before your first show, test the layout of your booth at home. We set ours up in the living room. We had an 8-by-12-foot space at the show, so we staged our card tables, lawn chairs, free-standing bookshelf, and folding screen (used to display the bags) in our living room. This let us figure out where to put everything and see if we needed all that junk.

Another way to be organized is to load your vehicle the night before. The shows we've done want us to be completely set up by 9 a.m. The time to load your car is not at 6 a.m. the morning of the show.

This is particularly important in our case because we have only one car, a little Ford Focus sedan. If we have to use the canopy, we have to haul everything in two trips, and that forces us to stay very local. If you're traveling any kind of distance, then you need a bigger vehicle. This is why vendors have big SUVs, panel vans, pickup trucks, or haul trailers. You must have everything you need already with you. You can't go back and get it midway through the day.

We can travel farther to indoor shows like the York Book Expo, where the organizers provide tables and chairs. We only have to make one trip to get all our stuff to the show. If your indoor venue provides tables, you're in luck. Remember to ask if chairs are provided; sometimes you get tables but not chairs. You may have to pay extra for their table or electricity, but if the fee is small enough, and the venue one you couldn't do otherwise, it may be worthwhile.

- **Have the right equipment.** Outdoor shows <u>require</u> a canopy. No exceptions. The venue may not tell you this. Instead, you'll find out the hard way as you sit there for hours in the blazing sun. Or worse, you'll sit there in the rain. Most craft shows are rain or shine so you need to be prepared. We've done a show where it rained on and off all day. Surprisingly, it was a profitable day because everyone who came was ready to shop and spend money. Canopies also mean that if summer afternoon thunderstorms crop up, you can save your merchandise from weather damage.

We bought our canopy for about $250 at Costco. It is bright white, decently sturdy, and came with side and back panels. We don't normally put up the panels, but on that rainy day, we were glad we had them. Get a white canopy because it reflects the heat better.

Good signage with consistent branding and color tells customers you're serious about your business.

Canopies are also useful for other events, such as girl scout cookie sales in parking lots or when providing composting information at the farmers' market. Our canopy gets used as often for something else as it does for a craft show.

Craft show canopies are not the same as the lightweight dining tarps seen at family reunion picnics. They are much sturdier. Also, invest in a set of weighted bags to attach to the canopy's legs. They hold the canopy in place in the wind. The vendors we've spoken to say high wind is much worse than rain. The weighted bags hold the canopy down, keeping it from becoming airborne. Your canopy may come with stakes and guy wires but some places won't let you use them. Either the vendors are too close together to use them, or you're setting up on asphalt.

Books, our stock in trade, have to be protected from wind and weather, so we bought special heavy canvas bags designed to be wrapped around the canopy's legs. I filled a whole lot of quart-size freezer bags with fine gravel and placed them into the canvas bags. The bags kept the gravel from getting water-logged. If one bag sprung a leak, the other bags still contained their gravel. At 40 pounds apiece, the weight bags work well, without being too heavy to manage, and they fit within the canopy when the side panels are installed.

Any heavy, reasonably small weights will work but be sure you can carry them, and they

We use both sides of our hangtags to advertise our books.

aren't a tripping hazard. We've seen vendors use sandbags, concrete blocks, salvaged truck gears, and barbell weights. They all work.

Have a sign for the front of your canopy. A sea of white canopies all look alike. The next show you go to, take a look around. Vendors who bought a custom-decorated canopy that displays their line of craft beer or handmade goat's milk soap really stand out. A long, skinny sign protected by clear plastic contac-paper is a good compromise on price. We got our Peschel Press sign from Staples for about $30.

It is bright, robin's egg blue with our name

and logo and it shows up nicely, stretched across the front top edge of our canopy.

- **Your business needs a name.** Ours is Peschel Press. My husband chose the name and designed our simple logo. Our name is simple, too, but it describes what we are in a one-line entry in a show brochure. Think carefully about your company name. You don't want to be obscure like, say, 'P & P Enterprises'. A name like that tells a potential customer nothing about what is being sold and so provides no reason for a customer to go searching for your booth. On the other hand, 'P & P's Cloth Grocery Bags', while clear, doesn't allow you to easily branch out into other craft areas. When you choose a name, do an online search to make sure you haven't chosen one that is already being used by someone else.

Your name and logo should also go on your merchandise. We make hangtags for our bags that show all the important information. We use both sides of the hangtags to do this. Blank hangtags are made by Avery; you can buy them at your local office supply store or online. We use the 2-by-3-1/2-inch size which is big enough to say everything we need to say without being too big and costing more. These tags come 96 to the box and, if you follow the directions carefully, you can print them yourself on your printer instead of paying someone else to do it. The cord attachment works nicely: unless the tag itself tears, the tags haven't come off on their own. They have to be cut off with scissors.

Our books have our name and logo wherever it's appropriate for a book to do so. If you're unsure where to attach a tag or logo onto your merchandise, look at what other vendors do and then see if it works for you.

We print the price on our bags as well as use a sign. Keep this in mind: if you price your merchandise on its hangtag, you'll have to replace the tag if you raise your prices. Nobody minds if you draw a red line through a price and write in a lower one but the other way won't work.

- **Pay attention to the customers.** That seems obvious, but I've been to too many shows where the person running the booth is paying close attention to a smartphone and not to the customer standing in the booth looking to hand over some money. Don't be that person. Think of what you want to say to people walking by. We always say hello and thank you for coming to the show. We don't do a hard sell. Does everyone stop in? No, but that's okay.

Over the years, we perfected our sales pitch about our books and what they cover. I also know how to talk about how I make the bags, choose the fabrics, and how well they hold up. Smile and be friendly. Customers who don't buy on the spot often come back later. Sometimes, they come back the following year.

Depending on your craft, you can attract customers by doing something interesting in your booth. I've seen vendors painting, carving, sewing, crocheting, throwing pots, or making jewelry. They give customers a reason to stop, watch, and ask questions.

- **Keep your booth attractive, neat, and well-organized.** Watch out for foot hazards as you don't need the hassle or the lawsuit. Your display units should stand securely so they don't wobble when someone is examining a bag.

Make sure you bring plenty of bags in an assortment of colors as you won't know what will sell. Arrange them attractively to draw customers into the booth. We've laid bags flat, hung them from the canopy, and hung them from chains attached to a folding screen. See what other people do and figure out what you can do to make displays without laying out money until you know, for sure, you'll be doing this often. We still use our card tables and lawn chairs because they work. Remember that you have to haul around display units so consider their weight and size.

We don't bring our laptops or my sewing machine to attract business. It's too much to lug around and would require an extra fee for an electric outlet.

Instead, I make and give away butterscotch crunchies; a powerhouse fusion of sugar, salt, and texture. These cookies are stellar and everyone who walks by is invited to enjoy one. After doing this for several years, we have people who remember us and stop by solely because of the cookie. We give the recipe to everyone who wants one. Since people don't throw away recipes, we thoughtfully provide a catalog of our books on the back side so a cookie baker can go to Amazon later to buy our books.

- **Be prepared to spend the entire day.** It can be exhausting, so be ready for that too, with coffee, aspirin, throat lozenges, sunscreen, snackies, plenty of water, and comfortable shoes.

- **Know how you're going to handle money.** We use a cashbox and keep a very close eye on it (another reason to <u>never</u> leave your booth unattended). We accept cash, checks (we've never been stiffed) and when we got a smartphone, we signed up for Square, which allows us to accept credit and debit cards. Previously, we posted a sign saying "Cash and Checks Only." I've seen vendors who insist on cash only. It's up to you, but "cash only" can limit your sales. The advantage of cash and checks (besides privacy all around) is that you keep all your money. Credit card and debit card companies charge you, the vendor, a small fee for the privilege of accepting the customer's card. So does Square. However, accepting Square means you can make sales you otherwise would have missed. That's certainly been our experience.

Keep careful track of what you sell and how much money you take in. Your accountant will need to know this when tax season rolls around. Have her explain to you what to do about sales taxes. You may want to fold the sales tax in your price so you don't have to calculate the tax and add it to the cost of your merchandise. That's what we do.

Have clear, easy to read signs. You want your customers to know who you are, what you sell, and how much your products cost. Our signage is simple because cloth grocery bags are one price and books are another. We also provide our book catalog (which we print ourselves), business cards, the butterscotch crunchie recipe, and our website information. Since we do most of our shows here in Hershey, when we see customers at one show, we tell them about the next show coming up and that we will have something new to display.

- **How should you choose shows?** We look first for shows that are close to home. Then we look for shows that have both juried and non-juried categories. A juried category means that you have to send photos and descriptions of your work so the venue holder can evaluate what you do and does it match what they want. Better arts and crafts shows nearly always do some jurying, because they want to keep out Chinese-made junk being passed off as locally made handicrafts. If you've ever been to a craft show full of poorly made Disney knock-offs and yard sale fodder, you've seen a non-juried show.

Because we sell our books along with my cloth grocery bags, a juried show with a non-juried component gives us a good chance to get customers who might buy books as well as the usual craft show items. A strictly art show won't take us. Books, despite our writing them ourselves, don't count and my cloth grocery bags, no matter how well designed and made, don't count as art, either.

The other show we attend is the aforementioned York Book Expo. The bags come along for the ride, and I do sell some, but the primary focus is on the books.

We started with the Hershey Winter Arts Show because I already knew about it, having shopped there in previous years. While at the show, I asked how to apply for the following year, they accepted us, and away we went. We heard about Art on Chocolate (since renamed Hershey ArtFest) getting started and applied and were accepted. The same thing happened with the York Book Expo. These shows are very local (down the street) or, in the case of the York Book Expo, come with tables, chairs, and are inside, making it easy to bring our stuff.

People on the craft show circuit range from doing a few shows a year like us, to one a month, to one every weekend. There are multiple shows running every weekend from spring to fall, with many Christmas shows as well. There are multiple listings online, organized by state. The lists don't overlap so you need to check several websites to get the contact information. Googling "craft show listings" will display the websites with the freshest information.

However, the easiest way to get started is to check what is already happening in your area. Ask around and attend the shows within 20 miles of you or less. Most of them advertise in your newspapers or in the upcoming events sections that radio stations and TV stations maintain. Your chamber of commerce and tourist bureau should also know what's going on. Many, many churches and social organizations also organize small bazaars and shows.

Visit a show, see if it looks like a good fit for you and ask the organizers. They will have a booth somewhere and the staff will be happy to answer questions. You may discover that they are always looking for new vendors, that they have a five-year waiting list, or that they want only a specific type of arts and crafts.

A small church bazaar is a good way to decide if you want to sell cloth grocery bags or whatever else you make. It will be very local, everyone will be friendly, and it will be small and not so overwhelming.

It should also be cheaper. Craft shows demand payment upfront for the space you rent. A one-day show like Hershey ArtFest wanted $85 for a 10-foot-by-10-foot space. A big, multi-day show will cost much, much more and you have to be there every single day, from open to close. Always ask how much it will cost first, before you apply.

- **Calculate your breakeven point.** In order to earn a profit, you have to sell enough cloth grocery bags to pay the booth fee, plus your fabric and labor costs, travel time, gas, meals, lodging, taxes, etc., before you can make actual money. Yet people do make money on the craft show circuit.

This is work. Not nine-to-five work but it is work. Your results depend entirely on how hard you work, how good your stuff is, how many shows you attend, and how lucky you get. Luck matters more than you think. We've done a dozen shows and each one has been different. You don't know how many people will show up, what they want to buy, or what the weather will be like. You won't know what your competition will be like either, until after you set up and walk around.

But if you are flexible and outgoing, it's fun! You get to talk to all kinds of people, ask them what they like and, if you are willing to listen, they will tell you what they are looking for. They will also tell you what they cannot find, which can be useful if you want to expand your craft business outside of cloth grocery bags.

Pay attention to what happens at a show and the next one will be a little easier and the one after that will be easier still. It will never be perfect, mind you, but you might make some money and you will certainly learn a lot about running a small business.

26. Know Your Competition

If you're making cloth grocery bags to sell, you need to know who and what you're competing against. Why should a customer fork over $10 for a cloth bag? You have to be able to make a case for your superior, reusable, locally made in the U.S., cloth, lead-free bags.

At the head of the competition are the "free" bags every store hands out. They aren't really free, as the store has to pay for them and then pass the costs along in the form of higher prices. This is something that many people are unaware of. In some areas, you have to pay a few pennies for each plastic or paper bag you use. The store is being honest when they charge you for the bags. Other municipalities have banned plastic bags so stores don't hand them out at all. Shoppers have to reach for alternatives, hopefully yours.

A customer may tell you that "free" bags from the store are the cheapest bags of all, as long as you remember to bring them back to the store when you shop. A plastic T-shirt bag or a brown paper bag can last through many uses if you're careful when you handle and store them.

People who are serious about thrift will use "free" bags until they rip to shreds and then they'll get more "free" bags on their next shopping trip.

You might reach these customers by emphasizing the environmental costs of plastic T-shirt bags. You can remind them that your cloth bags will not rip unexpectedly, flinging expensive groceries onto the ground, as reused grocery store bags are wont to do when they've been repeatedly overstressed.

These 99-cent bags will last longer than plastic bags, but they will eventually rip, tear, and unexpectedly dump your groceries on the ground.

The next step up in reusable shopping bags are those 99¢ wonders that every store sells nowadays. These bags will last far longer than plastic bags, but they still rip, tear, or otherwise unexpectedly dump their expensive contents onto the ground.

If a customer questions your cost per bag, help them to understand that your cloth bags can be hand-washed and repaired. You can't do either with a 99¢ bag. They are not made of cloth, but a plastic, cloth-like substance. When this rips, the bag is just as dead as a ripped plastic bag. If the straps tear free, the bag is useless. Moreover, the designs stenciled on the bags are often printed with lead. Lead is very toxic and the design can rub off onto the bag's contents along with every surface the bags touch.

Then you come to cheap, canvas bags. These may have a grocery store logo stenciled on the side, making sure everyone knows where you bought it. My example cost me $3.99 at my local grocery store.

It is a functional bag and far better made than one of those 99¢ polypropylene wonders. This bag can be repaired, and it can be hand-washed. The indifferent, stenciled design probably has

The straps on this $3.99 bag are secured only by a 1-inch-by-1 ½-inch rectangle at each end.

no lead in it.

This bag, though, compared to your cloth grocery bags, is not very wide. The seam margins are very narrow and finished only with serging. The seam margins are not sewn down, thus reinforcing the bag's structure. The straps are secured only by a 1-inch-by-1½-inch rectangle at each end.

If your customer is comparing your cloth bags to this type of reusable bag, remind them that you make your bags yourself, locally. The money goes to support your family. Your bags are sized and constructed better. Moreover, your bags do not come with a dreary store logo stenciled on the side. Instead, your bags have an interesting mix of patterns and solids to choose from. Your bags are made in limited runs. That gives some exclusivity. Your customer can rest easy knowing that her grocery bags are unique and unlikely to be mixed up with someone else's. Your cloth bags are stylish enough that they don't have to be reserved strictly for grocery store runs.

Then we come to more expensive reusable bags. These bags compete directly on cost, or they cost more than yours do.

I spotted this bag being advertised in Parade magazine. The baggu T-shirt bag is $10. The company says they're made of nylon. I will assume this not the nylon used for stockings and is instead the ripstop nylon used for windbreakers. They are made in China.

This shopping bag is patterned after a grocery store plastic T-shirt bag. It has no shaping of its own, other than the pair of gusset seams that force a simple sack into a three-dimensional bag. The straps are an integral part of the bag body, which your customer may not like if they want to carry the bag on their shoulder.

If you are selling your bags for $10 each, you can point out to the customer that you are right there, your bags are the same price, your

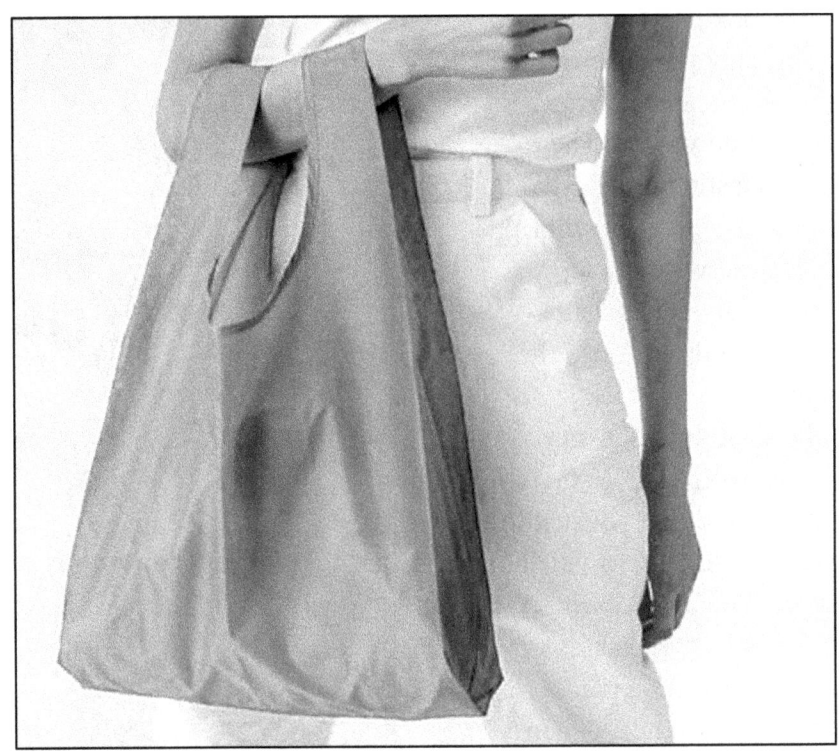

This nylon baggu T-shirt bag is stylish but has no shape and the straps are awkwardly placed.

bags are shaped to hold groceries, and your earnings go to support your children. Moreover, you make your bags yourself, locally.

Once you pass baggu's price point, cloth grocery bags get more and more expensive, twenty bucks apiece or even more. You can easily compete with those bags on price, being a local craftsperson, and on quality of construction.

There are plenty of other reusable bags out there suitable for groceries. Take a look at them online and in stores. Examine them closely, looking at how they are made and whether or not they can be repaired or washed. The more you know about your competition, the easier it will be to sell your customer on your own beautiful handmade bags that will last a lifetime.

27. Afterword

I wrote this book as much for my own use as for yours. I've sewed hundreds of grocery bags, yet if I didn't make any for a while, I couldn't remember how I did it! I'd have to look over finished ones, check my notes, and reconstruct the process.

Writing this book also helped me streamline the sewing process. I had to think about every step and if there was a better way to do it. I learned how to make boxed bags to expand the scope of the book, and I'm very glad I did. Boxed bags are easier and quicker to sew than tailored bags, once you learn their origami-like structure.

It has become very worthwhile to know how to make both styles as I can use my fabric stash more efficiently. I never used to piece fabric to make Frankenstein bags and now I do it all the time, eking out more bags with less waste fabric.

I hope this book will prove as useful to you. With it, you'll be able to replace all those plastic bags you use now, make useful, valued gifts, and even start a home-based business and make some money freeing other people from disposable bags.

The other advantage I hope you take away from this book is the concept of production sewing. If you are going to make a quantity of anything, whether scrubs and pjs or men's oxford shirts or band uniforms, you need to be efficient.

Think about how much fabric you require and sketch the layout of all those pattern pieces. Wider fabrics may let you be still more efficient with the layout, leaving less waste cloth behind.

Read the pattern assembly directions carefully and then work out a better way to sew all those garments. Your pattern won't address assembly line sewing so you have to figure out how to make ten of one thing. Complete all of one step on all your items before moving onto the next step.

Sewing systematically can save hours and hours of your time, just as an economical layout will save you serious money on the cloth. And don't forget your notions. If you use the same size buttons for all your oxford shirts, then you don't need to reset the size of your buttonhole foot. If you use the same trim throughout, you can buy it in quantity and spend less per yard.

Finally, I would like to thank my husband, who graciously agreed to edit and publish this book, my dear daughter who redrew my terrible sketches into much clearer drawings, and my beta sewers who figured out all the mistakes in my directions:

- Anne Simmons
- Dominic
- Jen Wilt
- Kaitlin Schreiber
  (www.humblestitch.com)
- Patty
- Vicky Burkholder
  (www.burkholv.wordpress.com)

I could not have written this book without them. They all made this a far better book than it otherwise would have been. The errors that remain are all mine.

Stitching Patterns

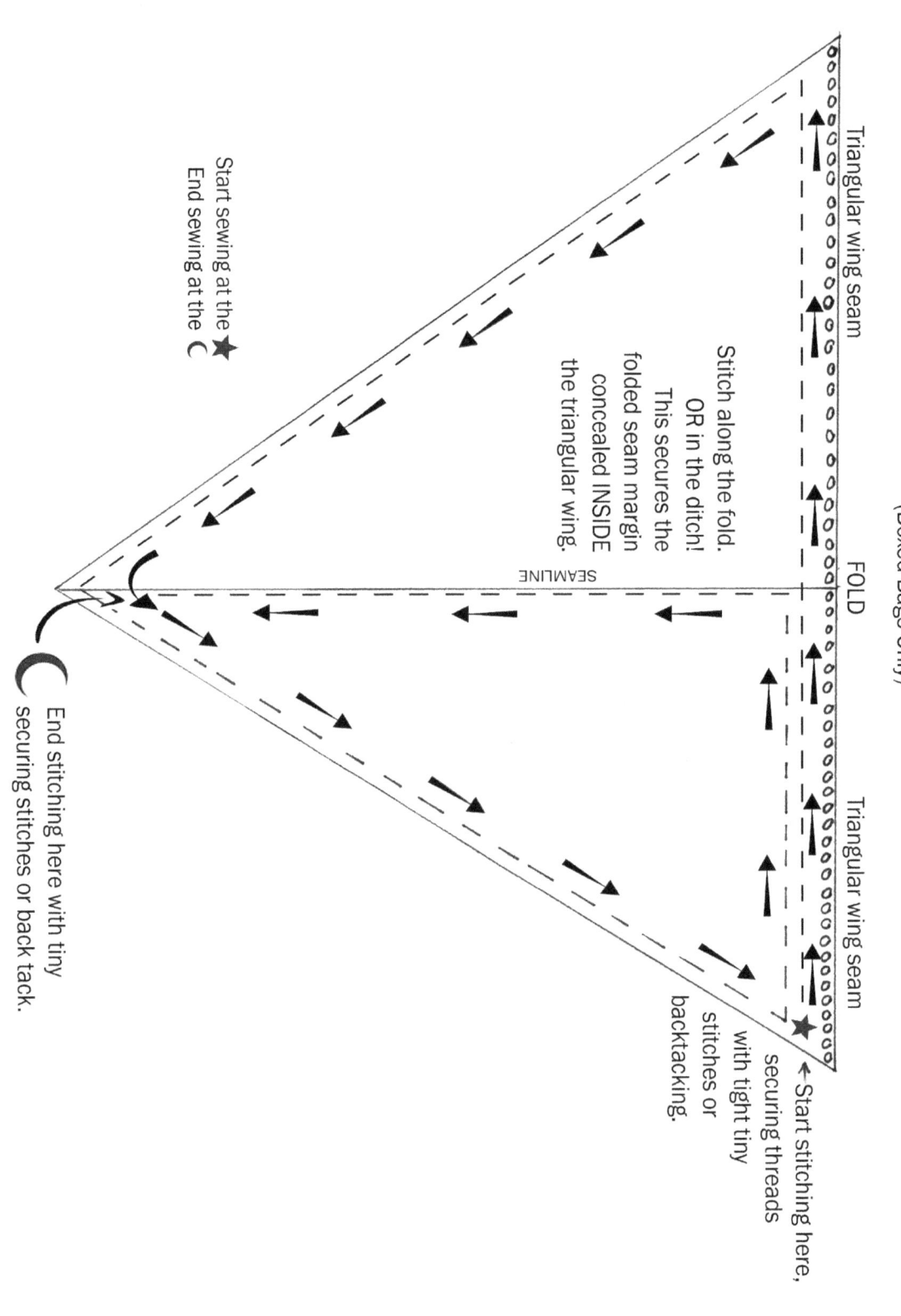

Stitching Patterns

Flange Stitch Diagram
(Boxed Bags Only)

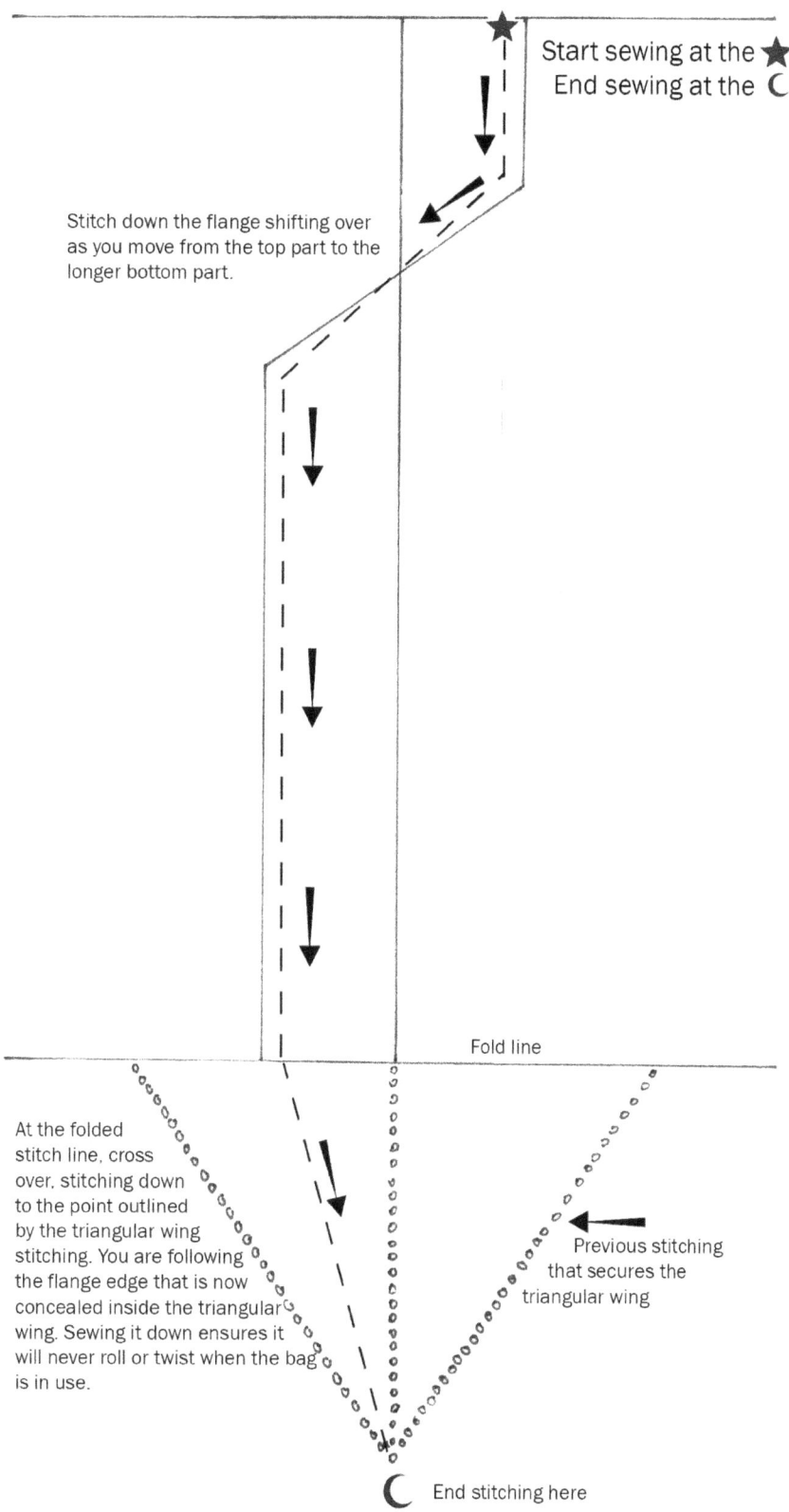

Start sewing at the ★
End sewing at the ☾

Stitch down the flange shifting over as you move from the top part to the longer bottom part.

Fold line

At the folded stitch line, cross over, stitching down to the point outlined by the triangular wing stitching. You are following the flange edge that is now concealed inside the triangular wing. Sewing it down ensures it will never roll or twist when the bag is in use.

Previous stitching that secures the triangular wing

☾ End stitching here

Stitching Patterns

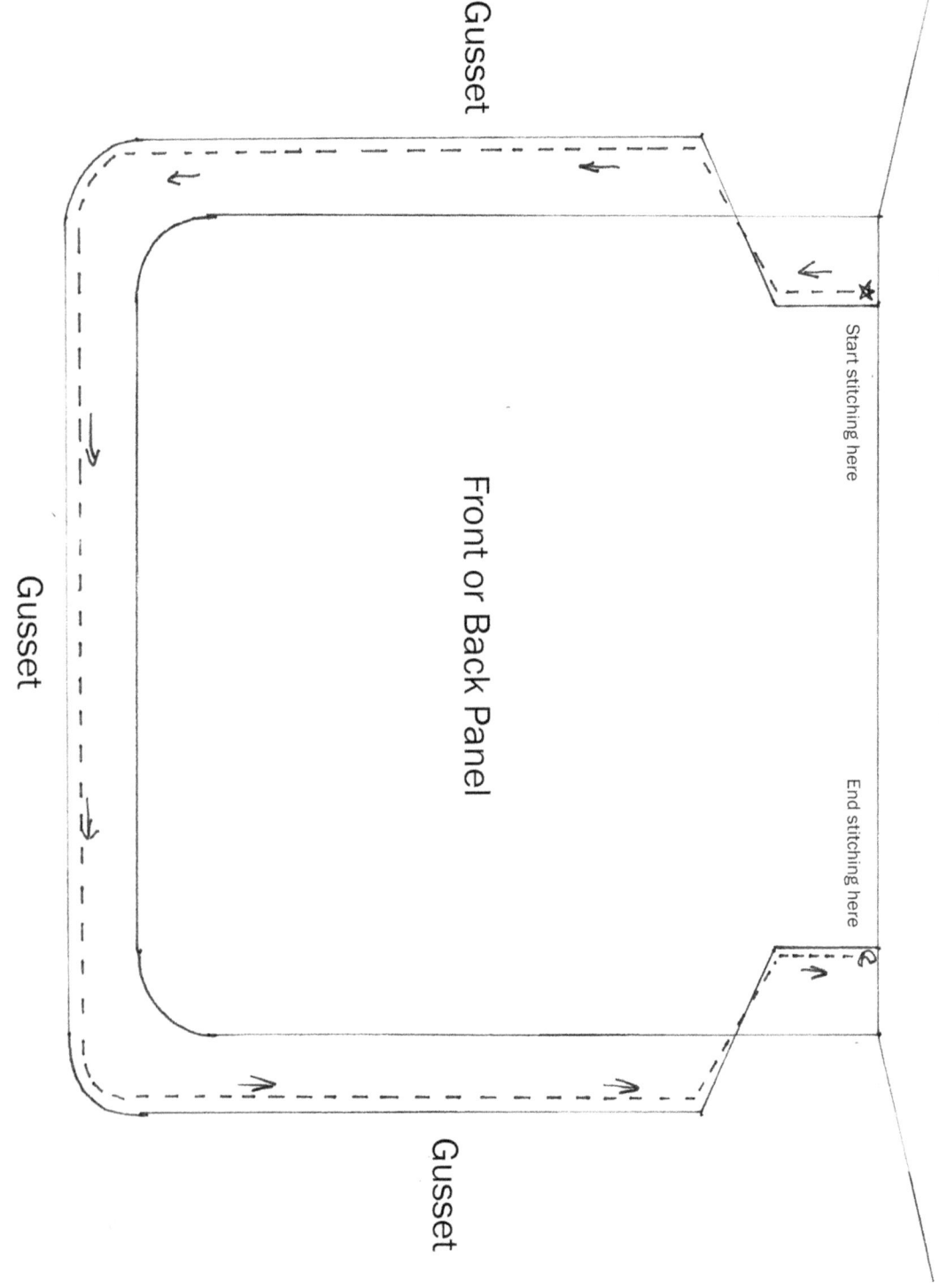

Stitching Patterns

Strap Stitching Diagram
(Boxed and Tailored Bags)

This is one continuous line of stitching giving an outer line that follows the left edge of the strap edge, encloses the raw bottom end with zigzagging, goes back up the right strap, goes across the width of the strap, back tracks a few stitches, then back down the left side of the strap 1/8 inch inside the 1st row of stitching.

At the bottom of the strap, switch back over to zigzagging, sew over and just above the previous set of zigzag to further cover and contain the strap's raw edge.

Then, sew a straight stitch back up the right side of the strap 1/8-inch inside the outer line. Go up to the top, back track down 1/2-inch, then stitch to the right edge, then across the strap to the left edge, then back across again to the right edge, securing your stitch.

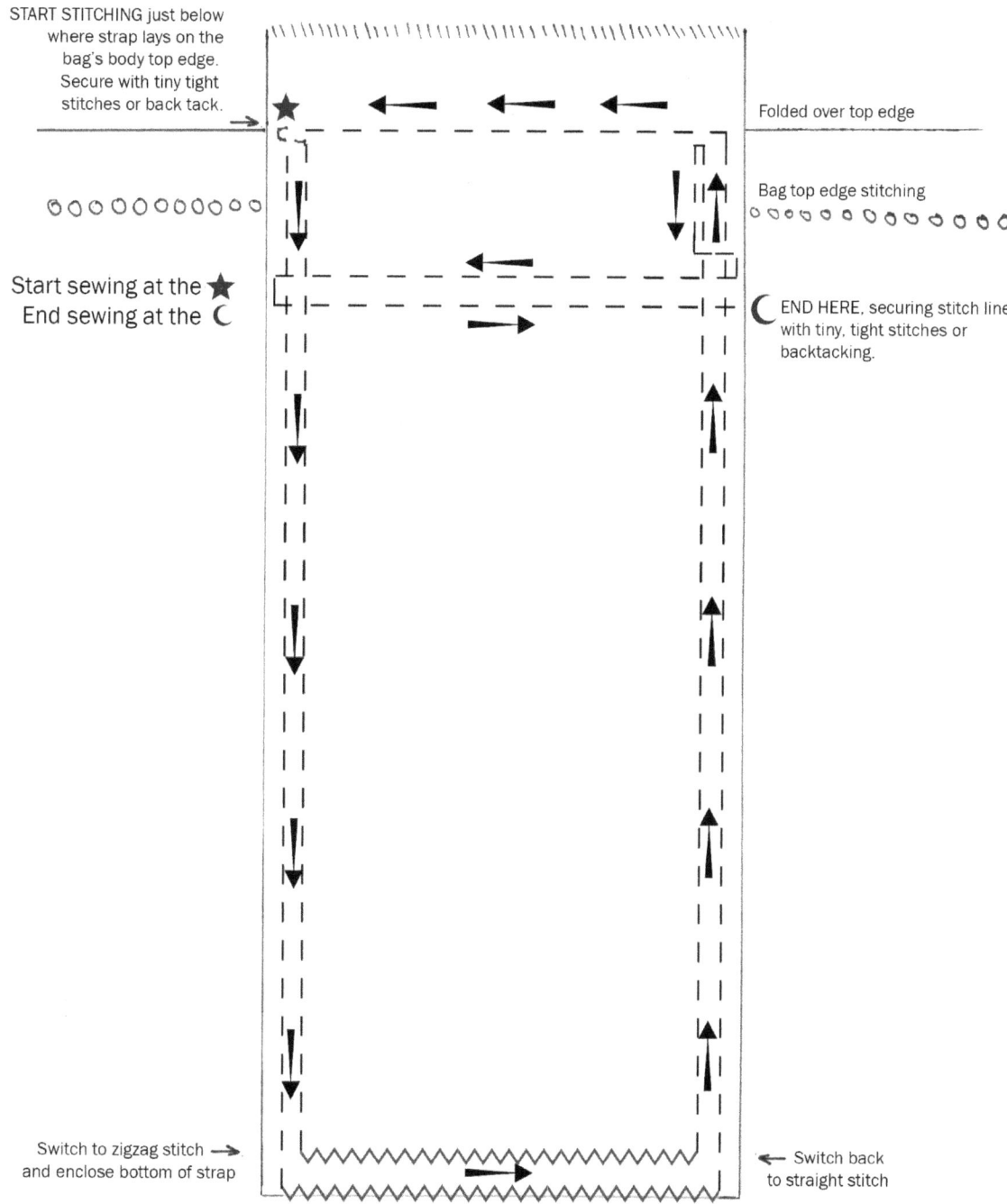

105

Stitching Patterns

Top edge of bag strap stitching
(Boxed and Tailored Bags)

Do a lot of back tracking at the top. It's faster, stronger and neater than starting and stopping separate lines of stitching.

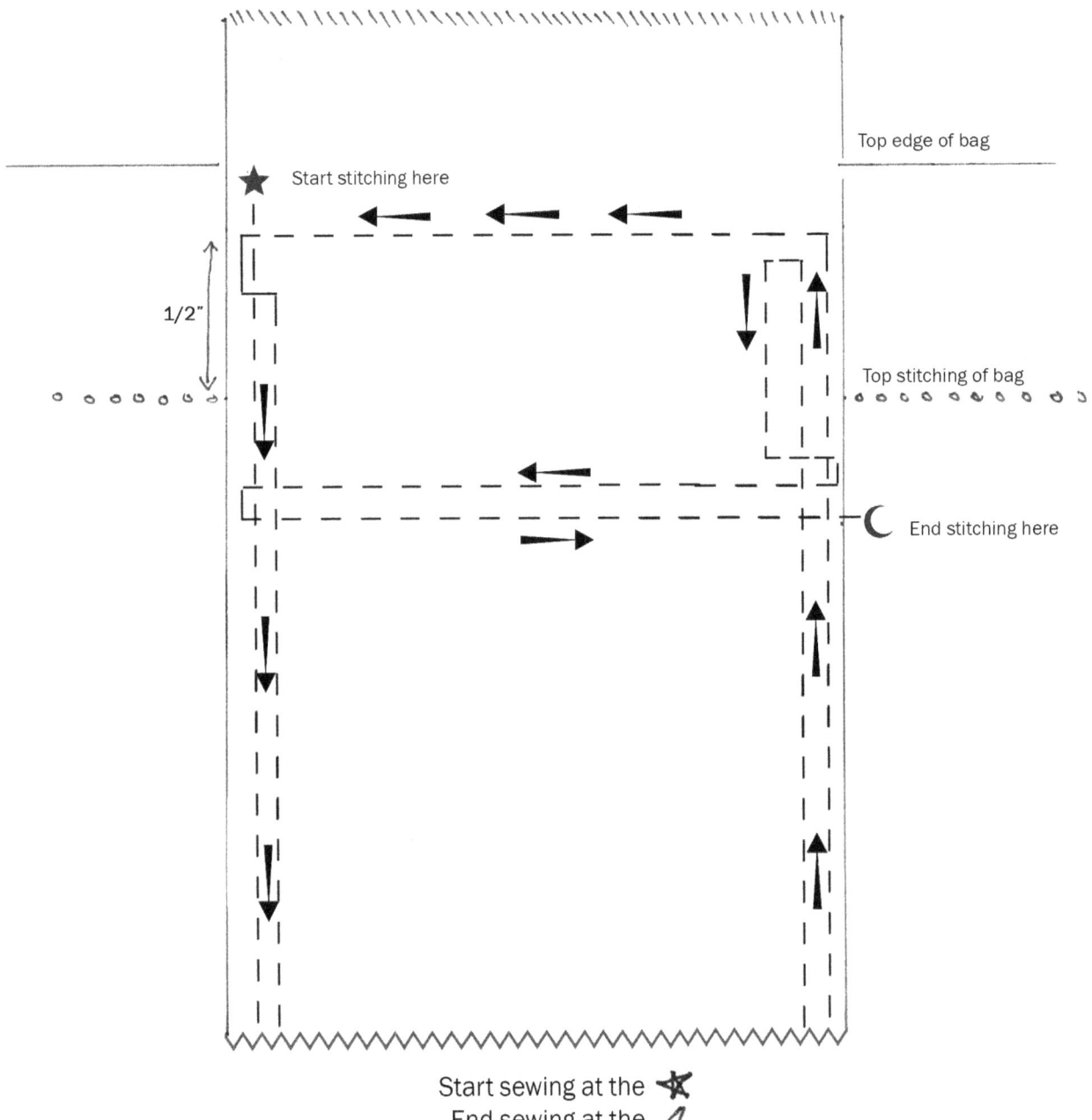

Stitching Patterns

Bottom edge of bag strap stitching
(Boxed and Tailored Bags)

The second set of zigzagging is slightly offset and higher than the first row. This better contains the raw edge AND spreads the stitching out so you don't get a huge lump of thread that catches the presser foot. Sew the second inner row of stitches (1/8-inch from the outer edge) keeping 1/8-inch distance until you near the bottom. At that point, my inner stitch line merges with my outer stitch line so I cover MORE of the bottom strap edge with zigzagging.

You don't HAVE to do this BUT the corners of the webbing are where it is MOST likely to fail. MORE zigzagging secures and covers the corners best.

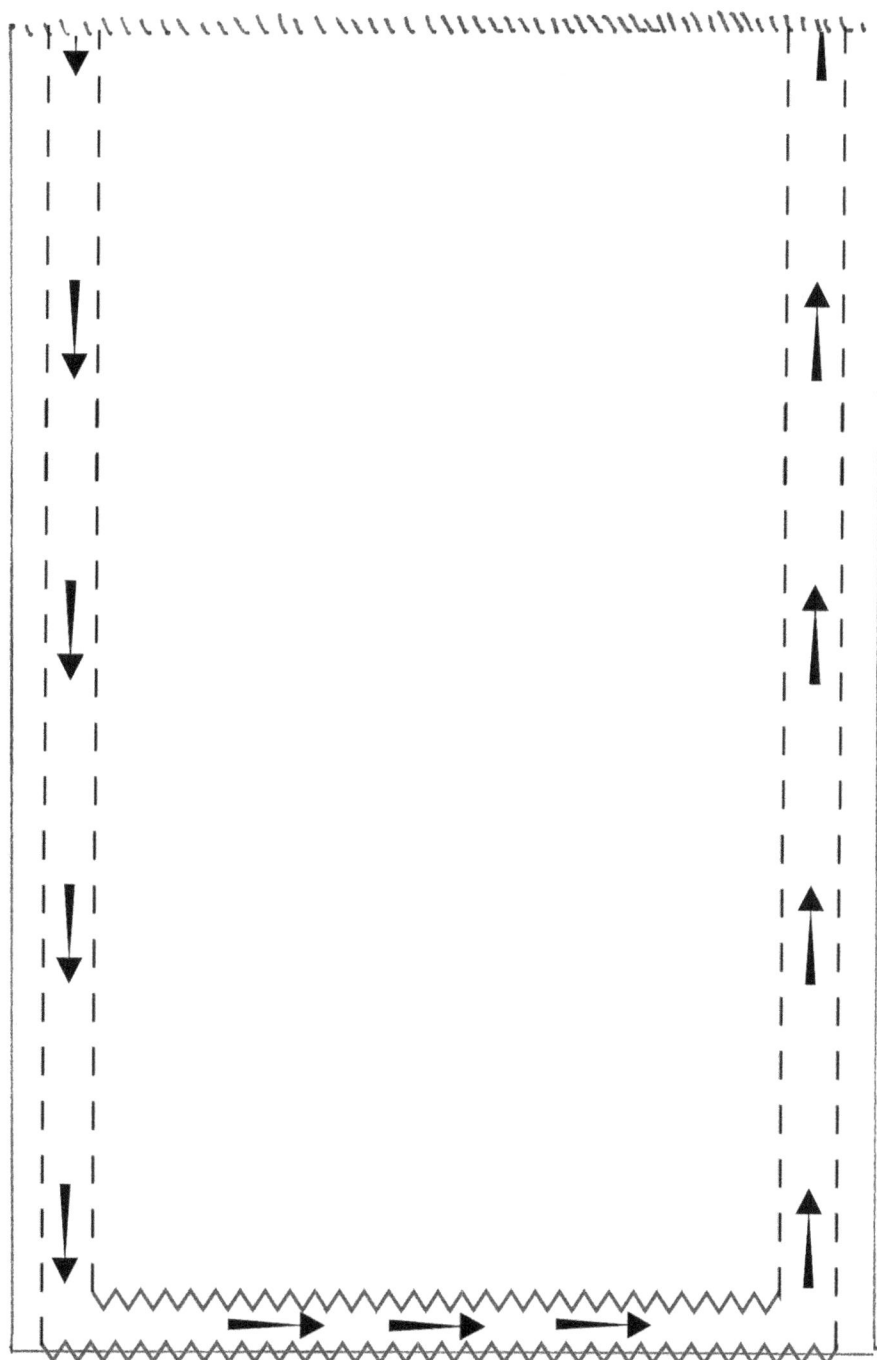

Stitching Patterns

How to Use the Pattern Layouts

I don't use paper patterns to sew either boxed or tailored bags. Instead, I use measurements. Look over the pattern layouts for both types of bags and what you see are regular rows of rectangles.

The tailored bags have more complicated layouts because each bag consists of three pieces: front panel, back panel, and gusset. Thus, each bag has to have three pieces cut out to sew the bag. The front and back panels are the same size and arrange easily into a grid on the cloth. The gussets are long, narrow rectangles and they don't always fit nicely onto the cloth.

All your panels are the same; either 13-by-15 inches or 14-by-16 inches.

Keep in mind that what matters the most in laying out gussets is their length. They all have to be the same and they have to be long enough to line up with the panels with some fabric left over to trim off. You have some leeway in their width so if you need to make your gussets a bit narrower to squeeze out another finished tailored bag, you can do that. Don't make your gussets narrower than seven (7) inches or wider than nine (9) inches. One makes a bag too narrow for gallons of milk and the other becomes squatty in shape.

The measurement charts will help you work out on paper how many rows of panels and gussets will fit in a given length of cloth and how to best orient them so you minimize cutting waste.

The boxed bags have a straightforward layout: rows of identical, large rectangles. One large panel (19-by-36) makes a single bag.

I work directly with the cloth, marking the widths of panels and gussets, and then cutting them apart. Or I use chalk markers, a yardstick, mark my fabric, snip, and rip it apart. Or, I use mark my cloth and pull threads.

Whatever bag style you chose always start the same way.

1. Straighten the leading, cut edge of the fabric. Always stick to the true grain so the bags don't twist in usage. To get the true, straight edge, pull threads until a single, pulled thread goes from selvedge to selvedge. Trim off the fringe you form. This is your starting side.

2. Iron the yardage so as to remove any distortions or wrinkles that will make your measuring and cutting less accurate.

3. Decide what type of bag you are going to make before cutting. If you chose tailored bags, decide on and stick with a size so any extra panels and gussets can be matched up later.

4. At this point, you can:

Lay the fabric out. Draw chalk lines. Cut apart the panels.

Lay the fabric out. Snip at the dividing line between a row of rectangles and rip the fabric. Divide the larger rectangle of ripped fabric into smaller panels as needed, ripping at each division.

Lay the fabric out. Snip at the dividing line between a row of rectangles and pull threads until you have a clear line. Cut along that line. Divide the larger rectangle of fabric into smaller panels as needed, pulling threads to do so, and then cutting along the line.

The advantage of chalk and a yardstick is you don't deform or stretch the fabric. The more complex layout for tailored bags often demands marking the fabric with chalk. The disadvantage is you may, over many sets of panels, become slightly off-grain. Cutting along chalk lines leads to possible whiskers on the edges of panels.

The advantage of a snip and ripping the fabric is it is fast and stays on-grain. The disadvantages are that you may deform or stretch the fabric along the ripped edge. You may also lose some fabric to kerf, when you distress the woven structure and more threads come loose. Also, not every fabric will lend itself to ripping. Some just refuse and you won't know until after you've tried.

The advantage of pulling threads is it is absolutely accurate and the panels remain absolutely on-grain with no distortion. There are no stray whiskers that you'll have to trim off later. The disadvantages of pulling threads are that it's slow, some fabrics won't cooperate because of the way they are woven, and you lose some cloth to kerf (but not as much you will when ripping).

Keep all three methods of marking and cutting panels in your repertoire. Let the cloth make the decision for you as to which method works best. As for me, whenever I can, I rip my cloth apart into panels because it's the fastest, yet still accurate method. I take the risk of deforming the edges of a panel, knowing that I'm going to press the edges at some time during the sewing process and they'll eventually be concealed within the seams.

One final tip. Ripping, like pulling threads, keeps the panels on-grain. However, if the design motif of the fabric was printed off-grain, ripping and pulling threads will make sure everyone knows. Chalk lines, despite the whiskers you'll have to trim off later, work better if your fabric's design was printed off-grain, because you can line up your markings with the design's own orientation and not with the woven grain. You may get some twist in the finished bags because you're off-grain, but they won't look twisted because the design is straight.

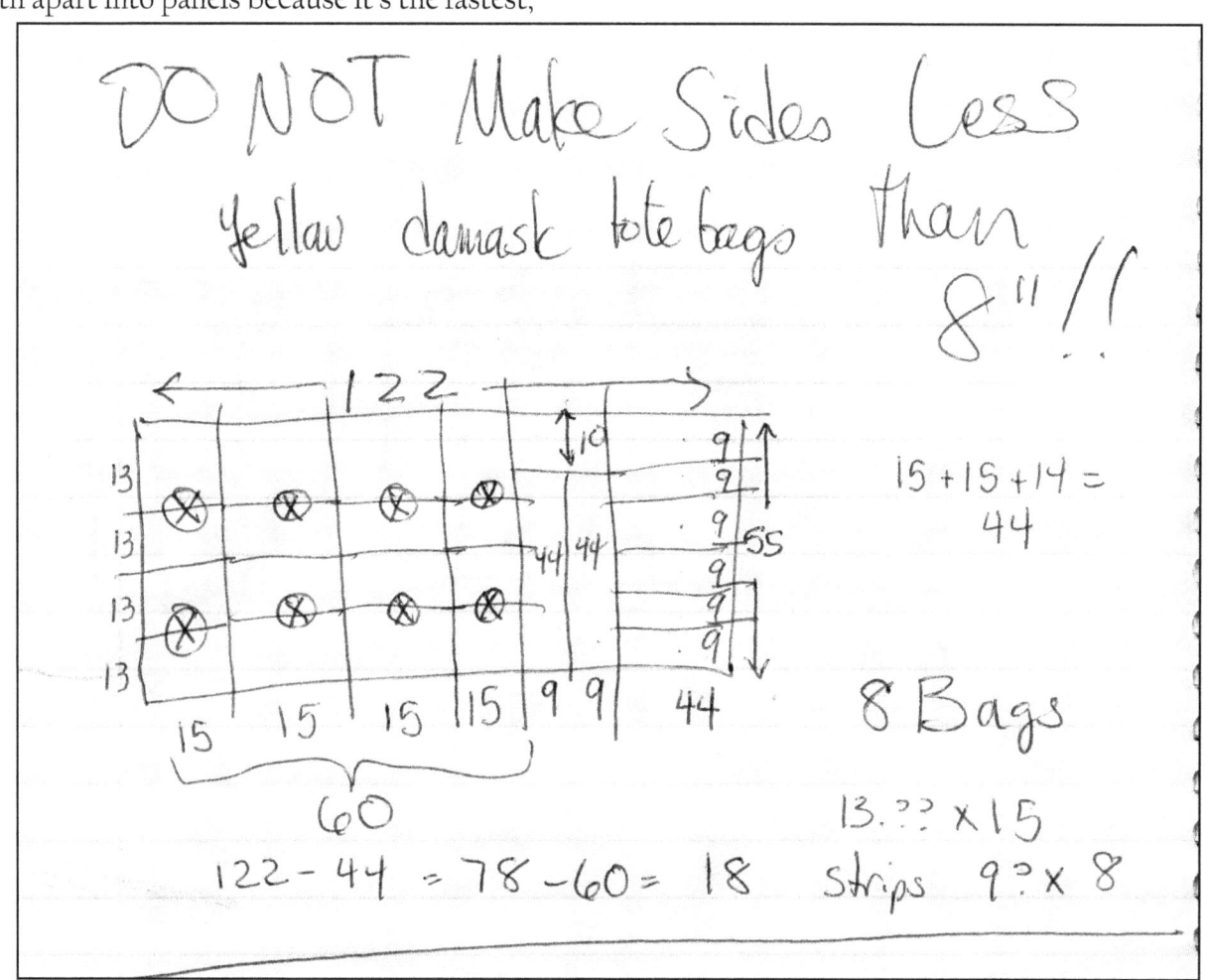

This shows my thinking process. The panel and gusset measurement charts on page 114 and 115 will make the math much easier! And, yes, I leave notes to myself rather than try to remember the details.

Stitching Patterns

Index to Charts

BOXED BAG LAYOUTS

Layouts: 45" by 36" and 216"	111
Layouts: 54" by 36" and 216"	112
Layouts: 60" by 36" and 216"	113

TAILORED BAG LAYOUTS

Panel Measurement Chart	114
Gusset Measurement Chart	115
45" by 36" and 50"	116
45" by 45", 86", and 108"	117
54" by 45" and 88"	118
45" by 67.5" and 206"	119
60" by 158" and 157.5"	120
45" by 71", 100", and 95"	121
45" by 150" and 200"	122
45" by 190"	123
54" by 44", 42", and 45"	124
54" by 84", 84", and 134"	125
54" by 176"	126
36" by 60" and 39" by 60"	127
60" by 66" and 47"	128
60" by 95" and 103"	129
60" by 140" and 190"	130
54" by 103" and 176"	131
60" by 45", 88", and 90"	132
60" by 103" and 133"	133
60" by 162"	134
60" by 236"	135
45" by 36", 49", and 110"	136
45" by 128" and 92"	137
54" by 52", 56", and 104"	138
54" by 96", 116", and 126"	139
54" by 142" and 198"	140
60" by 36", 64", and 72"	141
60" by 96", 104", and 112"	142
60" by 144" and 184"	143
60" by 110", 112", and 108"	144

19" x 36" panels, 45" wide

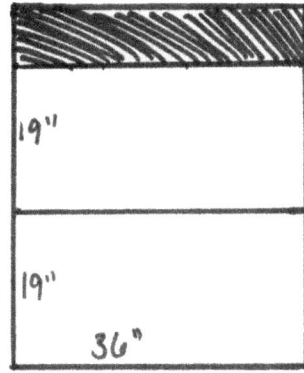

Two complete bags
from 1 yard
zero margin of error

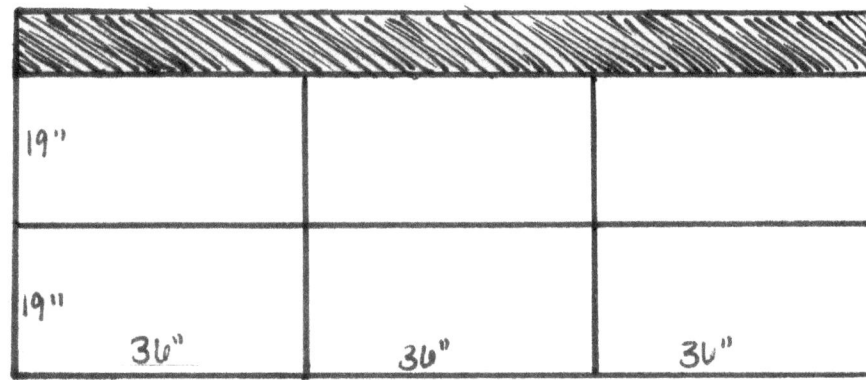

6 yards =
12 bags
zero margin
of error

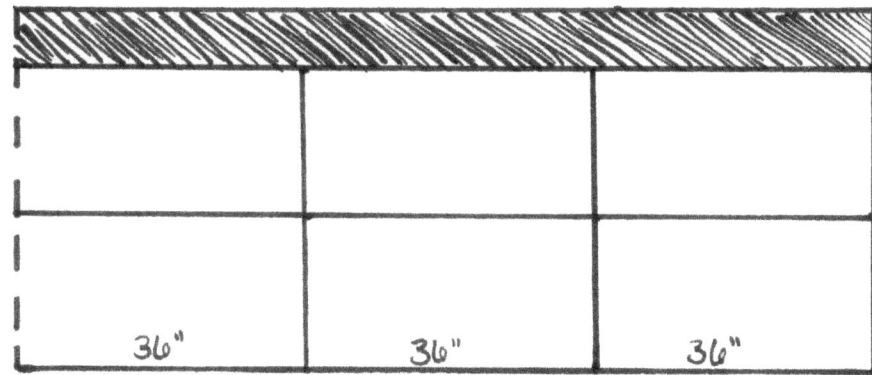

Boxed Bag Layouts

<u>19" x 36" panels, 54" wide</u>

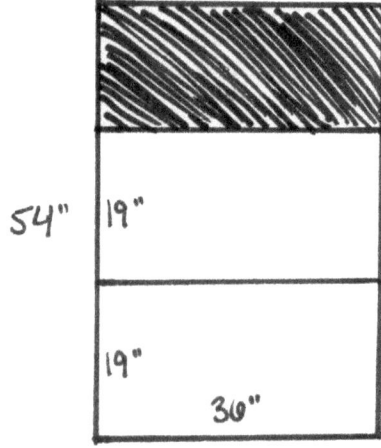

1 yard = 2 bags + waste

Use waste for straps, trim, or tailored panels

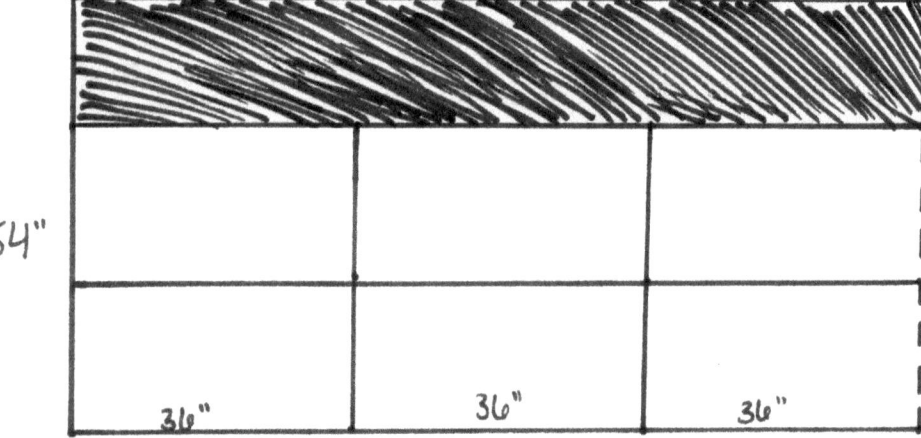

**6 yards =
12 boxed bags +
lots of waste**

Use waste for straps, trim, tailored bag panels, or gussets

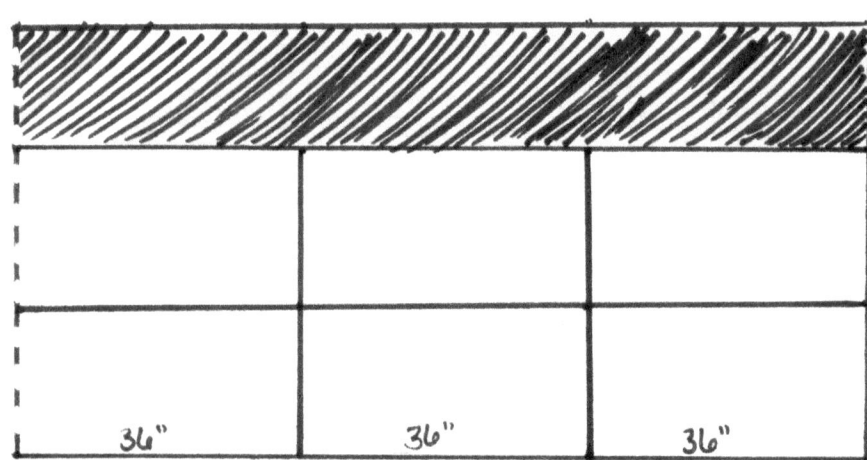

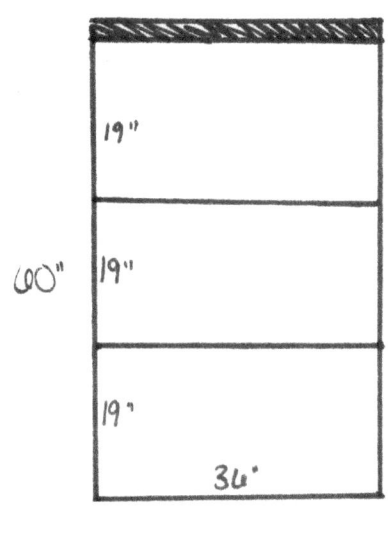

19" x 36" panels, 60" wide
All gussets are 43" long

1 yard = 3 bags
+ waste for trim lines

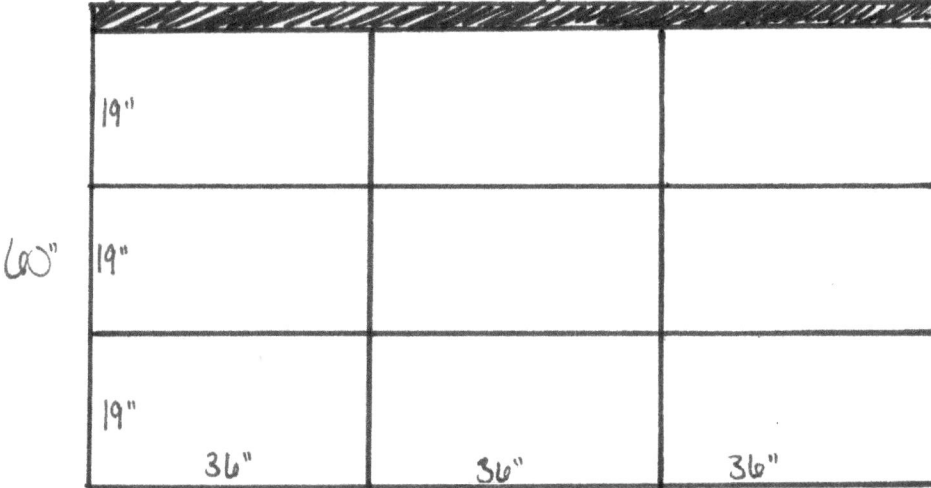

6 yards =
18 bags
zero cutting error

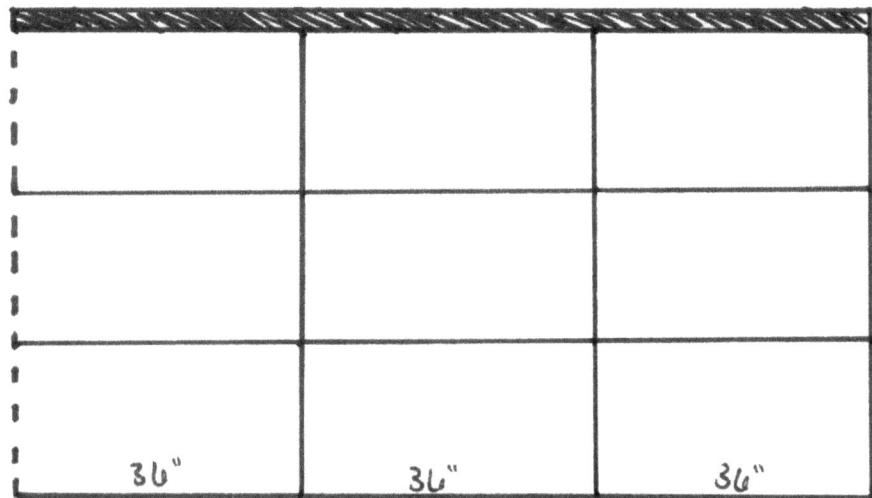

Tailored Bag Panel Measurement Chart

Panels

13 Inch	ONE YARD			13	13	13
	26	39	52	65	78	91
	TWO YARDS			13	13	13
	104	117	130	143	156	169
	THREE YARDS	FOUR YARDS	FIVE YARDS	13	13	13
	182	195	208			
	SIX YARDS					

14 Inch	ONE YARD			14	14	14
	28	42	56	70	84	98
	TWO YARDS			14	14	14
	112	126	140	154	168	182
	THREE YARDS	FOUR YARDS	FIVE YARDS	14	14	14
	196	210				
	SIX YARDS					

15 Inch	ONE YARD			15	15	15
	30	45	60	75	90	105
	TWO YARDS			15	15	15
	120	135	150	165	180	195
	THREE YARDS	FOUR YARDS	FIVE YARDS	15	15	
	210					
	SIX YARDS					

16 Inch	ONE YARD			16	16	16
	32	48	64	80	96	112
	TWO YARDS			16	16	16
	128	144	160	176	192	208
	THREE YARDS	FOUR YARDS	FIVE YARDS			
	SIX YARDS					

Gussets

7 Inch

ONE YARD					TWO YARDS					THREE YARDS					FOUR YARDS				
7	7	7	7	7	7	7	7	7	7	7	7	7	7	7	7	7	7	7	7
14	21	28	35	42	49	56	63	70	77	84	91	98	105	112	119	126	133	140	

8 Inch

ONE YARD					TWO YARDS					THREE YARDS					FOUR YARDS				
8	8	8	8	8	8	8	8	8	8	8	8	8	8	8	8	8	8	8	8
16	24	32	40	48	56	64	72	80	88	96	104	112	120	128	136	144			

9 Inch

ONE YARD					TWO YARDS					THREE YARDS					FOUR YARDS				
9	9	9	9	9	9	9	9	9	9	9	9	9	9	9	9	9	9		
18	27	36	45	54	63	72	81	90	99	108	117	126	135	144					

13" x 15" panels, 45" wide, without nap

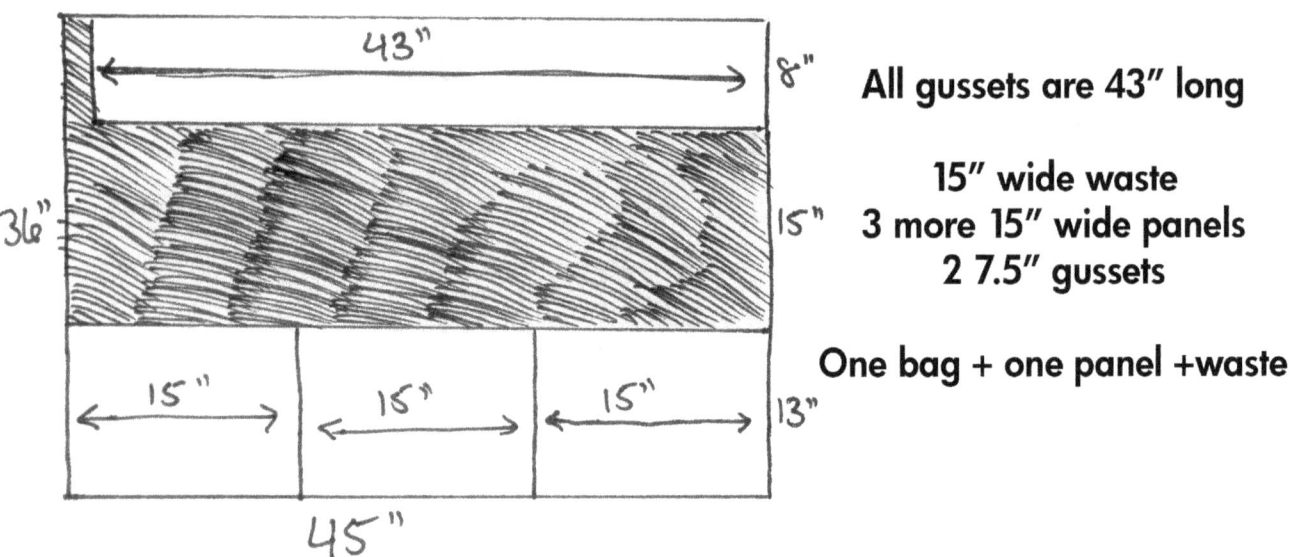

All gussets are 43" long

15" wide waste
3 more 15" wide panels
2 7.5" gussets

One bag + one panel + waste

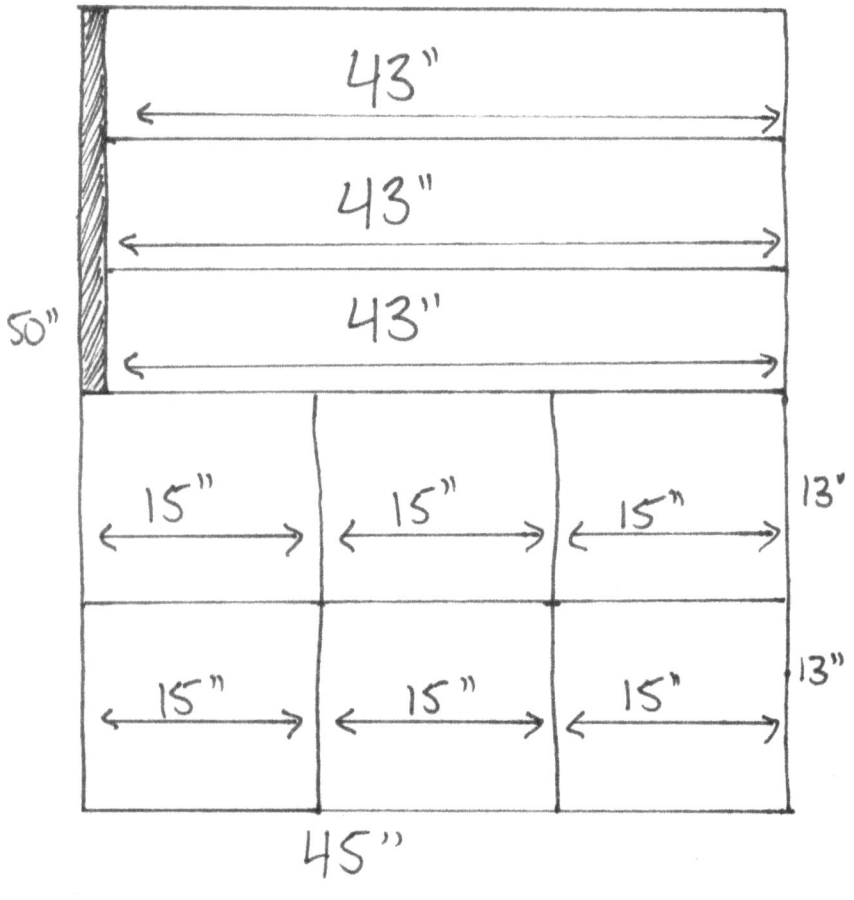

Gives three complete bags with a waste strip 24 x 2" wide. Plus some average for cutting margins.

13" x 15" panels, 45" wide, with nap

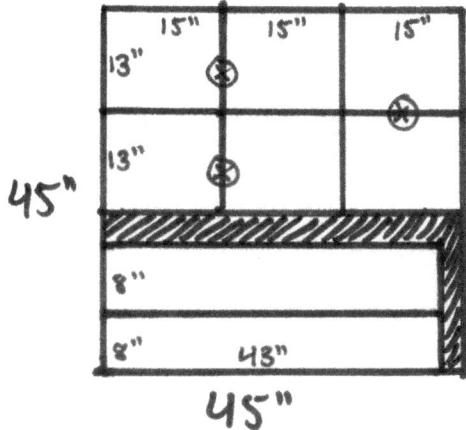

With nap layout you can use more fabric and have more gussets and panels

1 1/4 yards yields 2 bags with an extra pair of panels

All gussets are 43" long

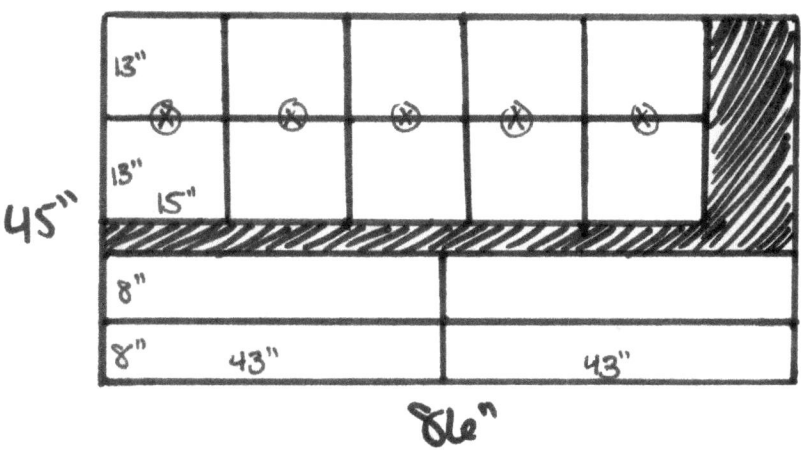

2 yards + 3/8 yard = 4 complete bags + 1 extra pair of panels + enough extra waste to piece a gusset or cut another panel that is cross grain

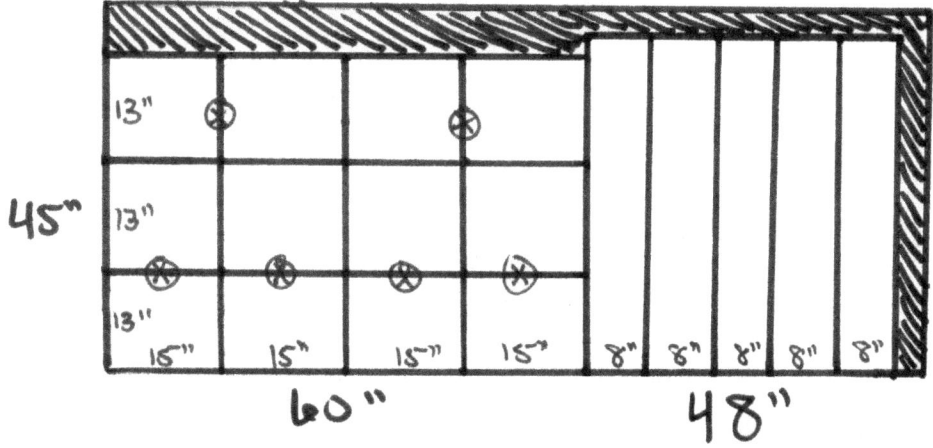

3 yards = 6 complete bags with/8" gussets that are cut cross grain

13" x 15" panels, 54" wide, with nap

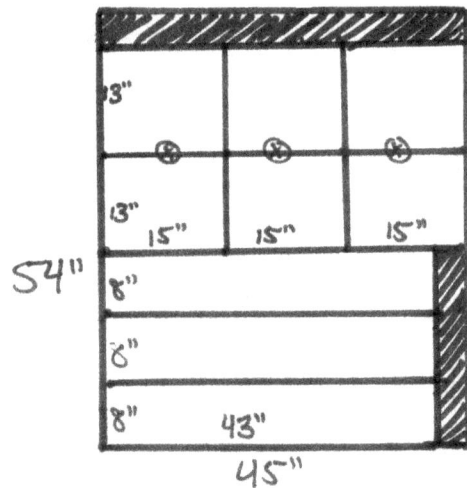

All gussets are 43" long

1 1/4 yards = 3 complete bags + waste

No cutting margin

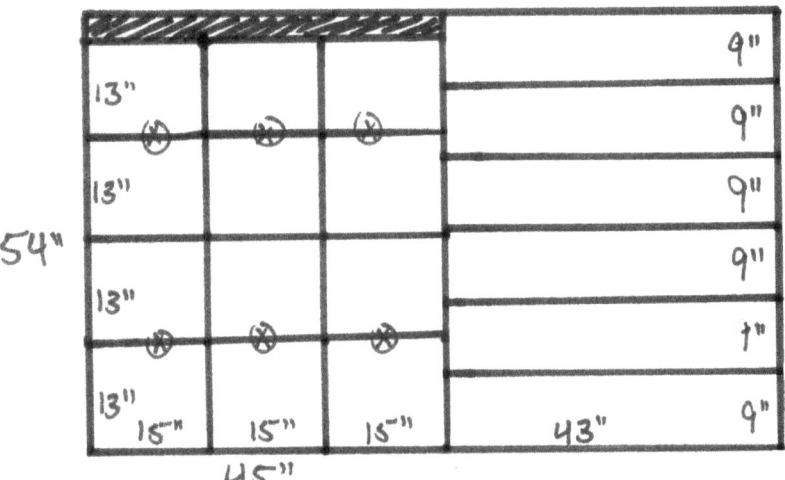

2 yards + 1/2 yard = 6 complete bags with wider gussets and less waste

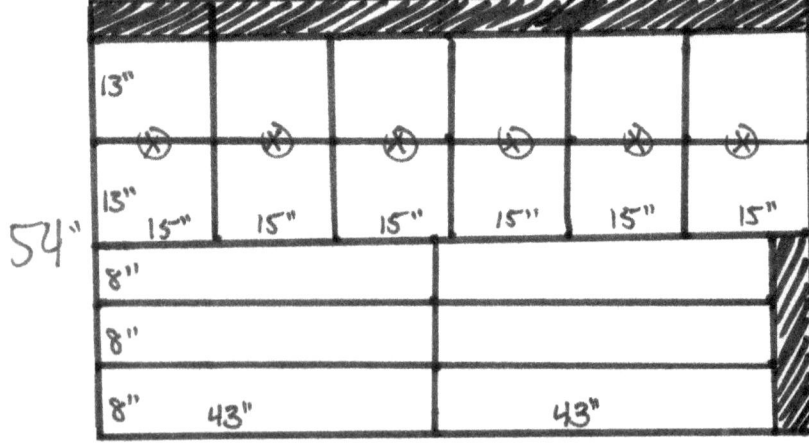

2 yards + 1/2 yard = 6 complete bags + waste

13" x 15" Tailored Bag Layouts

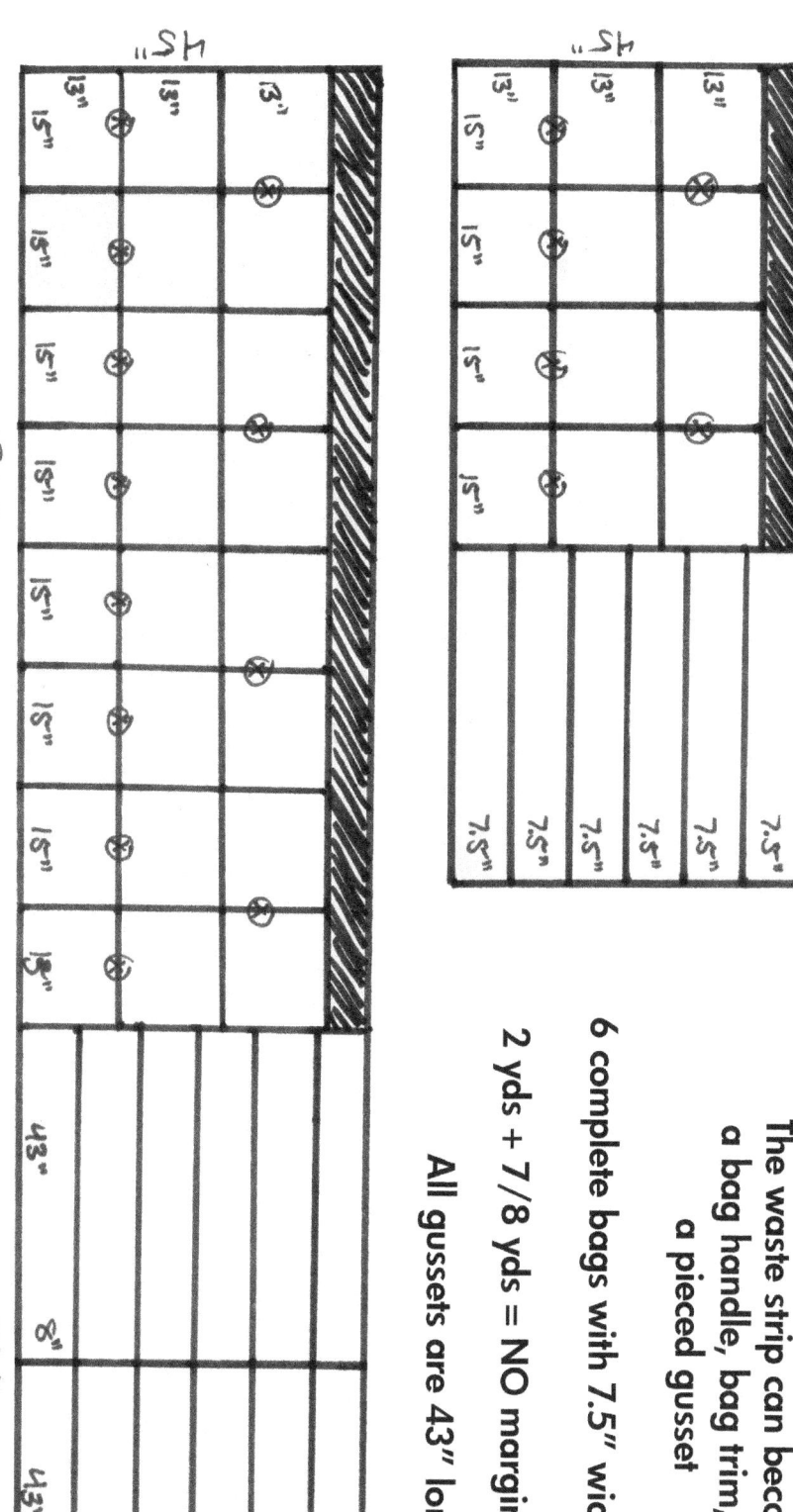

13" x 15", 45" wide, with nap

The waste strip can become a bag handle, bag trim, or a pieced gusset

6 complete bags with 7.5" wide gussets

2 yds + 7/8 yds = NO margin of error

All gussets are 43" long

5 yards + 3/4 yard (no margin) = 12 bags + 6 x 120" waste

13" x 15" Tailored Bag Layouts

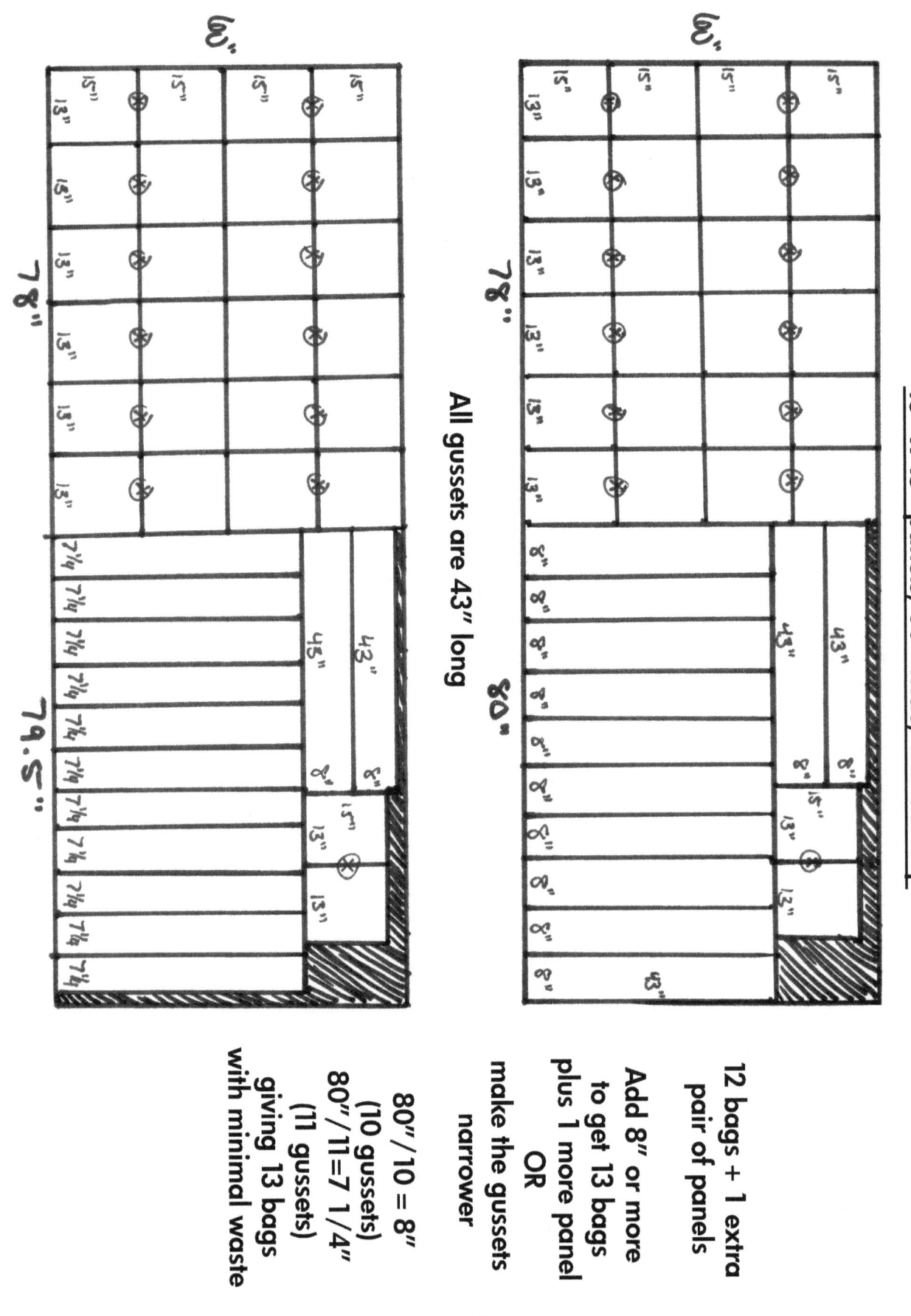

13" x 15" panels, 60" wide, without nap

All gussets are 43" long

12 bags + 1 extra pair of panels

Add 8" or more to get 13 bags plus 1 more panel

OR

make the gussets narrower

80"/10 = 8" (10 gussets)
80"/11 = 7 1/4" (11 gussets)
giving 13 bags with minimal waste

13" x 15" Tailored Bag Layouts

13" x 15" panels, 45" wide, without nap

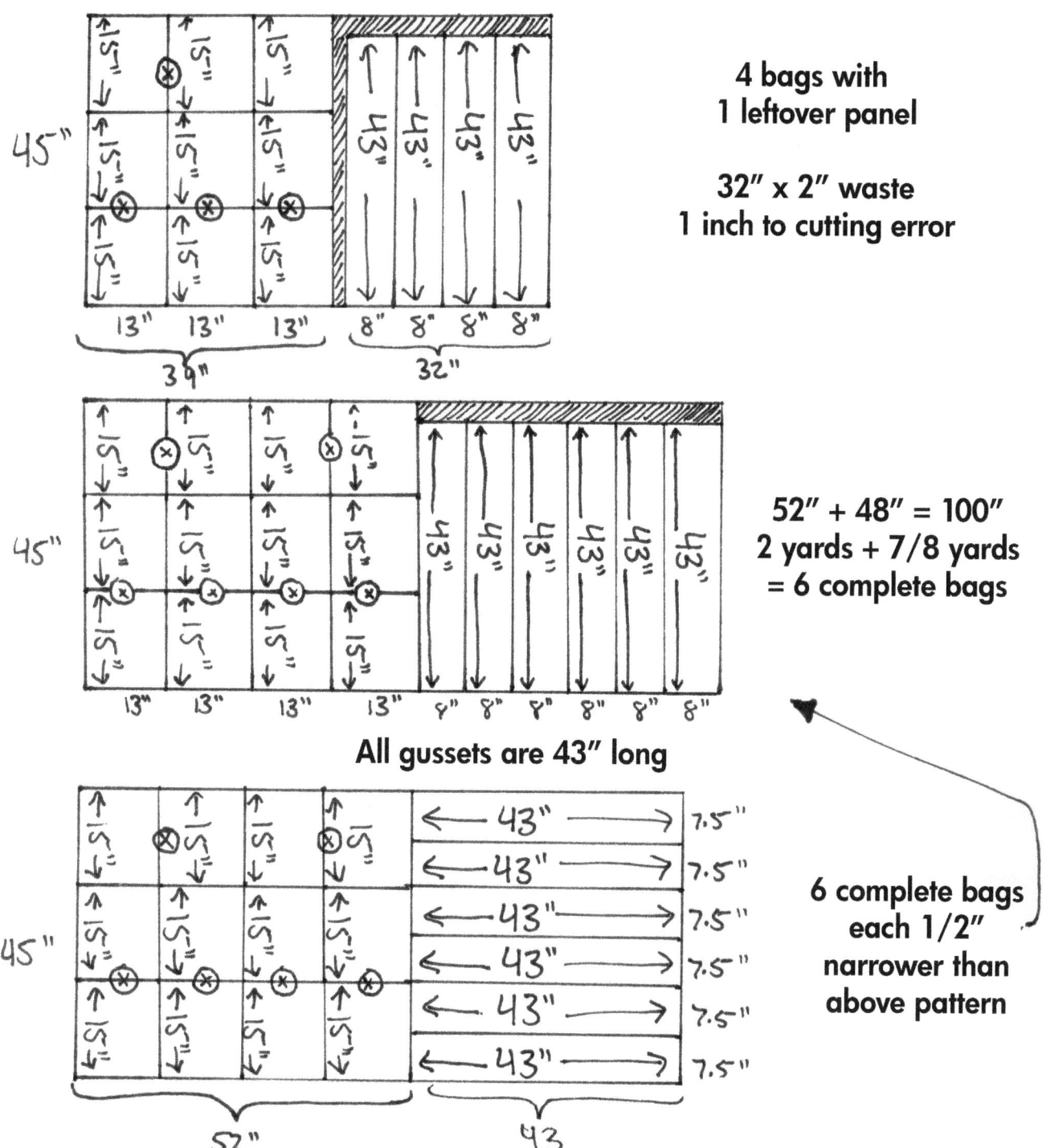

4 bags with
1 leftover panel

32" x 2" waste
1 inch to cutting error

52" + 48" = 100"
2 yards + 7/8 yards
= 6 complete bags

All gussets are 43" long

6 complete bags each 1/2" narrower than above pattern

95" or 2 3/4 yards leaves a few inches for error

13" x 15" Tailored Bag Layouts

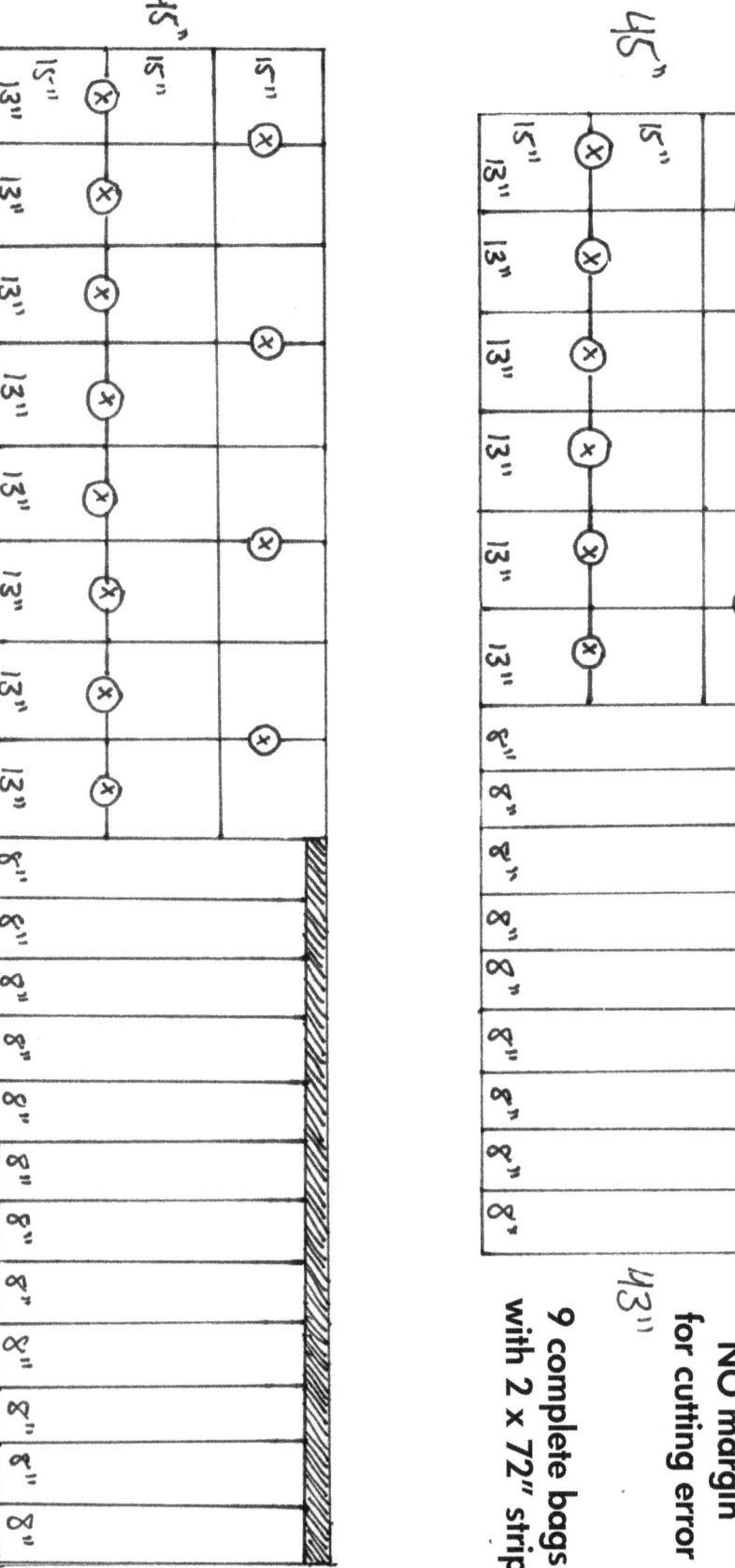

13" x 15" panels, 45" wide, without nap

<--- 2 x 72" waste
4 yards + 1/8 yard
NO margin
for cutting error

9 complete bags
with 2 x 72" strip

5 yards + 5/8 yard ---> 2" margin for error

12 complete bags + 2 x 96" waste strip

13" x 15" Tailored Bag Layouts

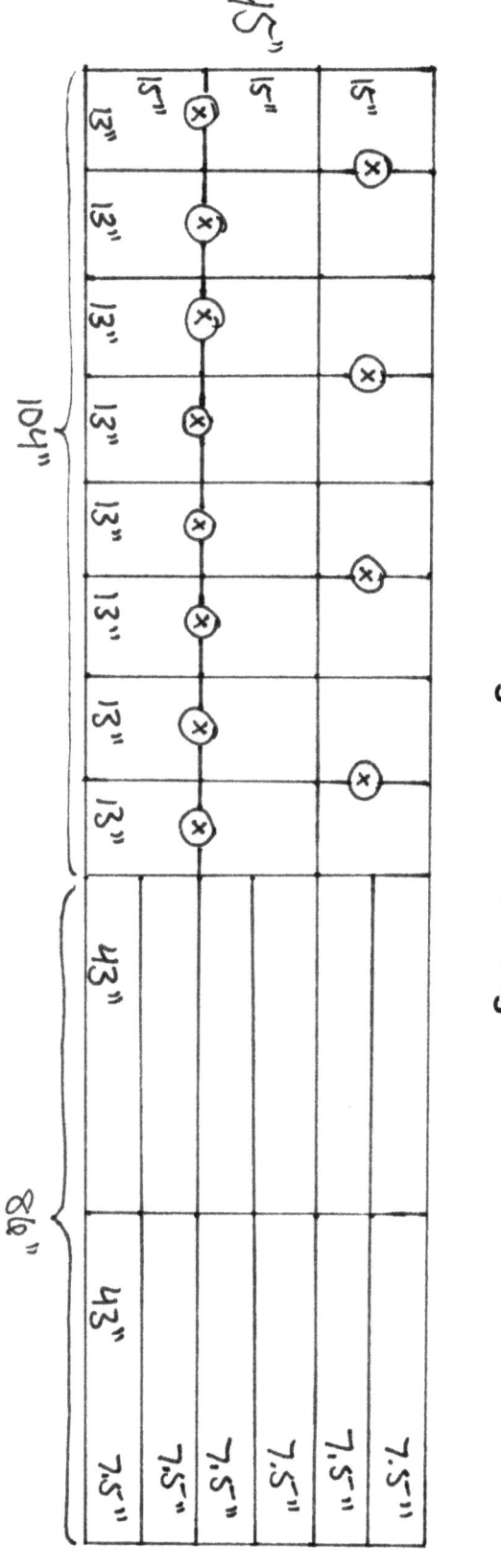

13" x 15" panels, 45" wide, without nap
All gussets are 43" long

5 yard + 3/8 yard = 12 complete bags
NO waste 7.5" gusset

13" x 15" Tailored Bag Layouts

13" x 15" panels, 54" wide without nap

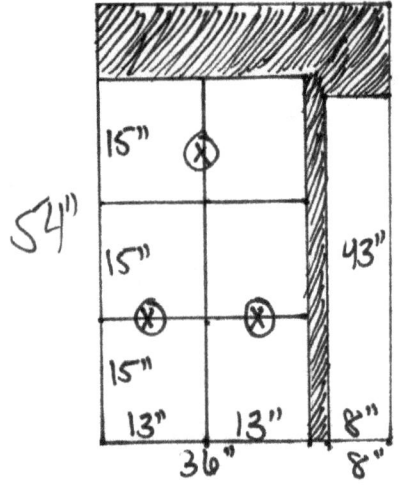

All gussets are 43" long

3 panels + 1 gusset
from 1 yard 54" wide
cloth + 3 waste sections

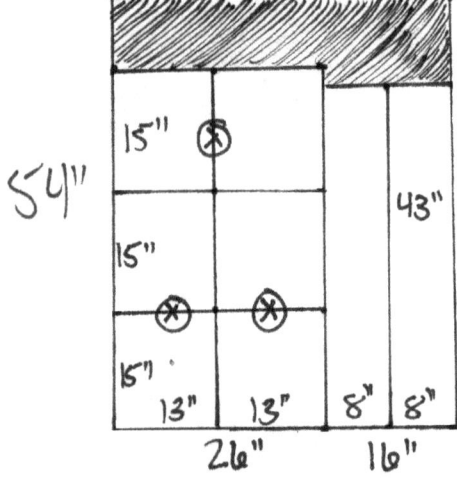

If you buy 42" wide cloth you have
NO margin for error.
You get 2 complete bags
plus 1 pair of panels
plus enough waste fabric
to piece the last gusset

1 yard + 1/4 yard = 36 + 9 = 45
to make the third bag

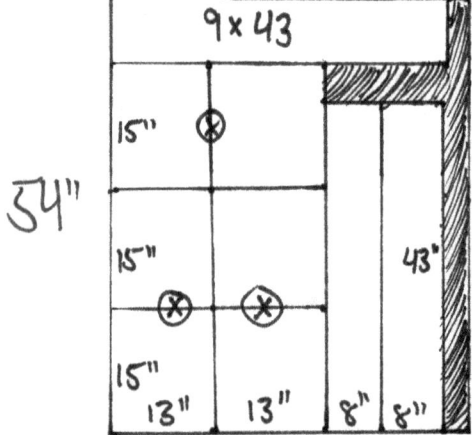

1 1/4 yards = 3 complete bags

13" x 15" panels, 54" wide without nap

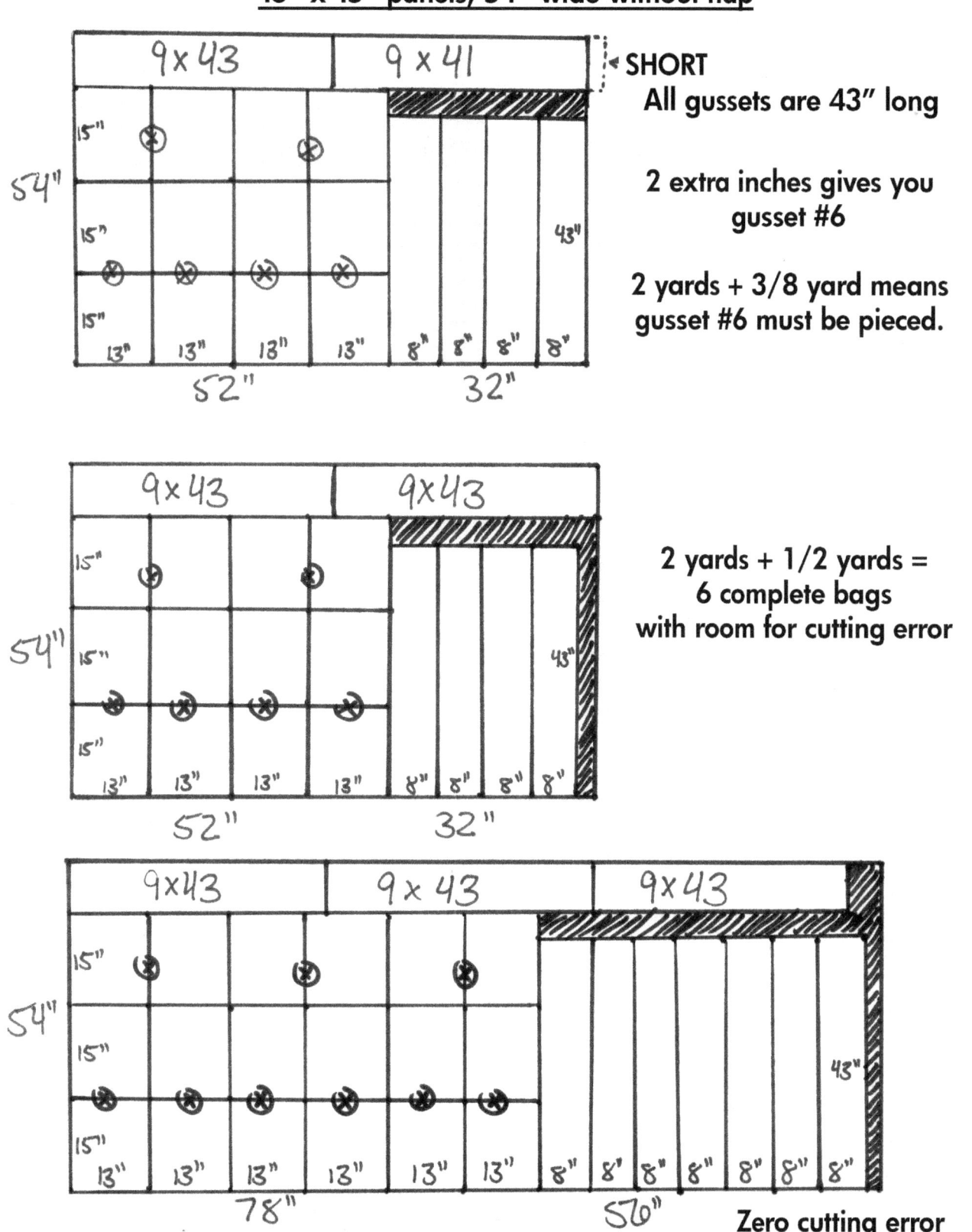

SHORT
All gussets are 43" long

2 extra inches gives you gusset #6

2 yards + 3/8 yard means gusset #6 must be pieced.

2 yards + 1/2 yards = 6 complete bags with room for cutting error

3 yards + 3/4 yard = 9 bags + 1 spare gusset + waste

Zero cutting error on panels and gussets

13" x 15" Tailored Bag Layouts

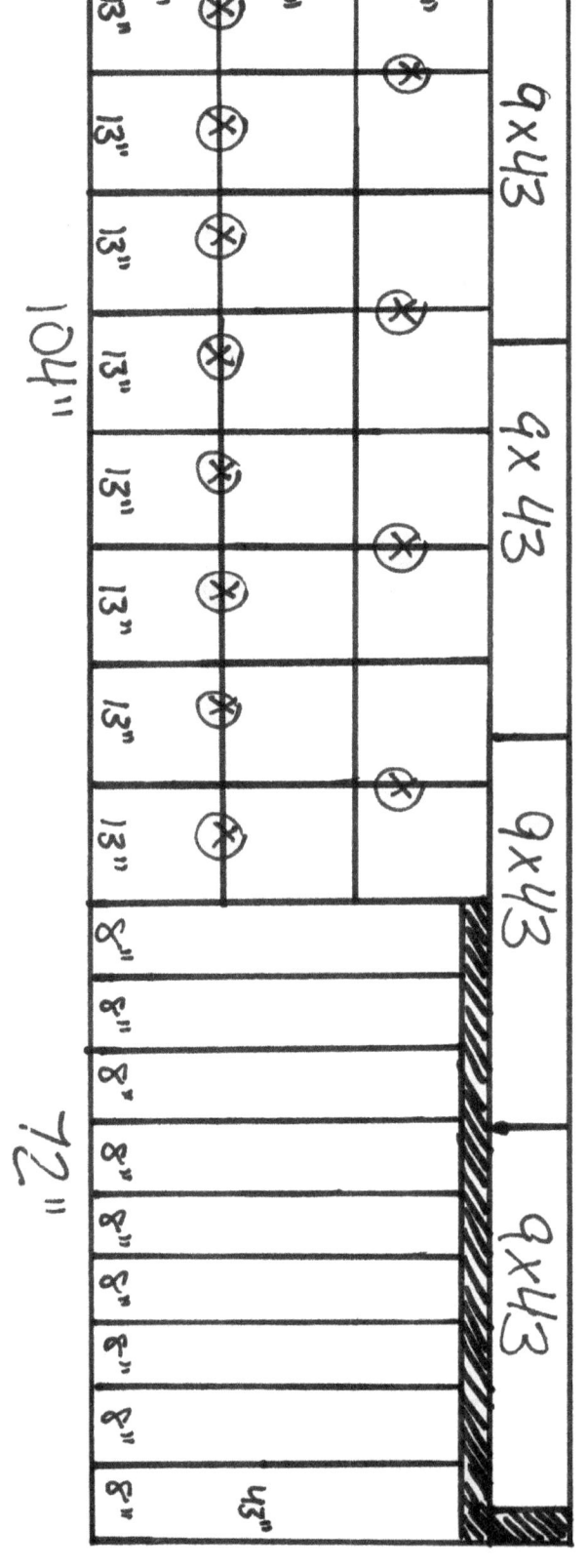

13" x 15" panels, 54" wide without nap

All gussets are 43" long

176" ---> 5 yards

12 bags + 1 extra gusset + 4 x 9 + 2 x 72 waste

13" x 15" panels, 60" wide with nap

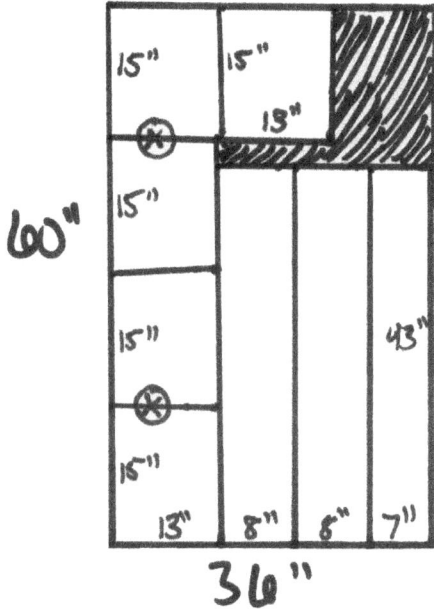

All gussets are 43" long

1 yard (60") = 2 complete bags + 1 extra panel + waste

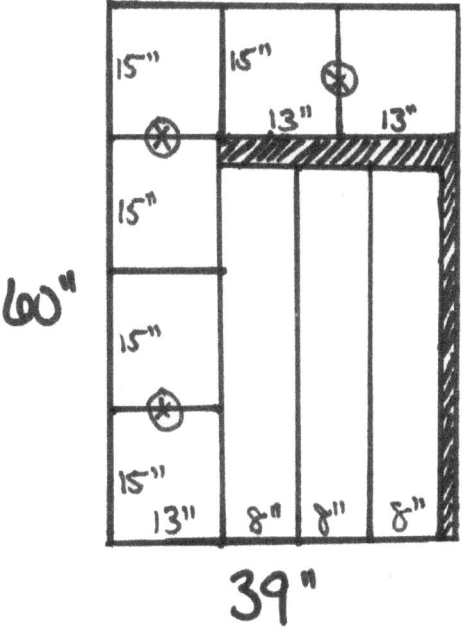

1 yard + 1/8 yard = 3 complete bags + waste

13" x 15" panels, 60" wide without nap

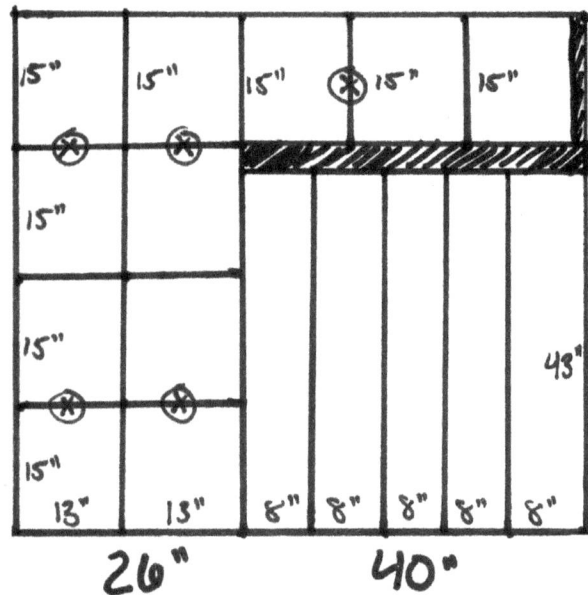

All gussets are 43" long

1 yard + 7/8 yard =
5 complete bags +
1 extra panel +
waste

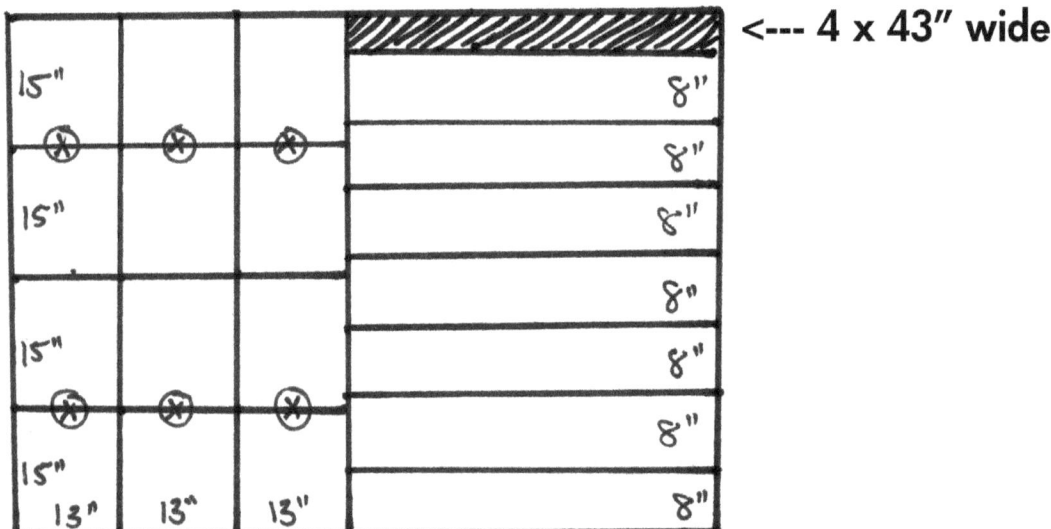

<--- 4 x 43" wide

2 yards + 3/8 yard = 6 complete bags + 1 spare gusset

13" x 15" Tailored Bag Layouts

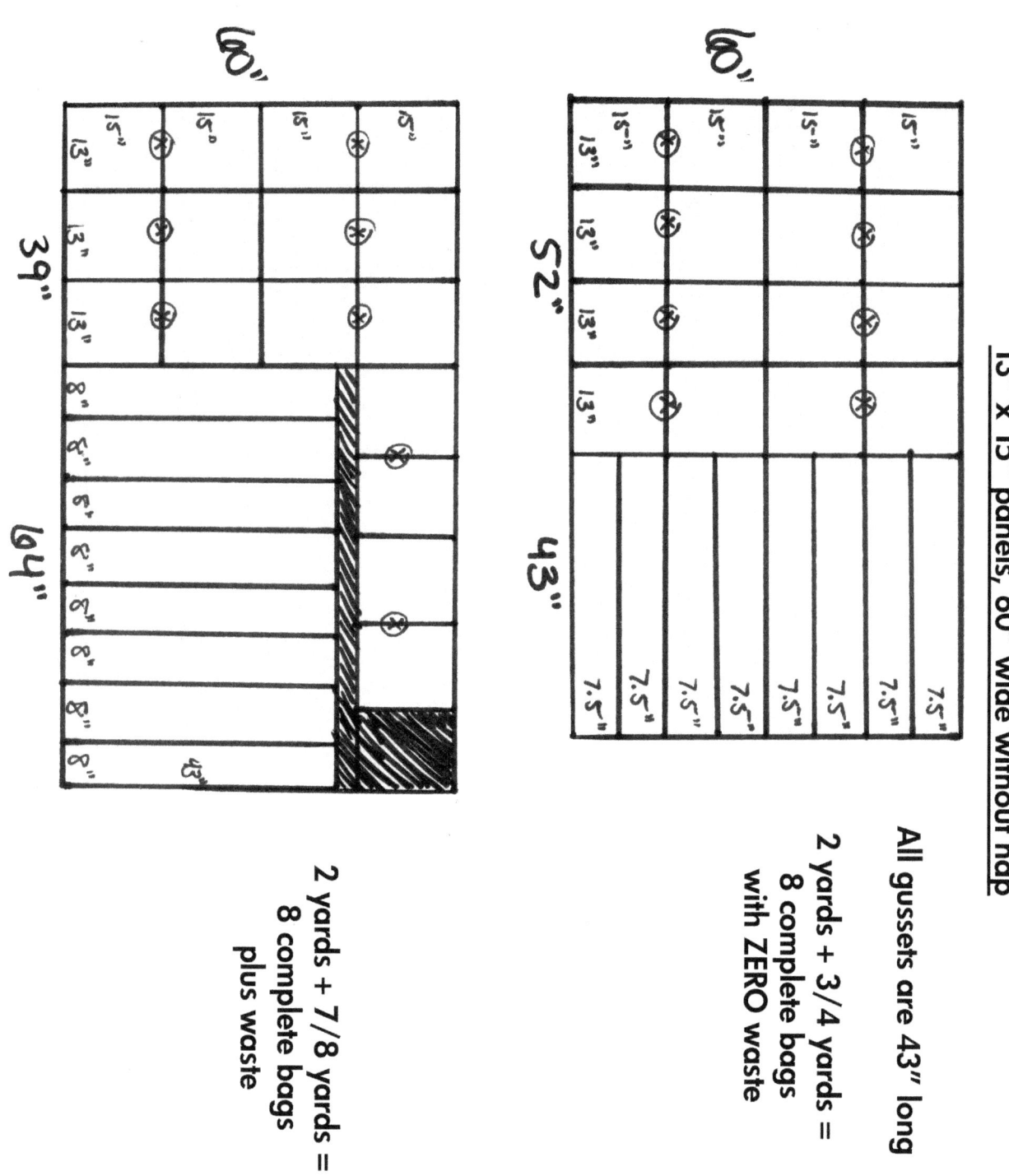

All gussets are 43" long

2 yards + 3/4 yards = 8 complete bags with ZERO waste

2 yards + 7/8 yards = 8 complete bags plus waste

13" x 15" Tailored Bag Layouts

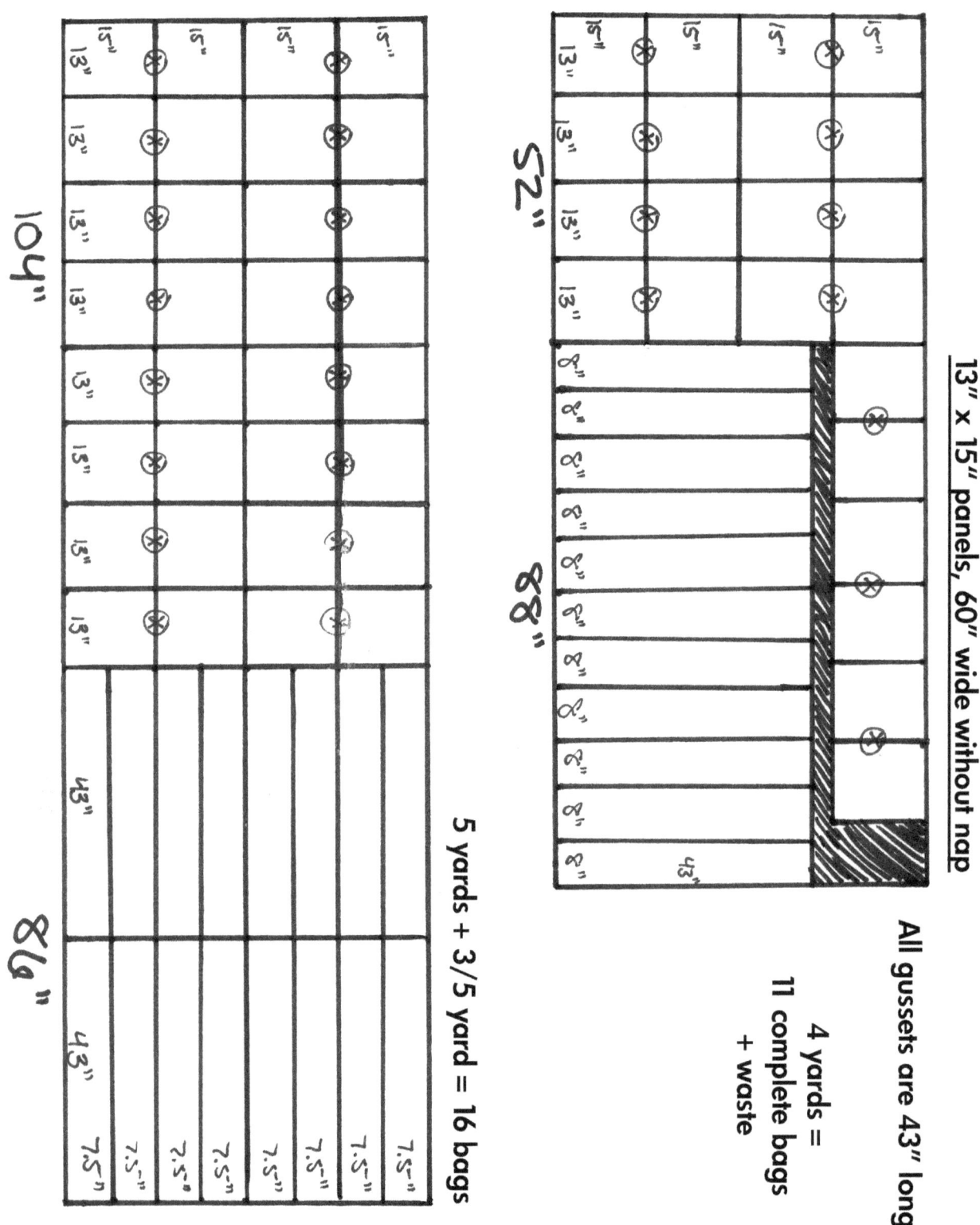

13" x 15" Tailored Bag Layouts

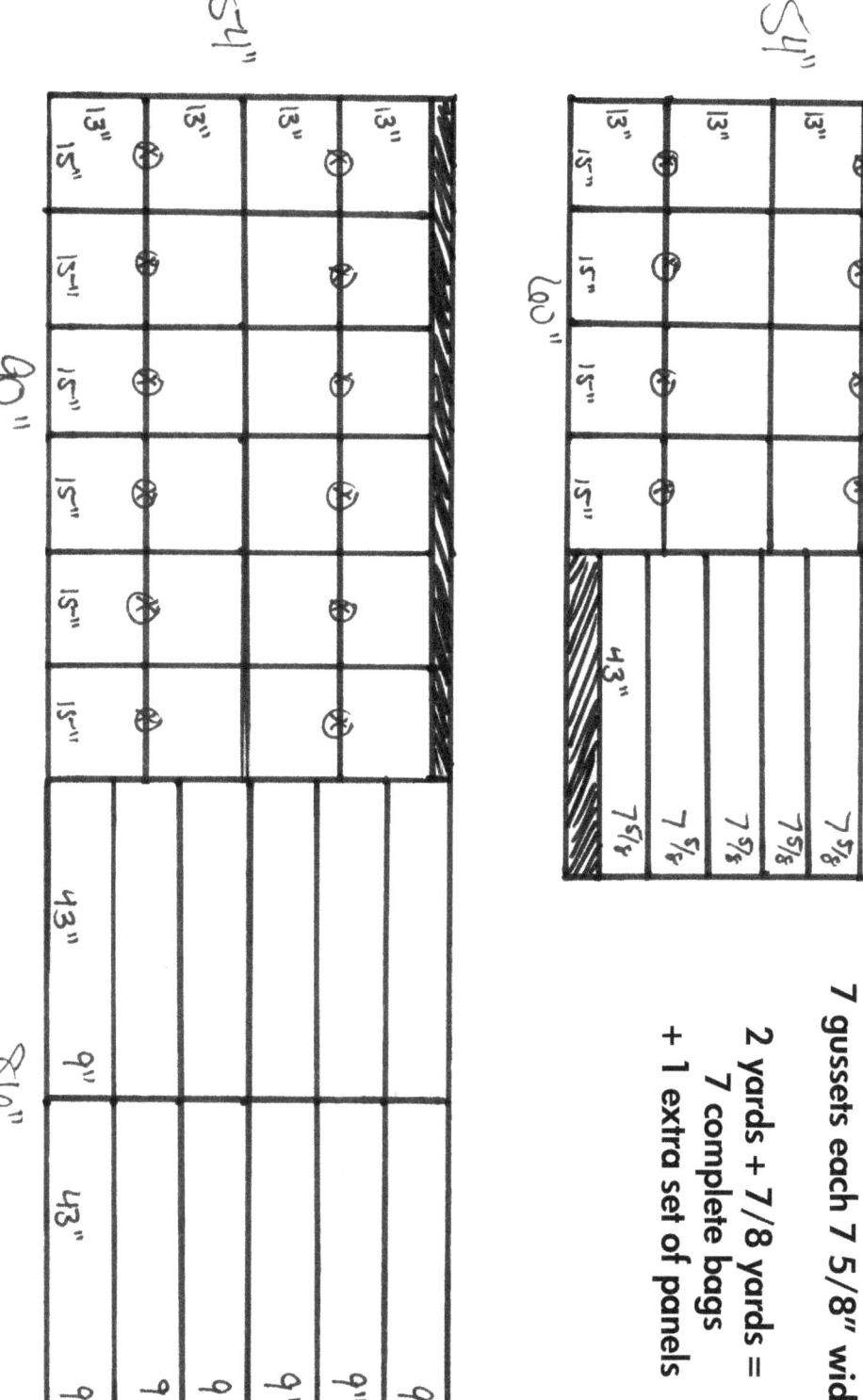

13" x 15" panels, 54" wide with nap

All gussets are 43" long

7 gussets each 7 5/8" wide

2 yards + 7/8 yards = 7 complete bags
+ 1 extra set of panels

5 yards = 12 complete bags with wider gussets

13" x 15" Tailored Bag Layouts

13" x 15" panels, 60" wide, with nap

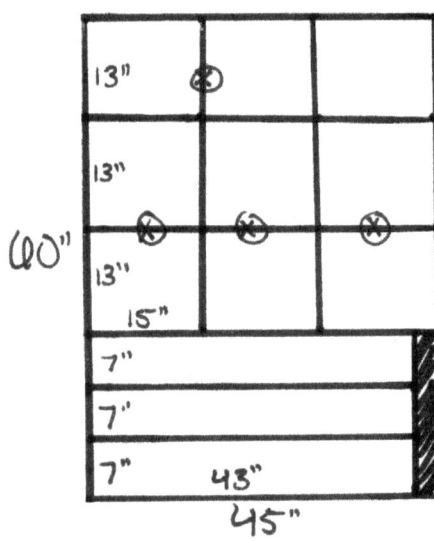

All gussets are 43" long

1 1/4 yards =
3 complete (narrower) bags
+ 3 spare panels

(No cutting margins)

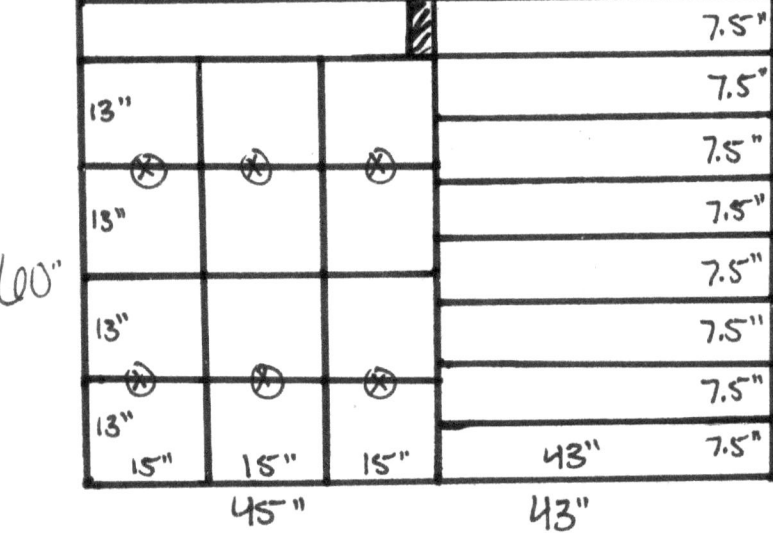

2 1/2 yards =
6 complete bags
+ 3 extra gussets

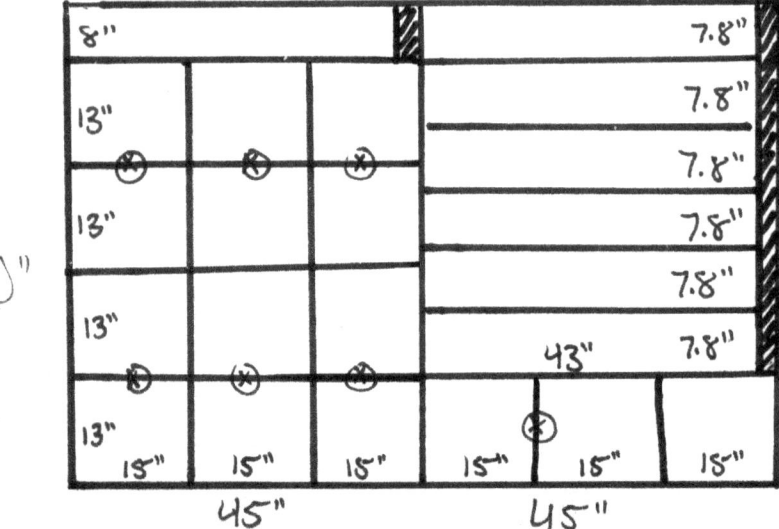

2 1/2 yards =
7 complete bags
+ 1 extra panel

13" x 15" Tailored Bag Layouts

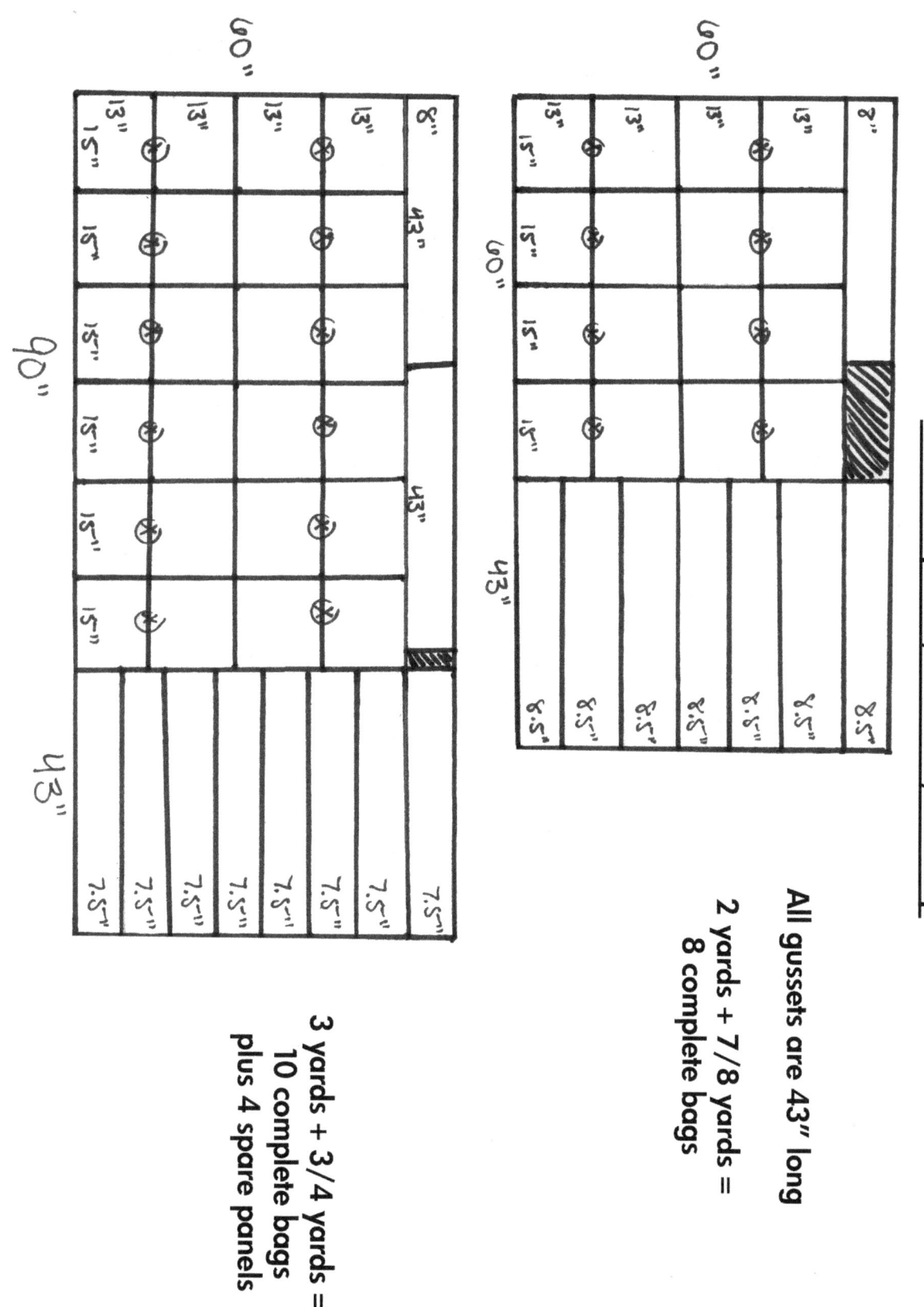

13" x 15" panels, 60" wide, with nap

All gussets are 43" long

2 yards + 7/8 yards =
8 complete bags

3 yards + 3/4 yards =
10 complete bags
plus 4 spare panels

13" x 15" Tailored Bag Layouts

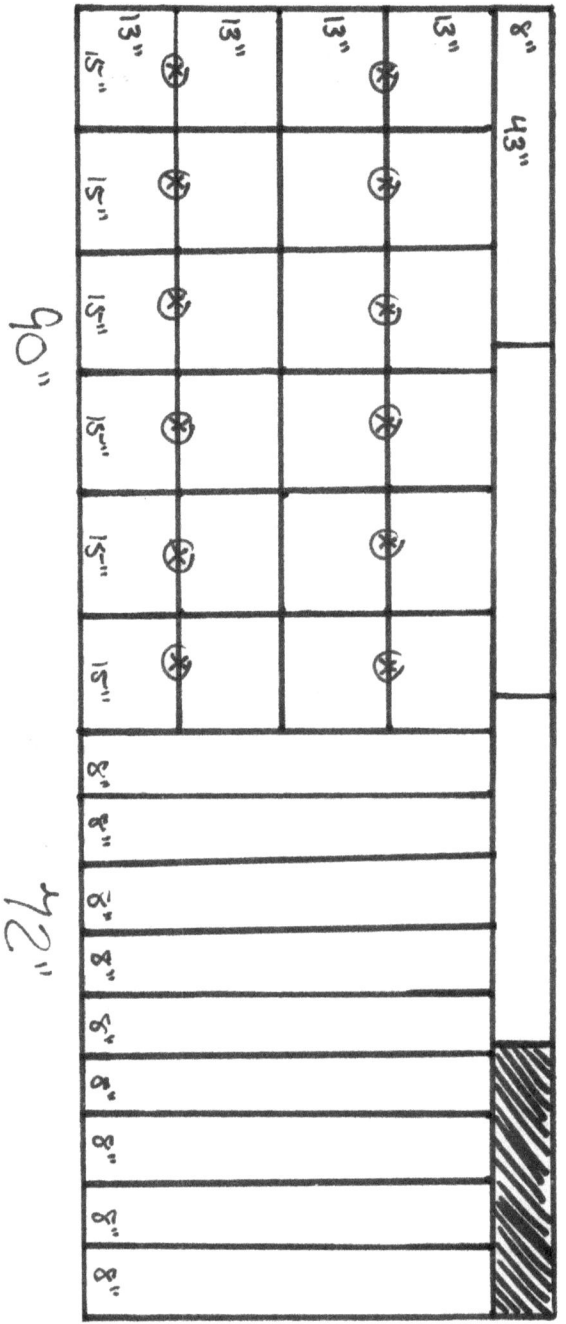

13" x 15" panels, 60" wide with nap
All gussets are 43" long

4 1/2 yards = 12 complete bags

(If you don't care about the nap for the gussets)

13" x 15" panels, 60" wide with nap
All gussets are 43" long

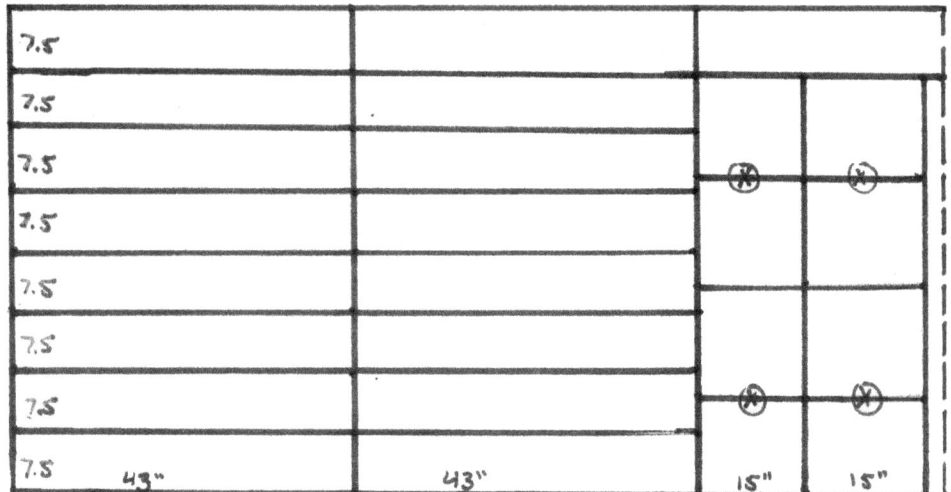

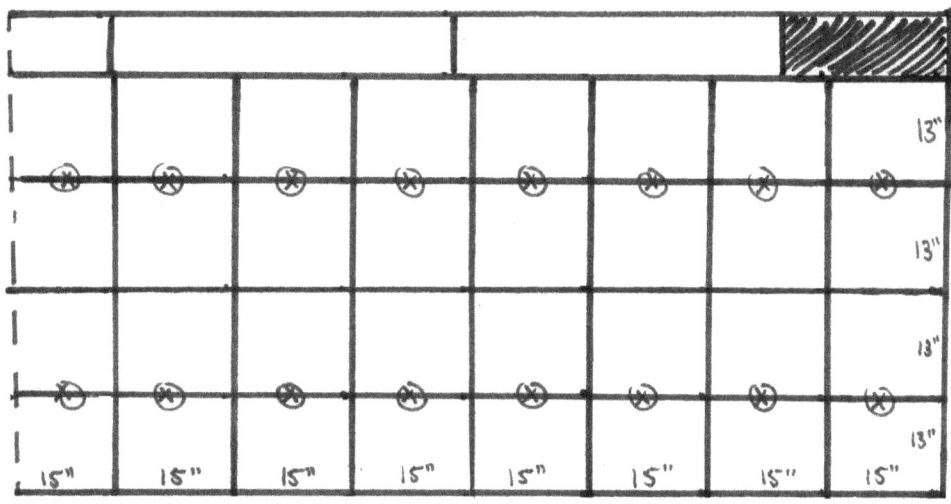

**6 yards + 5/8 yards =
19 complete bags + 1 pair of panels**

14" x 16" Tailored Bag Layouts

14" x 16" panels, 45" wide

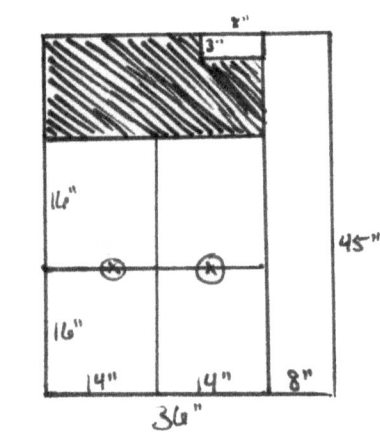

All gussets are 46" long

1 yard = 1 complete bag + 1 pieced gusset
+ 1 pair extra panels + waste

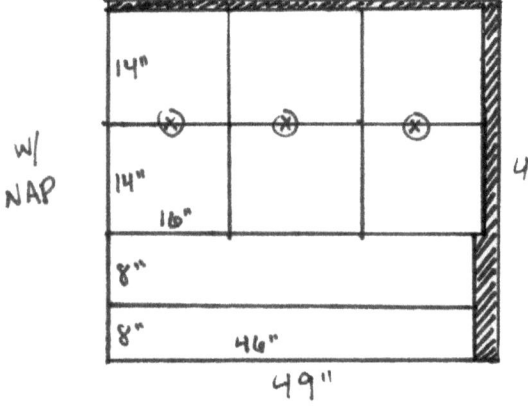

1 yard + 3/8 yards =
2 complete bags
+ 1 extra pair of panels

3 yards =
6 complete bags
(2" for error)

14" x 16" panels, 45" wide with nap

All gussets are 46" long

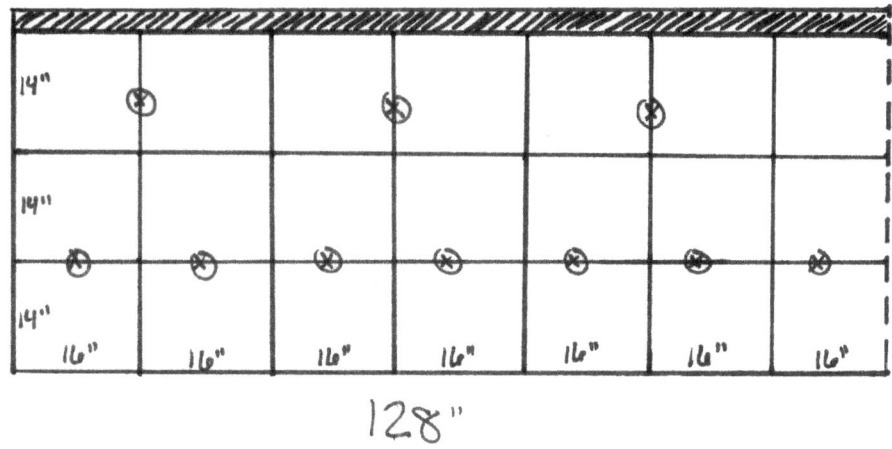

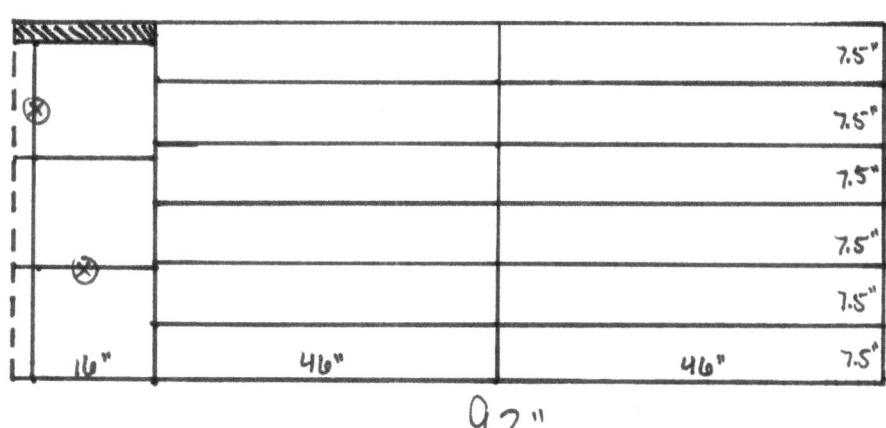

6 yards + 1/4 yard = 12 complete bags + 3 x 128 waste

14" x 16" panels, 54" wide

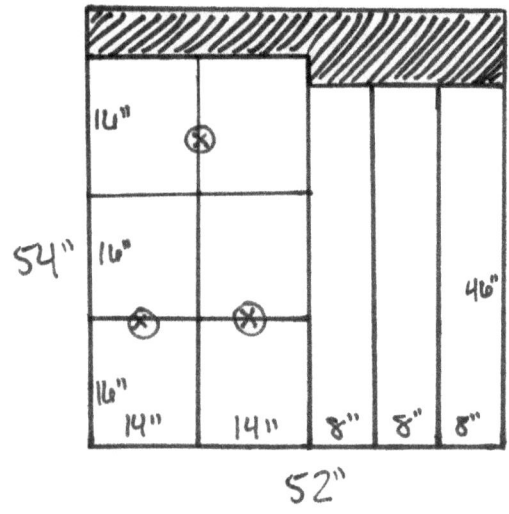

All gussets are 46" long

1 1/2 yards =
3 complete bags

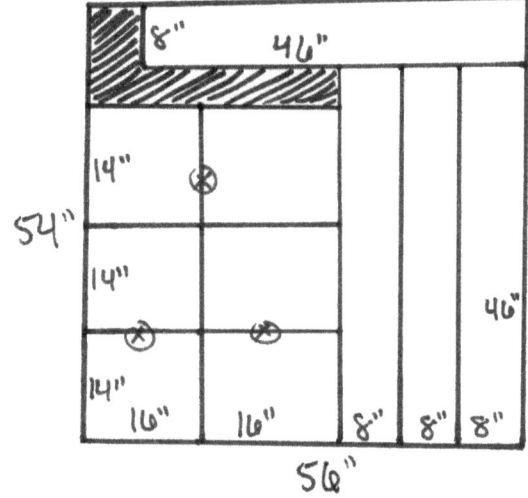

1 5/8 yards =
3 complete bags +
1 extra gusset

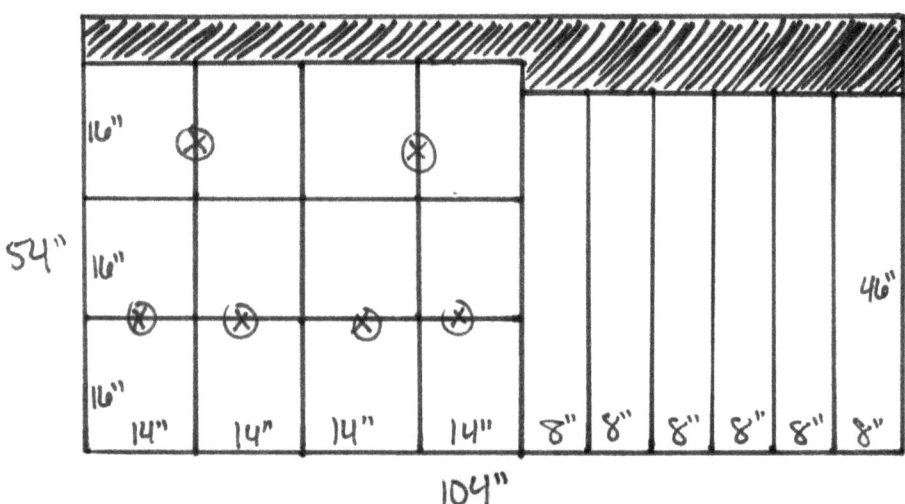

3 yards + cutting error = 6 complete bags + 1 extra gusset

14" x 16" Tailored Bag Layouts

14" x 16" panels, 54" wide

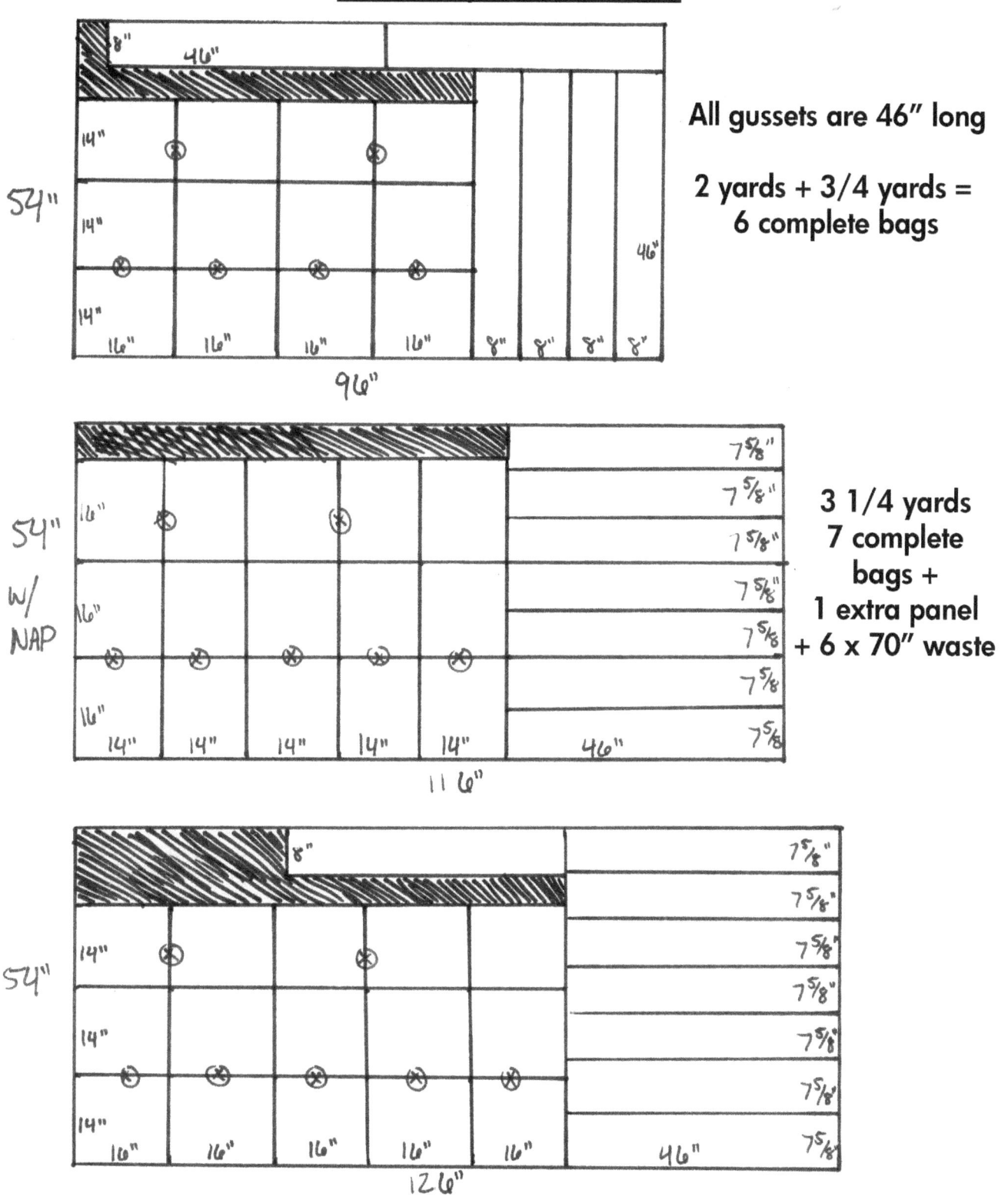

All gussets are 46" long

2 yards + 3/4 yards = 6 complete bags

3 1/4 yards
7 complete bags + 1 extra panel + 6 x 70" waste

3 1/2 yards = 7 bags, 1 extra gusset, 1 extra panel, & enough waste to piece panel #2 of bag #8

14" x 16" Tailored Bag Layouts

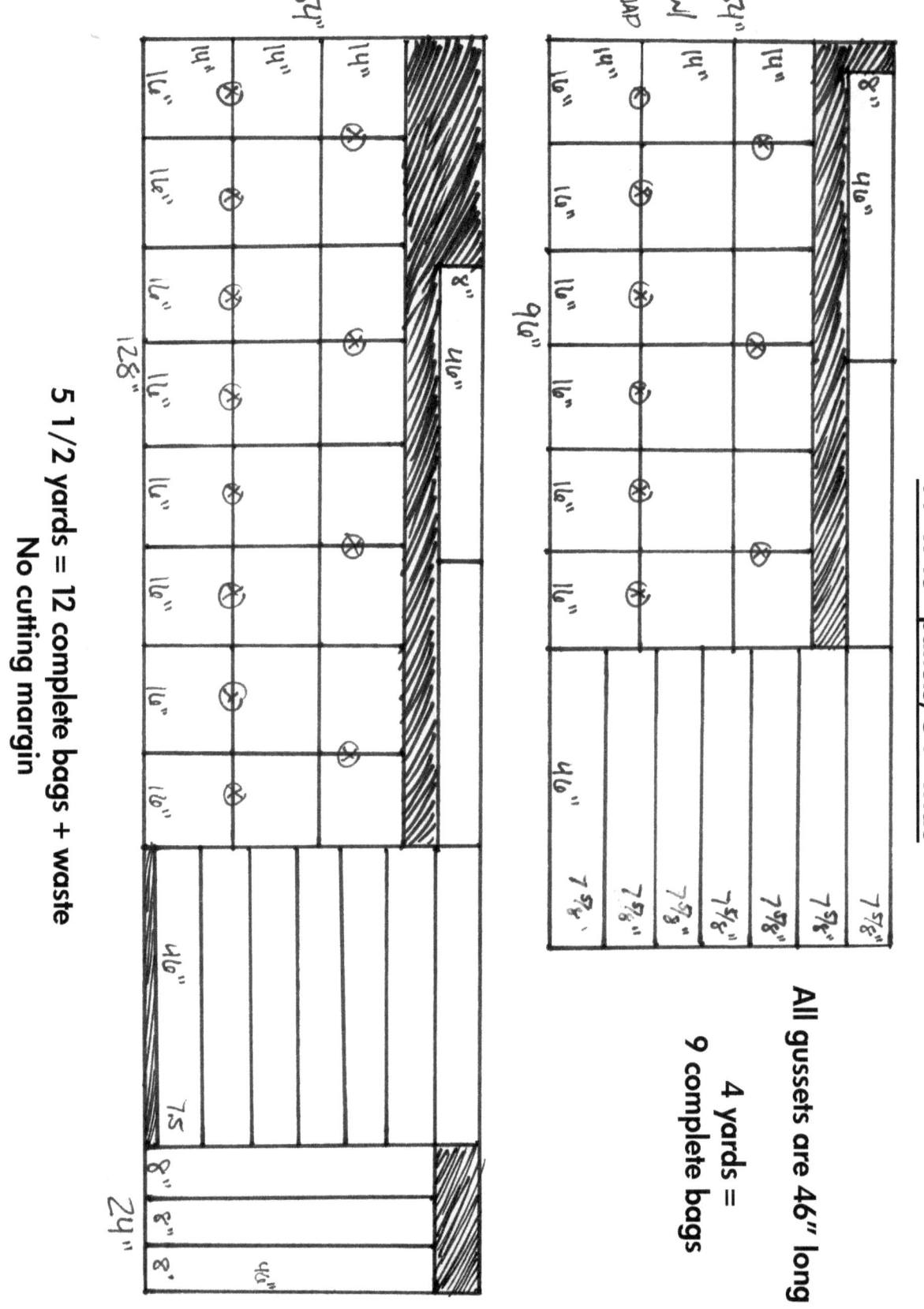

14" x 16" panels, 60" wide

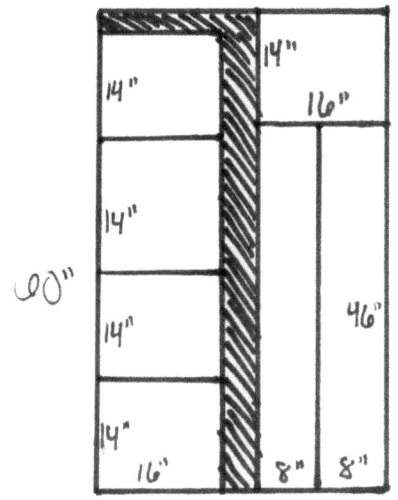

All gussets are 46" long

One yard =
2 complete bags +
1 spare panel +
waste

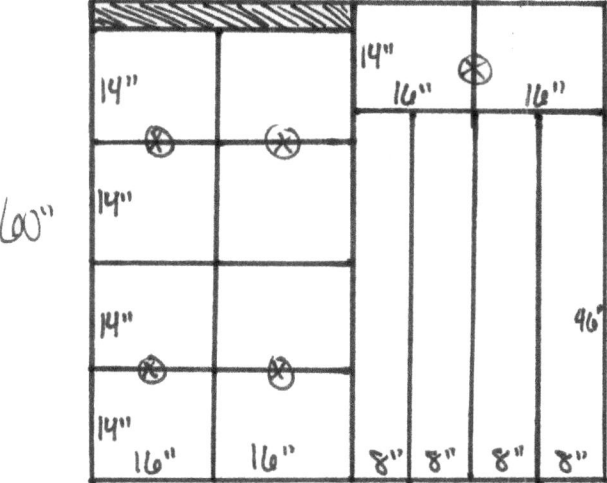

1 7/8 yards =
4 complete bags +
1 pair extra panels

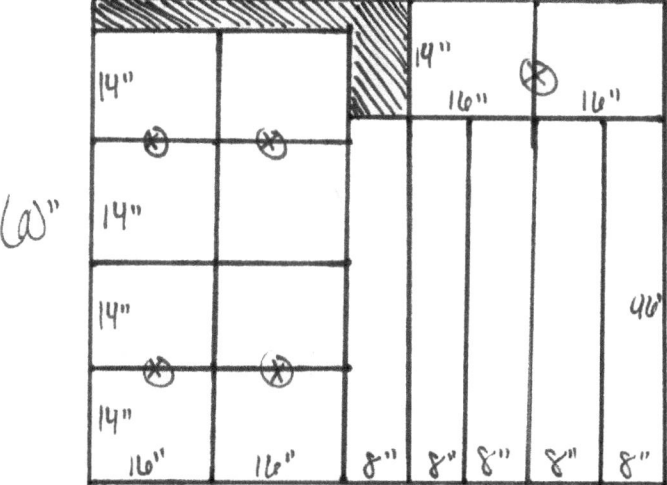

2 yards =
5 complete bags
no margin for error

14" x 16" panels, 60" wide

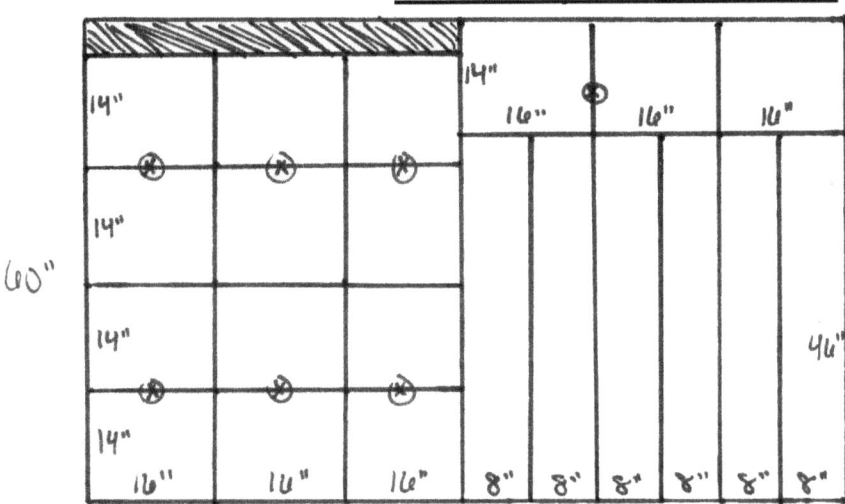

All gussets are 46" long

2 yards + 3/4 yards =
6 complete bags +
3 spare panels

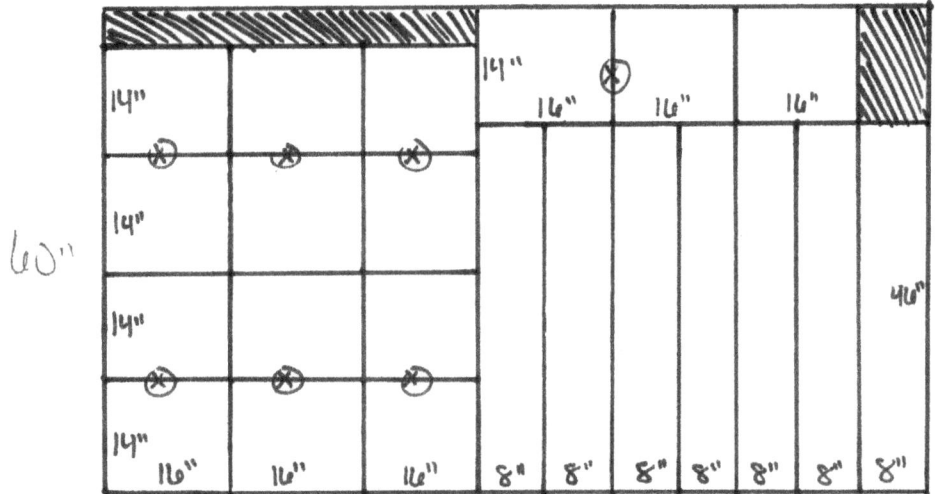

3 yards =
7 complete bags +
1 spare panel

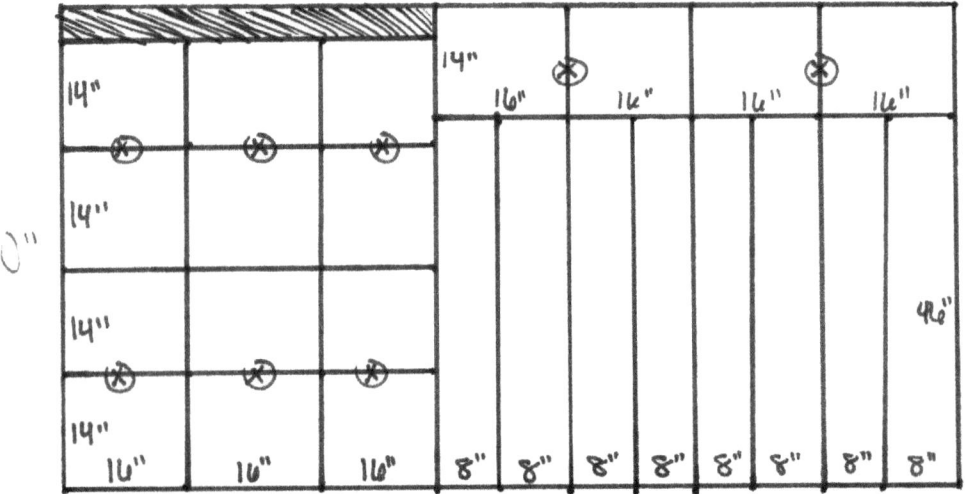

3 yards +
1/8 yards =
8 complete bags

Zero cutting margin

14" x 16" Tailored Bag Layouts

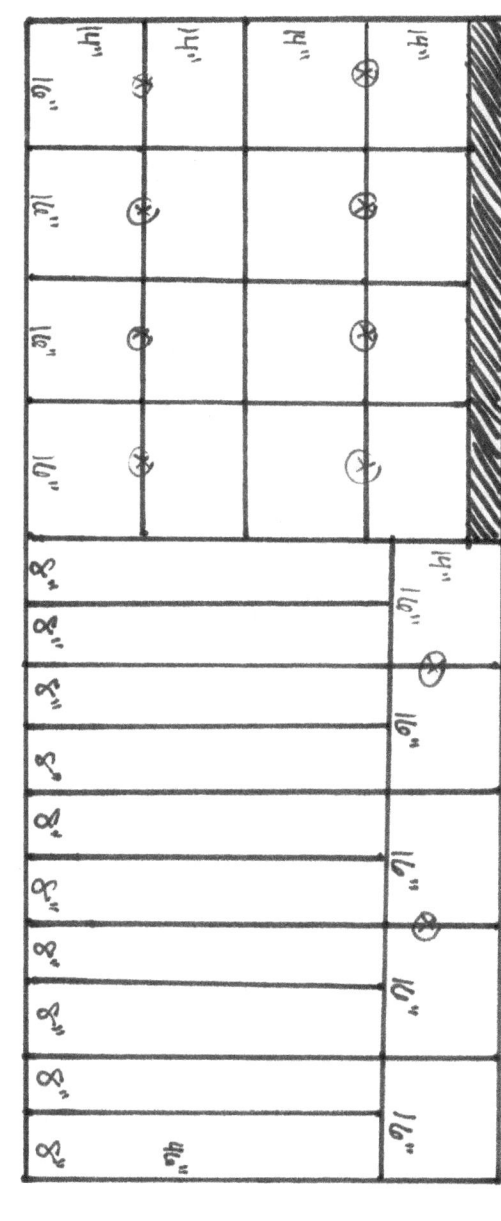

14" x 16" panels, 60" wide

All gussets are 46" long

4 yards = 10 complete bags + extra panel

No margin for error

5 yards + 1/8 yard = 13 complete bags

14" x 16" Tailored Bag Layouts

14" x 16" panels, 60" wide

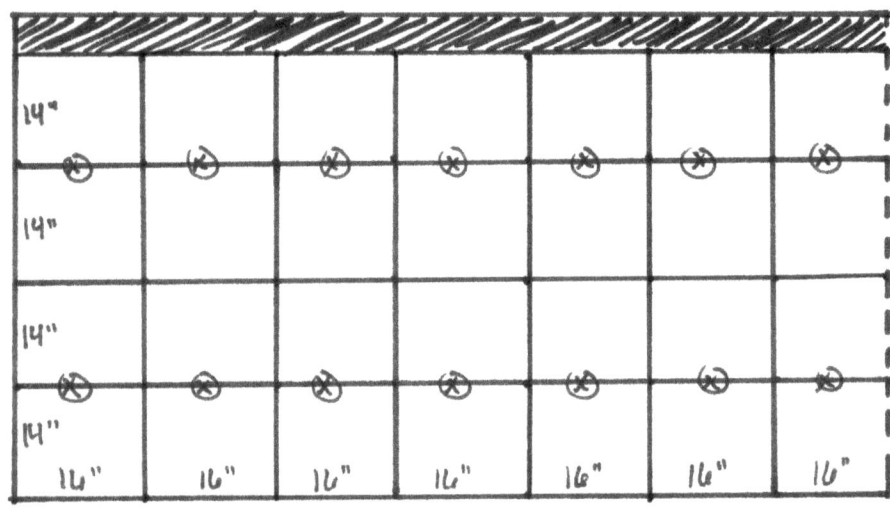

All gussets are 46" long

3 yards + 1/8 yards = 8 complete bags with 7.5 gussets

6 yards + 1/8 yards = 16 complete bags with 7.5 gussets

Zero margin for error

About the Author

Teresa Peschel lives with her husband, children, their dog Muffy, and a supervising cat named Olga in Hershey, Pa. It really is the sweetest place on earth and the air really does smell like chocolate. Her interests include thrifty living, keeping a small environmental footprint, making utilitarian objects beautiful, and getting ready for the hard times that are bearing down on us. "Sew Cloth Grocery Bags" fits all of those themes.

MORE FROM PESCHEL PRESS
Home of the History Behind the Mystery

The Complete, Annotated Series
Edited and Annotated by Bill Peschel

Return to your favorite novels by Agatha Christie & Dorothy L. Sayers, republished with plenty of extras, such as footnotes describing people, places, events, and idioms, and essays about the author, their creations, and historical events. They deepen your enjoyment and understanding of the novel and its world.

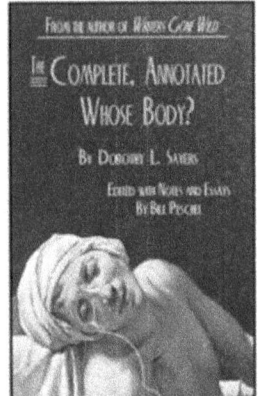

The Complete, Annotated Whose Body?

Dorothy L. Sayers

Her first novel featuring Lord Peter Wimsey comes with 3 maps of London, 10 essays on notorious crimes, anti-Semitism, Sayers and Wimsey, plus a timeline of his cases and Sayers' life. *282 pages.*

The Complete, Annotated Mysterious Affair at Styles

Agatha Christie

Hercule Poirot's debut, updated with revised art, explanation of the murder method, and essays on Poirot, Christie, strychnine, women during the war, plus chronology and book lists. *352 pages.*

The Complete, Annotated Deluxe Secret Adversary

Agatha Christie

Tommy and Tuppence battle socialists plotting to destroy England! This deluxe edition has illustrations from the newspaper edition, plus essays on thrillers, Christie's vanishing and more! *478 pages.*

Suburban Stockade
Strengthening Your Life Against an Uncertain Future

"Suburban Stockade" is Teresa Peschel's manifesto memoir about her quest to drop out of the rat race, embrace her peasant ancestry, and prepare her family for an uncertain future. She describes how our emphasis on a consumer economy and cheap goods blinded us to the personal and moral costs of economic growth. To pursue material wealth, we're taught to ignore the value of family, friends, and community, and the pleasures of a comfortable home and good food. Peschel dares you to build your suburban stockade by not playing the game where the rules are set by corporations and economists and rigged by politicians and the media.

Don't miss future Peschel Press books: Visit Peschelpress.com and sign up for our newsletter. We publish only when we have something to say and we will never sell or trade your personal information.

The Bride From Dairapaska

By Odessa Moon

In Trade Paperback and Ebook editions from Amazon and KINDLE UNLIMITED

The first book by Odessa Moon in the Steppes of Mars series,

On a terraformed Mars, young Debbie Miller was sent far from her rural village as part of a marriage compact between the rulers of two demesnes. A peasant who knew only obedience, she accepted her duty to bear her husband's children and work alongside him. But when they were sent to build a village in a barren patch of nowhere, her abusive husband forces her to take action. She flees with her children and their dog into the vast open steppes where dying was preferable to life with him.

Debbie only wanted to escape, but her encounter with the Steppes Riders, and especially Yannick of Kenyatta, unwittingly ignites changes that attract the attention of Mars' ruling families. Left to her own resources, Debbie must adapt to her new life and figure out how to defend her adopted people.

"The Steppes of Mars" series imagines a transformed world where a disaster on Earth decades ago cut off all contact with its wealth and resources. Experience a Mars where its genetically modified inhabitants have developed their own cultures, beliefs, and religions. A semi-feudal world where ruling families control vast demesnes under a central government at Barsoom. A world of limited resources where train travel is possible but cars and planes are not. A world of free-cities — open and domed — villages, vast fields and steppes, and people banding together to survive and thrive in this harsh new world.

The Bride from Dairapaska

- 357 pages.

- Available as trade paperback and Kindle ebook.

- First in a series; "The White Elephant of Panschin" comes in early 2020.

- Set on a terraformed planet in which societies develop a high-tech feudalism.

The Dictionary of Flowers and Gems

By Skye Kingsbury

In Trade Paperback and Ebook editions

Discover the language of flowers and the power of gemstones

Sunflowers for health and lavender for chastity;

Chrysanthemums for wealth and bachelor's buttons for celibacy.

For every emotion and feeling the Victorians used flowers, bushes, and trees to express it. Not just love, attraction, and desire, but also doubt, indifference, slander, and cruelty. They created beautiful bouquets and tussie mussies to express their connection to the natural world and feelings — not all of them pleasant — to each other.

We're rediscovering this bygone way to communicate our deepest thoughts and emotions and "A Dictionary of Flowers and Gems" can help. We've taken 2,000 plants, supplied their scientific name, and arranged them from **Aaron's Beard** ([*Hypericum calycinum*]: Invincibility, Protection) to **Zinnia, yellow** ([*Zinnia*]: Daily remembrance, Remembrance).

We also resorted the plants according to emotions, such as **Abandonment:** Anemone (Zephyr Flower), Field Anemone, Grape, Japanese Anemone (Windflower), Jasmine Anemone, Red Anemone, Wildflower Anemone, and **Zeal**: (Elderberry, Wake-robin (Arum)).

Finally, we created specialty lists to cover emotions such as courtship, love and affection, beauty, and refusal, making it easier to create themed bouquets and gardens. There

are also lists for color connections, birth month flowers and anniversary flowers, making this the most useful flower reference on the market.

A bonus section lists more than 400 gems and crystals and their associated powers and benefits. See which ones strengthen the chakras, encourage feelings of peace and calmness, radiate love, and fortify self-confidence.

"A Dictionary of Flowers and Gems" provides an easy-to-use reference for quick consultations for practitioners of the floral and gemstone arts.

The 223B Casebook Series

Collected and Annotated by Bill Peschel

Reprints of classic and newly discovered fanfiction written during Arthur Conan Doyle's lifetime,
With original art and extensive historical notes

The Early Punch Parodies of Sherlock Holmes

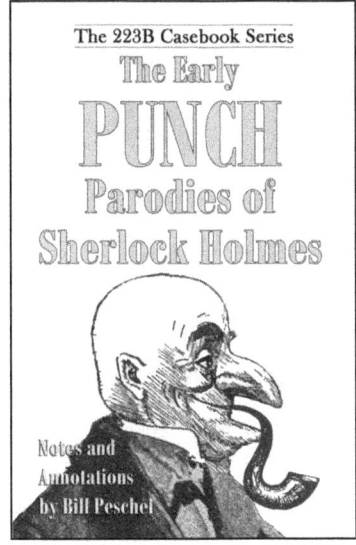

- More than 50 parodies, pastiches, book reviews, cartoons, and jokes from 1890 to 1928, culled from the pages of *Punch*, the classic British humor magazine.

- Includes 17-story cycle by R.C. Lehmann.

- Two parodies by P.G. Wodehouse and a story by Arthur Conan Doyle.

- Exclusive essays on *Punch*, Lehmann, Wodehouse, and an interview with Conan Doyle. Plus, a bonus story featuring Sherlock Holmes and Mark Twain! *281 pages.*

Victorian Parodies & Pastiches: 1888-1899
More than 60 pieces with stories by Arthur Conan Doyle, Robert Barr, Jack Butler Yeats, and J.M. Barrie. *279 pages.*

Edwardian Parodies & Pastiches I: 1900-1904
More than 55 pieces with stories by Mark Twain, Finley Peter Dunn, John Kendrick Bangs and P.G. Wodehouse. *390 pages.*

Edwardian Parodies & Pastiches II: 1905-1909
More than 40 pieces with stories by 'Banjo' Paterson, Max Beerbohm, Carolyn Wells, and Lincoln Steffens. *401 pages.*

Great War Parodies & Pastiches I: 1910-1914
More than 40 pieces with stories by O. Henry, Maurice Baring, Carolyn Wells, Edmund Pearson & Stephen Leacock. *362 pages.*

Great War Parodies & Pastiches II: 1915-1919
More than 35 pieces with stories by Ring Lardner, Carolyn Wells, John Kendrick Bags, and a young George Orwell. *390 pages.*

Jazz Age Parodies & Pastiches I: 1920-1924
More than 35 pieces with stories by Dashiell Hammett, James Thurber, Vincent Starrett, and Conan Doyle. *353 pages.*

Jazz Age Parodies & Pastiches II: 1925-1930
More than 42 pieces with stories by Edgar Wallace, Frederic Dorr Steele, Cory Ford, and August Derleth. *341 pages.*

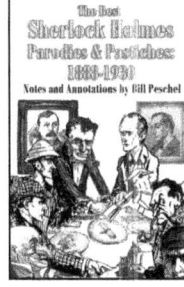

The Best Sherlock Holmes Parodies & Pastiches: 1888-1930
The best of the best! More than 33 pieces with stories by Wodehouse, O. Henry and James Thurber. *279 pages.*

The Casebook of Twain & Holmes
Bill Peschel
Seven new stories featuring Mark Twain in Sherlock Holmes' world. Guest appearances by Mycroft, Irene Adler, and John Watson! *230 pages.*

The Rugeley Poisoner Series
Edited and Annotated by Bill Peschel

The Illustrated Life and Career of William Palmer

(1856)

- Gossip about Palmer, racing scams, and London's stews.
- More than 50 restored woodcuts.
- Excerpts from Palmer's love letters.

225 pages.

The Times Report of the Trial of William Palmer

(1856)

- The *Times'* trial transcript edited, corrected, & annotated.
- More than 50 original woodcuts restored to better-than-new condition.
- An account of Palmer's execution and medical glossary

426 pages.

The Life and Career of Dr. William Palmer of Rugeley

(1925)

- Written by a doctor who interviewed witnesses and jurors.
- Rare photos and art.
- Essays on Palmer's impact on culture, strychnine, and Rugeley.

227 pages.

THE PESCHEL PRESS was created by Bill Peschel, a former journalist and co-holder of a Pulitzer Prize for his newspaper's coverage of the Joe Paterno case. In addition to the books listed here, Bill will publish original fiction by himself and others.

He lives with his family and animal menagerie in Hershey, where the air really does smell like chocolate.

www.ingramcontent.com/pod-product-compliance
Lightning Source LLC
Chambersburg PA
CBHW081158020426
42333CB00020B/2548